Death and Dying in America

Death and Dying in America

Andrea Fontana and Jennifer Reid Keene

polity

First published in 2009 by Polity Press

Polity Press
65 Bridge Street
Cambridge CB2 1UR, UK

Polity Press
350 Main Street
Malden, MA 02148, USA

ISBN-13: 978-0-7456-3914-7
ISBN-13: 978-0-7456-3915-4 (pb)

A catalogue record for this book is available from the British Library.

Typeset in 10.5 on 13 pt Swift
by Servis Filmsetting Ltd, Stockport, Cheshire
Printed and bound by MPG Books Group

For further information on Polity, visit our website: www.politybooks.com

Contents

Detailed contents

Acknowledgements

WE would like to thank Polity for reaching across the Atlantic and commissioning us to write this book. We especially appreciate Emma Longstaff and Jonathan Skerrett for their help, support, and suggestions. We owe a debt of gratitude to Caroline Richmond for a wonderful editing job. We would also like to recognize the anonymous reviewers who provided insightful and very helpful comments that enabled us significantly to improve the manuscript.

UNLV graduate students Daniel Sahl, Kerie Francis, and Allison Heard assisted with various parts of the project, and we would like to thank and recognize them for their work. Eric Lopez also helped gather sources for this text, and to him we are grateful. We also thank our supportive colleagues currently at UNLV and elsewhere.

Above all we would like to recognize and thank our spouses, our toughest editors, for their support and patience with us while we endeavored in this long journey.

We dedicate this monograph to our children, Dylan and Devin for Jennifer, and Nicole for Andrea. May they have long and joyous life journeys.

Andrea Fontana and Jennifer Reid Keene
Las Vegas, August 20, 2008

PART I

DEATH AND CULTURE

CHAPTER 01

An American View of Death

Introduction

Woody Allen once said that he was not afraid of death but that when it actually happened he did not want to be there. With that statement Allen captured one of the central principles of the American perception of death – we think it, we talk about it, we watch films, tell stories, and read books about it, but ultimately, as individuals and as a society, we still deny it and would prefer to avoid it. Even though death permeates our popular culture, rarely do we contemplate or plan for our own death. As much as we wish to avoid facing the reality of our own mortality, as a culture we are also obsessed with the notion of death and dying.

Thanatology – the study of death and dying – has long been a significant area for social researchers, who have produced a wide body of research and knowledge from philosophical, religious, psychological, historical, and sociological perspectives. Why, then, do we need another book on death and dying? As an answer to that question, consider the words of Emile Durkheim, one of the founders of sociology, who once said that the ways in which we bury our dead and mourn them is a reflection of the way we live (Durkheim, 1965). From a sociological perspective, death and mortality are indicators and outcomes of various social processes and the arrangements of social institutions. For example, death is related to many social phenomena, including health and healthcare, lifestyle, education, social interactions, political struggles, wars, and more. The answers to the questions of who dies (versus who lives) and under what circumstances people die can tell us a lot about a particular culture and society. Indeed, as we shall demonstrate, social patterns in death and dying in many ways mirror trends in other aspects of society. In this book, we focus specifically on death and dying in American society and how it relates to other social arrangements.

In contrast to those of some other industrialized nations, American society is strikingly heterogeneous, and as such we can expect to see wide differences in how and under what circumstances people die within the United States and between its various groups. Social stratification is a powerful organizing feature of society, and, just as we find inequality in the ways in which people live, we also find inequality in the ways in which people die. For example, sociologists have long recognized that social class is a defining feature of American society and one that serves to organize social relations. Social class has an effect on almost every aspect of society, from birth, through education and work, to retirement and even death.

One way to illustrate the relationship between social class and death in America is to consider trends in life expectancy over time and how it has varied across different groups. For example, in one study of trends from 1961 to 1999 the authors found that life expectancy for both women and men increased, but that "there was a steady increase in mortality inequality across the U.S. counties between 1983 and 1999, resulting from stagnation or increase in mortality among the worse-off segments of the population" (Ezzati et al., 2008: 557). Life expectancy continues to increase in most industrialized nations. However, American lifestyles and persistent social inequality have ensured that "female mortality increased in a large number of [American] counties, primarily because of chronic diseases related to smoking, overweight and obesity, and high blood pressure" (ibid.). In searching for explanations for these trends, sociologists attribute the causes to less affluent groups' poor diet, lack of education, financial stress, safety, unemployment, dangerous labor conditions, and other factors that stem from social stratification.

In this book we use sociological, anthropological, philosophical, and historical research to present the salient features of dying and death, with an emphasis on the American understanding and experience. At its most basic level, death is both an individual as well as an extremely social experience. While it is true that each of us will ultimately die alone, and that no one else can die for us, the social context in which death takes place, the lasting effects of an individual's death on survivors, and the social stratification processes that predict who dies when and how are all profoundly social in nature. Although there is a great deal of variation in how people deal with death, the social processes that affect who lives and who dies, and under what circumstances, are not random but are instead the product of large-scale institutionalized social systems.

 The overall goal of this text is to examine death and dying as an individual as well as a social experience. To that end, we consider various aspects of death and dying in America with attention to both macro-level (i.e., social institutions or large social systems) and micro-level (i.e., individual) phenomena and experiences. For each topic that we cover, we consider how large-scale, macro-level social processes relate to who dies, how they die, and the collective meanings given to their deaths and examine the individual experience of dying, as well as the implications for survivors.

The connection between micro- and macro-level social processes is a central theme in sociology. Durkheim was also a pioneer who stressed the need to examine the link between macro- and micro-phenomena, and his first attempt to make this connection was actually on the subject of death. In one of the first scholarly undertakings to provide an empirical explanation for a social phenomenon that was usually regarded as purely psychological or individualistic, Durkheim sought to find a social explanation for individual suicides by looking at suicide rates across different groups (Coser, 1977). Although suicide appeared to be a solemnly individual experience, he was able to show that social groups that were characterized by greater cohesiveness and social integration had lower rates of suicide than groups whose members were less cohesive and integrated (Durkheim, 1951). Durkheim also revealed that changes in individuals' social integration can affect suicide rates. During World War II, for instance, when people were united around the war effort and patriotism was high, American suicide rates declined significantly.

Durkheim's study was important and groundbreaking because it showed that group properties (suicide rates) were independent of individual traits and that seemingly individual phenomena such as suicide must be studied within the larger level group context in which it occurs (Coser, 1977). Ultimately, he demonstrated that individuals are profoundly linked to the groups in which they are members and that group membership is a powerful social force that directly impacts individual lives. For our sociological study of death, the implication of Durkheim's work is that he showed how death is not a simply random process that individuals experience alone, but rather is an outcome of social forces linking individuals to the larger society in which they live.

The historical forces that have shaped death in other cultures, Europe in particular, also shape death in American culture. However, the heterogeneity of the United States means that how death is played out in this country is linked to the cultural and historical contexts that have influenced death in other cultures and in other parts of the world. Because American society is so diverse it has a unique culture surrounding death that sets it apart from that in more homogeneous societies. Death in American society is in some ways similar to death in other industrialized nations, yet it also has clear differences. For example, the fact that the US is the only industrialized nation that does not guarantee its citizens healthcare is one feature that distinguishes this country from others and has implications for healthcare inequality throughout the life course and the quality of end-of-life care that individuals receive. This is an important point considering how diverse American society is in terms of race and ethnicity, socioeconomic status, nativity and citizenship status, and more.

These differences across individuals and groups within America are linked to differences in access to and use of healthcare services (Fuchs, 1998) which help determine who dies and under what circumstances.[1] In addition, American attitudes about religion and morality have implications for the ways in which people may choose to die and the legal rights that they have surrounding those decisions. These moralistic debates about death have become increasingly politicized in American popular culture over time and are a consistent theme in our popular and political discourses. For example, in contrast to some European countries, physician-assisted suicide is a highly controversial topic in America and remains illegal in the majority of the states; legal and political debates about it draw on religious, moral, and ethical arguments.

While America is a unique country in many ways, it also has plenty in common with other similarly industrialized nations. Consider that the causes of death are intricately linked to the larger organization of society, including its socioeconomic status. Taking a macro-level view of society, social demographers often categorize countries in terms of their relative wealth and power, and we see patterns in death and disease across countries of different status. High-income countries, such as the United States and Britain, were among the first to industrialize and typically have lower rates of infant mortality (death) and morbidity (disease), lower fertility levels (births), and longer life expectancy than lower income countries. We can see predictable similarities in the incidence of death and disease across these nations. Low-income countries, such as those in eastern, western, and sub-Saharan Africa, and some countries in East Asia, South Asia, Eastern and Central Europe, and Haiti and Nicaragua in the West, have mostly agricultural economies and are characterized by higher rates of infant mortality and morbidity, high fertility levels, and shorter life expectancy than highly industrialized and affluent countries.

In addition to differences in quality of life and mortality between high- and low-income countries, we see patterns in the leading causes of death. Indeed, currently the leading cause of death in high-income countries is heart disease, while in low-income countries it is HIV/AIDS, with malaria and tuberculosis also in the top ten (UC Atlas of Global Inequality, 2007). This is no accident. As we stated above, the socioeconomic status of nations has implications for their citizens' health, disease, and survival. Citizens in poorer countries tend to have unsanitary, unreliable water supplies, substandard housing conditions, less access to medical services, inadequate diets, and high mortality rates. In addition, in sub-Saharan Africa, for example, where HIV/AIDS is a rampant problem, many countries simply cannot afford to buy expensive medicines and therefore have predictably high rates of mortality.

As countries become increasingly affluent, the means by which people die change over time. As medical science, sanitation, and public health infrastructures have progressed in the industrialized world, countries' mortality rates have declined, and people are less likely to die from infectious diseases than from acute illnesses and conditions. In the United States, they are likely to live for longer periods with chronic conditions that can last for decades (arthritis and diabetes, for example). At the same time, however, those countries whose economies are still largely agriculturally based and have few resources for medical care or public health measures remain afflicted by infectious diseases.

Themes and organization of the book

In this book we cover the various aspects of death and dying and draw on scholarship from several social science disciplines, including sociology, history, philosophy, and psychology. As we cover the various topics we emphasize several themes that reoccur throughout our discussions. First, we draw on the various disciplines' contributions to the study of thanatology in order to illustrate fully how the many aspects of death and dying occur at both the macro- (societal) and the micro- (individual) level. Second, this link between the macro- and the micro-level necessarily means that patterns of inequality that are institutionalized at the societal level will translate into patterns of inequality in the individual experience of death and dying. Readers will find that the theme of social stratification and inequality repeats itself again and again throughout this text. Third, in keeping with the imperatives of late capitalist culture in the United States (Jameson, 1991), the topics of consumerism and commercialism also reveal themselves in many of our discussions.

The remaining chapters in this text cover nine broad topics related to the study of death and dying. Our goal is not to give readers a complete digest of all of the various research on each particular topic but rather to provide an overview using the most relevant classical and the most cutting-edge recent studies available. Further, we aim to provide readers with an understanding of how the various aspects of death and dying play out at both macro- and micro-level.

The text is divided into four thematic sections. The first section deals with the cultural aspects of death. Chapter 2 presents demographic factors related to large-scale trends in death and dying as well as the historical and cultural elements that have changed perceptions of death in Europe and America. The second section emphasizes death itself and its repercussions. Chapter 3 describes the places and environments where Americans die and has a strong emphasis on hospices (healthcare facilities for the terminally ill), hospice care, and the hospice movement (which was born in Europe). In chapter 4 we discuss controversial issues surrounding death and dying, including social inequality as it relates to who dies and under what circumstances as well as the debates surrounding euthanasia and physician-assisted suicide. Chapter 5 focuses on funeral rituals and also addresses the diverse and, at times, bizarre ways in which people dispose of the body of the deceased.

Part III of the book consists of two chapters addressing both individual and collective death. In chapter 6 we focus on death among children and the implications for surviving parents' and siblings' bereavement, and we also discuss children's conceptions of death and mortality. The concern of chapter 7 is with issues regarding mass death resulting from acts of epidemics, natural disasters, and war, as well as death as a result of violence, including death arising from accidents, homicide, and suicide. In the final section of the book we discuss the ways in which dying people as well as survivors cope with death. In chapter 8 we cover how those in the medical establishment deal with the delicate task of explaining to patients that they are dying. Chapter 9 examines the grieving process that survivors experience, and we also discuss the specific processes associated with bereavement and widowhood. The final substantive chapter of the book focuses on the various belief systems that guide how people think about life after death, and we specifically discuss religious, scientific, and extrasensory experiences, and philosophical beliefs. Finally, we offer a concluding chapter to reiterate our themes and sum up our main points about the American experience of death and dying.

CHAPTER 02

Changing Demographic and Cultural Aspects of Death

Introduction

THE ways in which individuals and societies relate to dying and to death have real consequences for our everyday lives at both the micro- and the macro-level. This is true because how we think about (or ignore) death partly determines how we think about living. For instance, Americans are apt to spend more time planning a vacation than they do thinking about their end-of-life preferences or their desires for their funeral. Simultaneously, the way we live affects our beliefs about death and the cultural expressions and artifacts that we employ for the dying and the dead. Indeed, American consumerism ensures that an entire industry has evolved to meet the demand for various funeral and afterlife accoutrements.

Perceptions of death and dying have changed over time and vary across societies. With the passage of time even the same behaviors regarding death take on totally different meanings at different historical moments. For example, it was no great concern to his contemporaries that Hamlet, the brooding prince of Denmark, wandered about carrying a skull in his hand, yet should Hamlet have lived in our century he would have been regarded as rather peculiar for carrying the very same skull.

In this chapter we first examine demographic trends and changes in the leading causes of death. Then we turn to the changing cultural image of death in Western culture and its influence on European societies. One of the main themes is that death and dying used to take place in communal, public settings with little medical intervention. Over time, however, the environment of death became a private event, while doctors assumed control over the patient and their life and death decisions. Finally, we examine the commercialization of healthcare in today's America and its implications for death and dying.

The demographics of death and dying

Life span and life expectancy

Social demographers are concerned with three primary social processes that occur in society: fertility, mortality, and migration. The first two are particularly important for our historical discussion of death. Fertility refers to the birthrate while mortality refers to the relative frequency of deaths in a population. (Mortality is not to be confused with morbidity, which is the incidence of disease.) Migration refers to the movement of people from one country or locality to another. Scholars who study population changes at the macro-level are concerned with how these three processes interact and determine the characteristics of particular populations, especially in terms of age structure (i.e., how many old people there are compared with how many young people) and other socioeconomic characteristics.

Scholars have also noted the relationship between migration and mortality. In his classic work *Plagues and Peoples*, William H. McNeill (1976) illustrated how trade, exploration, and migration have often helped spread disease and, in turn, death. One poignant example is the triumph of Cortez over the Aztecs in 1520. As the Spanish army was attacking the Aztec capital, Tenochtitlan, the Aztec people were also being overrun by smallpox brought over by the Spaniards. This spread of Old World diseases to the New World is a recurrent theme in American history and helped ensure that European immigrants were able to take over and colonize the Americas, typically by devastating indigenous populations, who had no resistance to these viruses. McNeill (1993: 30) notes that "the whole history of our country and the Americas at large, centering as it does around the repopulation of the land by immigrants from Europe and Africa, is a function of the disease disequilibrium that existed after 1500 between the Old and the New World." He also explains that the pattern was the opposite for Europeans attempting to colonize Africa, where they were confronted with and died from diseases and viruses to which Africans were already acclimated.

Related to these population indicators are two other important characteristics that social scientists use to evaluate and describe populations: life span and life expectancy. Life span refers to the longest number of years that any member of a species has been known to live according to the available biological information about that species, and it applies to an entire species without regard to individual members' geography or other subcategories. Scientists currently believe that the human life span is about 120 years (Perls and Fretts, 2001). Life expectancy is slightly different and captures the average age at which members of a population die. In other words, life expectancy is the average age at death for a given population. It is calculated statistically and can be determined for an overall population as well as for various subgroups within a population who may have differing hereditary factors, physical conditions, and socioeconomic opportunities and constraints.

Life expectancy in the United States has altered as medical technology has improved and other socioeconomic conditions have changed. As we can see in table 2.1, at the turn of the twentieth century life expectancy was about 51 for women and 48 for men. Compare those ages with women and men's life expectancies in 1949–51, which were about 71 and 66, respectively. Finally, in 2004, life expectancy at birth was 77.8 years for the whole US population and was 80.4 years for women and 75.2 for men (Miniño et al., 2007). We can see from these numbers how the life course has expanded for both women and men over time and how, on average, people in the United States are living increasingly longer. Gender and race differences are also apparent from this table. On average, women outlive men in every case, while African-American men have had the lowest life expectancy throughout the past century, and that trend persists into the 2000s. Social gerontologists and social demographers argue that differences in life expectancy across demographic groups are attributable to historical and lifelong variation in access to resources and opportunities for various groups in society.

It remains important, however, to remember that these numbers are for the United States and that life expectancies for women and men in other countries are different. Life expectancy in the United States is comparable to that in other industrialized nations such as those of Western Europe, but in less-developed nations it is much lower and varies from country to country. For example, in 1998, life expectancy in North America was 76, and in Western Europe 78; in contrast, in Latin America and the Caribbean it was 69, in the Near East and North Africa 68, in Asia 65, and in Sub-Saharan Africa only 49 years (US Census Bureau, 1999).

The demographic transition

When we think about historical changes in death and dying and how and why life expectancies have increased over time, it is useful to consider a long-established theory about historical macro-level changes in population dynamics. The demographic transition is a socioeconomic process that explains how countries shift from high fertility and high mortality to low fertility and low mortality as they develop from traditional pre-industrial to modern industrialized societies (Lee, 2003).

Table 2.1 Life expectancy for the overall US population and by gender and race over time

	1900–2	1909–11	1919–21	1929–31	1939–41	1949–51	1959–61	1969–71	1979–81	1989–91	2003	2004
All	49.24	51.49	56.40	59.20	63.62	68.07	69.89	70.75	73.88	75.37	77.4	77.8
Women	50.70	53.24	57.40	60.90	65.89	70.96	73.24	74.64	77.62	78.81	80.0	80.4
Men	47.88	49.86	55.50	57.71	61.60	65.47	66.80	67.04	70.11	71.83	74.7	75.2
White people	49.64	51.90	57.42	60.86	64.92	69.02	70.73	71.62	74.53	76.13	77.9	78.3
White women	51.08	53.62	58.53	62.67	67.29	72.03	74.19	75.49	78.22	79.45	80.4	80.8
White men	48.23	50.23	56.34	59.12	62.81	66.31	67.55	67.94	70.82	72.72	75.3	75.7
African Americans	33.80	35.87	47.03	48.53	53.85	60.73	63.91	64.11	68.52	69.16	72.6	73.1
African-American women	35.04	37.67	46.92	49.51	55.56	62.70	66.47	68.32	72.88	73.73	75.9	76.3
African-American men	32.54	34.05	47.14	47.55	52.26	58.91	61.48	60.00	64.10	64.47	68.9	69.5

Sources: Arias (2006), table 11; Miniño et al. (2007).

The demographic transition occurs in three phases (Lee, 2003). The first phase applies to pre-industrial, agricultural societies with low medical technology. During this phase, women begin having children at a young age and have many pregnancies, although a lot of infants and children die from various acute and infectious diseases. Thus, the fertility rate and infant mortality are both high and relatively few people live into old age. During the second phase, improvements in medical technology and sanitation help depress infant and maternal mortality, and therefore death rates begin to decline and the population increases. In the final stage, deaths caused by infectious diseases and acute illnesses decline, and most people die from extended or chronic conditions that persist over time (ibid.; Martin and Kinsella, 1994). In the postmodern era, some have noted the inherent ethnocentricity of demographic transition theory, since it has been based on the progression of advanced industrialized countries where the majority of the population is white (Coale, 1986).

The epidemiologic transition

This transition from societies characterized by high fertility and high mortality to ones characterized by low fertility and low mortality also mirrors historical changes in the leading cause of death over time. Epidemiologic transition theory argues that, as societies become increasingly modern and industrialized, their social, health, and economic conditions improve; and these changes have implications for how people die (Olshaunsky and Ault, 1986). As conditions get better, the leading cause of death shifts from infectious and parasitic diseases, which most often infect and kill infants and young people, to degenerative diseases, which most frequently affect people during middle and old age. Thus, over time, death gets redistributed from the young to the old (ibid.).

Historical studies of the United States and other developed countries show that the epidemiologic transition occurs in three distinct phases: the Age of Pestilence and Famine, the Age of Receding Pandemics, and the Age of Degenerative and Manmade Diseases (McLeroy and Crump, 1994; Omran, 1974). During the first phase, which in the United States would be from the early 1600s through the late 1800s, death rates were high. Endemic diseases, malnutrition, and epidemics of infectious diseases ravaged significant portions of the population. The second phase occurred beginning in the late 1800s as the incidence of epidemics began to decline, and the major cause of death shifted to indigenous infectious diseases. For example, in 1900 the two leading causes were tuberculosis, and pneumonia combined with influenza (McLeroy and Crump, 1994). However, in

2004 they were heart disease, cancer, stroke, and lower respiratory diseases (Miniño et al., 2007). This final shift from infectious diseases to chronic and acute illnesses is what characterizes the third phase of the epidemiologic transition.

While increased medical technology seems to be an obvious explanation for these changes in what kills people, scholars argue that it is not so simple. Some historical epidemiological research has shown that the decline in infectious diseases began to occur even before scientists developed effective vaccines or treatments (McKinlay and McKinlay, 1977), and that the decrease in deaths from infectious diseases is more strongly related to improvements in social and living conditions, including housing, sanitation, and nutrition (Breslow, 1990; McKinlay and McKinlay, 1977; McLeroy and Crump, 1994).

Death in the Western world

In this section we rely primarily on the work of two distinguished scholars: Ivan Illich (1926-2002) who was an Austrian philosopher and social critic whose work provides a view of the changing perceptions of death in European history, and Philippe Ariès (1914-1984), who was a noted French historian of the family and also wrote extensively about changing Western attitudes to death. Both Illich and Ariès provide a sense of the dominant perspectives on death and dying in Europe at different historical points and how the dominant views about death influenced individuals and societies during each period. To explain the evolution of death, both authors relied on multiple sources, including folktales, stories, and especially paintings, and their histori-cal accounts capture and describe the relationship between culture and death.

Both authors outlined the historical "stages" of perceptions of death and show how over time death changed from a communal, public setting, in which individuals and their loved ones had more control over the process of dying, to a completely different way of dealing with death, in a private, obscured, medicalized hospital environment in which doctors and medical staff are in control and the individual has little or no power. Within this changing context, the focus shifted from the dying person's concerns to those of standardized medical procedures in which the doctor and staff domi-nate. Furthermore, the new context of death requires that everyone involved is aware of the commercial and financial costs of the dying process. All of these factors have implications for who dies and under what circumstances.

Illich's stages of natural death

Illich describes death in European history as "the white man's image of death" (that is, as expressed in Western culture), which he sarcastically refers to as "natural death" (1976: 175). Natural death is an idealized type of death that has moved through distinct phases throughout European history. Ultimately, he shows that what has been considered a natural death has changed over time.

The first stage of natural death that Illich identifies is the *dance of the dead*. This is exemplified by the pagan tradition of dancing on tombs in cemeteries, a practice which the Catholic Church condemned for hundreds of years. Beginning approximately in the fourth century, dancing upon the dead symbolized a reaffirmation of life in pagan societies and was a way of expressing the individual joy of being alive while those below your feet were dead. In the late fourteenth century the dance became more introspective and less of a celebration. Paintings from this period portrayed the living dancing with a corpse in which "each partner is a mirror image of the other in dress and feature. In the shape of his body Everyman carries his own death with him and dances with it through his life" (Illich, 1976: 177). The dance with the dead was a gloomy reminder of one's mortality rather than a celebration of one's own life.

The second stage is the *dance of death*, which typified the idea of natural death during the fifteenth and sixteenth centuries. In paintings from this period, death is pictured as a skeleton rather than a person. The dance of death is between a living person and a "naked" skeleton. Illich argued that this type of dance was evidence that the dominant view about death was that it no longer follows us through life but only takes over the final moment. The skeleton symbolized the grim reaper, mowing down everyone regardless of wealth and status, making us all the same in the face of death. This view of natural death invokes a stronger image of finality than dancing with a person with flesh. According to Illich, this image led to a view of the body as an object and of death as a natural event ending the cycle of life, and gradually removing the influence of supernatural figures that had been prevalent in the Middle Ages.

The next stage of natural death is called *bourgeois death* and was dominant in the seventeenth and eighteenth centuries. This view of death specifically invokes social class status and its relationship to who dies and under what circumstances. The social historian Karl Marx identified two main social classes in capitalist societies, the bourgeoisie (the owners of the means of production) and the proletariat (the workers) (Marx, [1867] 1967). During this time, social class played an important role in social views of death, and also the role of medicine in staving off death. In this view, the bourgeoisie would enjoy the fruits of their ownership and would achieve greater financial security in old age than the workers. Because of their wealth and status, they would also face fewer health problems in later life because they engaged in less strenuous, sedentary work throughout their lives. With more wealth, the bourgeoisie would also have greater access to medical care and physicians' interventions. During this time physicians were gaining status as well as new skills as medical science advanced, and were therefore increasing their abilities to intervene and prolong life. Thus, the grim reaper's distribution of egalitarian death was quickly dismissed by bourgeois death.

Next, Illich related *death and medicine* by showing how medicine and its practitioners took control of dying and reshaped the image of death. Beginning in the nineteenth century, bolstered by the advances of sciences, the early development of the modern hospital, and the leap forward of medical technology, physicians took charge of the process, stepping in between a patient and death and redefining death as a medical event with specific clinical symptoms. At that period doctors dealt primarily with fighting pestilence (such as bubonic plague) and consumption (pulmonary tuberculosis). Medical control over death grew in the middle of the twentieth century as more advanced technology became increasingly available to doctors.

Finally, according to Illich, in the late part of the twentieth century death took place primarily while patients were under intensive care in hospitals. In this context, doctors control the circumstances and environment of death and cater to hospitals' procedures regarding the process of dying. This change fostered a trend toward the medicalization of life in which we become "patients" from birth to death. For example, it used to be normal and routine for babies to be born at home under the care of a midwife. Now home births are a distinct minority in the United States: most babies are born in hospital settings with constant fetal monitoring, mothers' labors are spurred on with drugs, labor pains are masked with intensive drugs and anesthesia, and the rates of Caesarean sections are at an all-time high. Birth was once a natural experience in which women's bodies (not doctors) were trusted to take over and deliver their babies. Now the birth process is highly medicalized, very expensive, and routinized, so that women have very limited choices about how births will proceed unless they seek out alternative types of care through midwives or birthing centers (many of which are not covered by health insurance). The same trends toward medicalization and routinization can be applied to the process of death. Death takes place in hospitals, under intensive care, with extensive medical interventions requiring expensive technology.

Just as the process of birth has become a medical and commercial business, so has the process of death.

Ariès' vision of death from the Middle Ages to the present

Ariès and Illich employ similar conceptions of death as they describe the historical evolution of views about death and dying, and their typologies are complementary. Ariès focuses on Europe from the Middle Ages to the present. According to him, the first view of death was *tamed death*, since the dying individuals accepted it calmly, knowing there was nothing to be done about it. People in the early Middle Ages (*c.* 500–*c.* 1100 AD) tended to be aware of their impending death, either through signs of their changing physical condition or through a premonition. Although people were not eager to die, they did not try to stave off death, as we do today. When they realized that their hour had come, they died simply, without much fanfare. If out in the fields, the dying person would prepare by lying down, facing up, so as to look toward heaven. In this Christian context, the dying person often turned toward the East, toward Jerusalem. He or she would pray, admit past guilt for sins committed, and then wait quietly, in silence, for death to come.

During this time, death was a public, communal affair. It usually took place in the bedchamber, where family, friends, and neighbors would come and go freely. Children were always allowed to be present, and not excluded as they are today. After the death, women in the family and from the community would wash and prepare the body for burial. This home-spun way of dying in which family members and the larger community were present was the norm. This public display of death continued until the end of the eighteenth century when physicians began to discover the principles of hygiene and the potential problem of infection in overcrowded conditions. The environment of death was rather austere and people did not carry on with great displays of emotion. During this era, death was familiar to everyone; it evoked no great fear since it was part of everyday life.

Death was all around, life expectancy was low, infant mortality was high. Today we tend to associate death with old age, but in the Middle Ages it was associated with youth. Medical practitioners were few and they could do little for patients, given the limited development of science. Family members (women) were the ones who usually practiced home medicine and attended to the sick and the dying. People also raised and killed their own food, adding to their familiarity with death.

Ariès' second stage is called *one's own death*. Religion has been a major force in shaping beliefs about death and dying, and in Europe and the West, Christianity has been a profound influence. According

Table 2.2 Summary of Illich and Ariès' stages of death in Western societies			
Stages of death	Historical period	Characteristics	Sociological relevance
Illich			
Dance of the dead	(300–1300)	Dancing on tombs with corpse to express the joy of life	Death is with us through life
Dance of death	(1400–1500)	Dancing with skeletons	Death is at the end of life
Bourgeois death	(1600–1700)	Death is forestalled with help of medicine	Death is related to social class
Death and medicine	(1800–2000)	Death is moved to hospitals	Doctors control death
Ariès			
Tamed death	(500–1100)	Death is a public affair	Death is accepted as natural; nothing can be done about it
One's own death	(1200–1400)	Death becomes personal	Living a virtuous life will be rewarded afterwards
Thy death	(1500–1700)	Death seen as a "break" from everyday life, like love	Romantic, emotional
Forbidden death	(1800–2000)	Death is moved to hospitals	Technical, private

Source: Derived from Illich (1976) and Ariès (1974).

to Ariès, before the twelfth century, Christians believed that the dead simply went to sleep until the day of the Second Coming of Jesus, when they would awaken in Paradise. In this view, the individual's fate was intimately tied to that of their group or society; resurrection took place collectively rather than individually.

By analyzing paintings of *The Last Judgment*, scholars noticed that in the twelfth century subtle modifications in the painting changed the meaning of death and made it more personal, suggesting that now the individual's actions in life would determine his or her fate after death (Ariès, 1974: 31). In the twelfth century, paintings of *The Last Judgment* began to show the separation of the just from the damned, depicting Christ sitting in judgment, the resurrection of the just to Heaven and the falling of the damned into Hell (Ariès, 1981: 99). Moving on to the thirteenth century, Christ is shown seated as a judge surrounded by his court, the apostles. In this version of the same painting, each person is judged according to his or her own deeds, not at the time of death but at the end of time. By the fourteenth and fifteenth centuries time is compressed, and paintings show the dying person being judged at his or her deathbed. Supernatural figures appear to the dying above his or her head, on one side God and his court, on the other side demons led by Satan. The dying person is judged and can sway the judgment by his or her demeanor, by dying in the appropriate manner.

A whole new perspective on how to die emerged in the fifteenth and sixteenth centuries with the *ars moriendi* (the art of dying). This is a body of Christian literature that provides practical guidelines for people who are dying and to those who are attending to the dying (both clergy and laypeople). These texts outlined prayers, attitudes, and actions that would lead individuals to a "good death" and salvation. They emphasize the importance of lifelong preparation in piety, respect for the Lord, and doing good deeds, while also stressing the need to resist temptation and despair in the final moment. With the guidance outlined in these texts the dominant view of death became much more individual, as people were to be judged alone and the judgment was tied to the dying person's biography and their behavior in the face of death.

In Ariès' model, the third phase takes on a concern for other people's death rather than simply one's own and is called *thy death* (*la mort de toi*). Between the sixteenth and eighteenth centuries, death gradually changed from a familiar everyday event to a break from life. Death, like love, evokes extraordinary feelings and emotions, and it breaks from the monotony of mundane life. In the art and literature of this period, writers and artists began coupling death with love. One poignant example of this is the mixture of eternal love and tragic death in Shakespeare's story of Romeo and Juliet.

In the late eighteenth century, the Romantic movement swept across the arts and literature throughout Europe. Romanticism emphasized individuality, feelings, and emotions, both beautiful and morbid. In this context, perceptions and expectations about dying became highly emotional and romanticized. Now, people's outward displays of mourning and the experience of death became greatly exaggerated (in contrast to previous norms and expectations), with a great deal of crying and even fainting. Where once death was an event to be expected and accepted, it now became something to fear. Ariès (1974: 68) argued that, with these changing perceptions of death, individual people had a more difficult experience accepting the loss of friends and intimates than they had had at any previous time.

The fourth and last of Ariès' stages is *forbidden death*. This conception of death is similar to the way that Illich described the medicalization of death. In the twentieth century, dying moved from the home and bedroom to the hospital bed. According to Ariès, individuals now die alone in a foreign setting and have little control over the process, which has been usurped by the medical team. This trend began in the nineteenth century and persists today. At the same time, death changed from a romantic event to a medical and technical phenomenon. In order to avoid the highly charged emotional outbursts associated with Romanticism, death became a private event, shrouded in secrecy. Now medical professionals dictated the circumstances of death; the public, communal aspects of death and dying faded and were replaced by a private, medical model. One explanation for this shift is that, with the social and economic changes associated with the Enlightenment and increasing industrialization, people began to fear death again. Coupled with this was a rise in the status of doctors and the medical profession in general as well as increasingly popular beliefs about the saving powers of medical technology (Starr, 1982). The demise of Romanticism and the rise of medicalization also meant that private deaths helped spare the emotions of the dying person and their survivors; rather than requiring melodramatic displays about death, they shifted their faith to doctors and their healing powers. All of these social changes helped move death from a communal to a private setting.

Both Ariès and Illich end their analyses of the historical changes in death and dying in the middle of the 1970s. At that time, both were vehemently critical of how American society had commercialized healthcare and the dying process and had turned control over to physicians and hospitals. We now take up a discussion of the relationship between medicine and death that picks up where Ariès and Illich left off.

Medicine and dying today

Patients' rights

The 1970s was an important decade in which various social and economic processes were converging that affected the medical profession and individuals' access to healthcare. Americans were growing increasingly unhappy with the state of healthcare and in 1974 the federal government eventually passed the Employee Retirement Income Security Act (ERISA), which established minimum standards for voluntarily established pension and health plans and provided minimum protection for individuals covered under these plans (US Department of Labor, 2008). ERISA required that healthcare plans provide patients with information about the costs and benefits of their plans as well as establish a grievance and appeals process.

ERISA has been amended various times since its creation. Two important additions include the Consolidated Omnibus Budget Reconciliation Act (COBRA) and Health Insurance Portability and Accountability Act (HIPAA). COBRA enables eligible workers and their families to pay to continue their health insurance coverage through their former employer after they lose their job (US Department of

Labor, 2008). The effect of COBRA is to allow some workers to extend their employer-provided health benefits until, all being well, they find another job with health benefits. COBRA is important because it is one of the only mechanisms American workers have to help ensure that the loss of a job does not automatically mean the loss of important health benefits (since the vast majority of Americans with health insurance are covered through their employers). HIPAA provides protections for workers and their families who have preexisting conditions that, if disclosed, might enable potential employers or health insurance companies to discriminate against them and deny coverage (ibid.). Even with these amendments, ERISA is limited in the degree to which it empowers individual patients to challenge their health insurance companies and attain the benefits they need.

This struggle to advocate for patients' rights continued into the twenty-first century. In 1998, President Bill Clinton attempted to get Congress to pass the Patient's Bill of Rights, but was unsuccessful. In 2001 Democratic (Edward Kennedy and John Edwards) and Republican (John McCain) senators joined together and proposed the Bipartisan Patient Protection Act, which eventually passed the Senate (Pear, 2001), although the bill was strongly opposed by the majority of Republicans. Its key components were to establish federal guidelines for health insurance and allow patients to file suit in order to enforce their rights (ibid.). The bill was significantly revised in the House of Representatives and became arguably weaker as a means of ensuring that patients could advocate legally for their healthcare rights. Ultimately, the House passed a much less effective version that essentially insulated employers and health insurance companies from litigation and met with President Bush's approval.

Just as patients' rights and security started to become an issue during the 1970s, the Dying Person's Bill of Rights was created to try and strengthen patients' control over how they die, and to provide dying people with a way to assert their dignity and humanity (Ferrell and Coyle, 2002). While this statement is not actual legislation, it is a document that various healthcare organizations recognize and employ as part of their mission statements. The Dying Person's Bill of Rights asserts that dying people have the right not to die alone, not to die in pain, and to participate in decisions surrounding their care, among other claims. Although not ratified by the government, this statement continues to serve as a guide for people and organizations that work with dying patients and who are concerned with managing patients' pain, which is called palliative care.

To better understand the significance of this statement of the Dying Person's Bill of Rights, consider the opposite of each of its directives. It may seem like common sense to many of us that people have a right not to die in pain or alone or that, of course, they are entitled to participate in how they are cared for. However, as with many of these kinds of declaration, the fact that medical professionals felt the need to create such a document is evidence that these were not actually taken-for-granted assumptions, but instead are a confirmation that medical providers needed to be reminded about how to take care of those who are most vulnerable and in need.

Rising healthcare costs

Over the past several decades, the American medical system has come under scrutiny for its high cost and failure to deliver medicine to the needy (Magner, 2005; Starr, 1982). In the 1980s, under Ronald Reagan's presidency, the United States government decentralized a great number of federal programs, allegedly seeking to reduce the influence of the federal government on Americans' lives and economic situations. This philosophy did not work for healthcare, however, and instead encouraged a corporate approach to healthcare provision. This free-market competition philosophy has created a complex, unwieldy healthcare system that has seen costs spiraling upward. Indeed, the United States spends 13.25 of its gross domestic product on health, more than any other developed country (Freund et al., 2003). Given its high cost, however, we would expect that the system would not only provide the best medicine available in the world, but would also be available to the majority of its citizens. Instead, the United States has a highly stratified and fractured healthcare system where the most affluent people who are able to pay out of pocket for services are the most advantaged, those who have employer-sponsored health insurance are better off than many, and older citizens who are eligible for government-provided health insurance (Medicare) are taken care of to some extent, while many people are left without health insurance of any kind. These kinds of differences in access to (and use of) healthcare are motivated by financial constraints and have implications for who lives and who dies.

Over three decades have passed since Ariès and Illich identified the dramatic changes in the relationship between medicine and death. In the process, various solutions have been put forth to fix the healthcare crisis and address the growing costs, including national health insurance, health maintenance organizations (HMOs), increased hospital regulation, and more rigorous control of drugs and the drug industry (Fuchs, 1998), but none has proved to be the magic bullet that would solve all of America's healthcare problems. Instead, we have much evidence of growing healthcare inequality, and even some universal healthcare models in Europe are being criticized and facing financial and social crises in the delivery of medicine.

Profitability and healthcare

Medicine in America has gradually turned into big business; we no longer simply provide medical care but we also market it. Some argue that insurance companies, drug manufacturers, and HMOs have stymied the freedom and power of physicians, even as physicians have long fought to establish and maintain their power and prestige as professionals (Starr, 1982). Medical decisions are strongly influenced by financial elements, sometimes in very troubling ways (Freund et al., 2003), as physicians are increasingly driven by profit. Consider the following example:

> Dr. Overdyke [a knee replacement surgeon] has said that he used the Sulzer implant because it was the best available. But Louisiana state officials say he had another incentive as well: the $175,000 a year that he stood to make from contracts from the company. The contracts called for him to consult on product design and "promote and educate other surgeons" on the virtues of the Sulzer products. (Abelson, 2005: 1)

In the years 2000 and 2001, until the doctor's agreement with the company was discovered, Dr Overdyke and all of his residents used exclusively the Sulzer product for knee replacements.

We also see evidence of doctors' profit motives in the kinds of practices they choose to enter. For example, cosmetic surgery is a hugely profitable and growing segment of the healthcare system (Singer, 2006), while the need for geriatricians and doctors specializing in the care of older persons (a much less profitable, more integrated and complex, and less sexy area of specialization) goes unmet, even with the dramatic aging of the baby boom generation (Gawande, 2007). In 2005, American doctors performed 455,000 liposuction operations, the most popular cosmetic procedure (Singer, 2006).

These trends apply to the development of new medicines as well. Some argue that there is no direct correlation between the need for medicines and the development of new drugs. The pharmaceutical industry, the largest funder of medical research in the United States, increasingly focuses its efforts on new 'lifestyle' drugs that are designed to treat illnesses that are the result of how people live – drugs to stop smoking, to treat erectile dysfunction, or hair loss, and to encourage weight loss (Lexchin, 2001).

Healthcare costs, social inequality, and death

In terms of social inequality, how we spend money on medical research reflects our values as a society and the economic structure of our medical system. Other examples of the influence of financial incentives and medicine deal directly with dying individuals and those faced with terminal diseases. Some might argue that the money spent on research and treatment for very specialized types of diseases that affect a small proportion of the population could be spent on researching cures for diseases that afflict larger social groups – from this perspective, the well-being of the larger group is more valuable than that of the smaller group. One example of this disjuncture is the case of sickle-cell anemia, which in the United States affects primarily African Americans and Hispanics. One in 500 African Americans and one in 1,000 to 1,400 Hispanic Americans have sickle-cell (CDC, 2008). Research on this disease has long been underfunded and the disease remains without a cure (Fuchs, 1998), while research on other diseases such as multiple myeloma (a cancer of the plasma cells), which afflicts about 16,000 people per year (Memorial Sloan-Kettering, 2008), has seen research money skyrocket through private philanthropic organizations (Groopman, 2008).

The cancer drug Abraxane, for example, was recently marketed as a new prescription for fighting late-stage breast cancer. The drug is extremely expensive, costing $4,200 per dose. An independent review of the drug that was published in a medical journal concluded that the "new" Abraxane was actually just a new marketing scheme for an old cancer drug, and the doctor marketing it was becoming a billionaire from the sales. As medical journals have pointed out, Abraxane does not prolong the life of the patients and the side effects from the old and new versions of the drug are similar. The marketing strategy is working, however, as desperate breast cancer patients insist on Abraxane as a last-ditch effort when chemotherapy fails. The high price of this particular drug is one more aspect of our broken healthcare system that serves to drive up costs overall.

Under the current system, doctors have no real incentives to keep prices down or to avoid new treatments on the basis of cost (Berenson, 2006). In a real-world market, healthcare consumers would be put off by the price of cutting-edge cancer drugs, and would likely reject them or attempt to agitate for lower prices, especially when the new drugs are only marginally more effective than previous incarnations. Yet, with patients and healthcare providers largely shielded from the actual costs of new drugs, there is little incentive to demand reform. Ultimately, the relationship between marketing, profits, and medicine blurs the line between healthcare that is effective and healthcare that is profitable. For those patients who are facing terminal illnesses or who are without health insurance at all, these conflicts of interest may have real consequences for who dies and who lives.

Medical advances have afforded us the luxury of living longer and healthier lives and postponing death until much later in the life course. As we have previously discussed, life expectancy for all groups has increased dramatically over the past century. Even with all of the advances in medical science, access to and use of healthcare is not equally distributed throughout American society, and we therefore must consider how to allocate the medical resources that we do have. These kinds of choices ultimately determine who lives and who dies, and under what circumstances. For instance, even though we might believe that everyone should be treated as equal, we must also face the difficult questions about who deserves and receives the most cutting-edge and expensive life-saving interventions. Particularly at the end, when doctors are able to employ costly medical procedures that may extend a person's life for a short time, we might also need to consider whether the expense and long-term prognosis of the procedure are worth it for the greater good of society (Fuchs, 1998). Of course, when we are talking about ourselves or a loved one we most often would argue that doctors should do whatever it takes to save a life – without regard for the expense. When we think about it in the abstract, however, our views about how to disseminate scarce medical resources may be different. When we consider how the resources used to save one life might have a more meaningful impact if those same resources were used to save 100 people's lives, the choices we face become much more difficult.

Conclusion

The emphasis in this chapter has been on the changing cultural perceptions of death over time. We began with a discussion of some of the basic demographic indicators of the health of a society and examined improvements in life expectancy. For all groups life expectancy has increased dramatically; nonetheless, we still see that, on average, women can expect to outlive men and that some groups in society do not have life expectancies as long as others. At the same time we have witnessed major shifts in the leading causes of death from infectious to chronic conditions, such that people now live longer than ever and have healthier life spans, even when they have chronic conditions that last for decades. These demographic changes are an important background to the historical changes in how people thought about and conceptualized death, as both Ariès and Illich describe.

Both authors trace the cultural perceptions of death in Europe from 300 AD to modern days. One of the dominant themes in their work is the shift in death as a public affair, open to everyone, to a private affair, closed to children and the larger community. Another trend apparent in their analyses is the increasing salience of social class in determining how people die. Ariès and Illich also reached similar conclusions about the state of death and dying in the late twentieth century and demonstrated that, like other aspects of life, death and dying had come to be controlled by physicians and hospitals and dominated by an increasingly consumeristic ethos.

Based on Ariès' and Illich's conclusions about the dominance of doctors in decisions and procedures about death, we finally discussed the financial and economic imperatives driving healthcare and medicine today and how those incentives influence individuals' access to and use of healthcare, and – ultimately – who receives medical resources and who does not. In examining these issues, we are left to consider the final question of who lives and who dies.

PART II

DEATH AND ITS AFTERMATH

Where Dying Takes Place

Introduction

Up until the nineteenth century most people died at home. The door to the bedchamber was open and the dying process was public for everyone to see. However, in the nineteenth century, cultural events and scientific discoveries changed how and where they died. Romanticism, a cultural mode that pervaded both Europe and the United States of America, placed a strong emphasis on emotions and feelings. It thus changed the dying process from being serene and resigned to one charged with highly emotional expressions of grief. Scientific discoveries of germs and a better understanding of infection led physicians to close the doors of the bedroom to the public for hygienic reasons and made dying a private affair (see chapter 2).

The medicalization of life in the twentieth century moved the locus of dying from the home to the hospital. Now the majority of Americans died as in-patients in hospitals (Flory et al., 2004). Hospitals are institutions which are geared to provide acute care for their patients but tend to lack individualized care. The social historian Illich (1976) was one of the first to criticize the American healthcare system and its relationship to death. Indeed, he argued that Americans were dying anonymously in the large bureaucratic and consumer-driven setting that is the modern-day hospital.

In the 1960s the nascent growth of hospice programs attempted to remedy these problems. Hospices are organizations that focus on end-of-life care and dignity with death. The majority aim to help people die at home or in a home-like environment. In the context of the medicalization of death, the hospice movement was an attempt to return individuality and dignity to the dying process that broke radically with the mainstream American medical establishment. But, in the 1980s, changes in Medicare, Medicaid, and private medical insurance established a reimbursement structure for hospice programs, which thus came to be seen as a cost-effective alternative to intensive care and were co-opted into mainstream American medicine.

In this chapter we begin by showing where Americans would prefer to die. We follow by providing data on where Americans actually die. We then look at the hospice movement and its effect on dying in America. We will trace the birth and development of the hospice as a concept and the variety of options for those in hospice programs.

Preferred places of death

The available studies on where people prefer to die bemoan the extremely limited availability of data available and are mostly concerned with terminally ill patients, usually those dying from cancer. Nonetheless, some research has asked people about their preferred places of death. A 1996 Gallup poll indicated that nine out of ten Americans would prefer to die at home (Gallup Organization, 1997). Americans live longer and frequently die of chronic diseases (see chapter 1), since most deaths take place among people between sixty-five and eighty-nine years of age (Fried et al., 1999). The last stages of life can bring about psychosocial problems for the patient and the family and may prove to be a financial drain for the patient, for the family, and for the healthcare system.

A qualitative study relied on a very small sample of twenty-five women suffering from stage IV breast cancer (Hays et al., 1999) but, despite its limitations, it is illustrative of the feelings and choices available to Americans facing death. The study showed that 64 percent of their subjects would prefer to die at home. This choice was conditional on the family's ability to provide palliative care and symptom control without becoming full-time caregivers. A minority of the women indicated a preference to die either in a hospital or in a chronic care facility. This group was concerned about the ability to receive proper symptom control at home and feared that if they died at home it would have lasting psychological effects on the family, and especially the children.

Fried and his colleagues (1999) suggest that studies seeking patients' preference for their site of terminal care may neglect an important issue: the type of disability preceding death and the care required for it. In this study, a number of the subjects were strongly concerned with greater likelihood of institutional settings to be able to provide more adequate symptom control: "When you're that bad, go [to the hospital]. This way you're right there. If you need them [the nurses], they're there" (1999: 111). The burden that a death at home would cause to the family was also an important factor. As one subject said, "They usually put you in a convalescent home if you are so sick that there is no help for you . . . you wouldn't want to be a burden on your family" (ibid.).

Another important factor in choosing a place to die is the relationship between patients and their primary care physician. Gramelspacher and his colleagues (1997) studied inner-city patients and internal medicine faculty members. They expected and indeed found differences between patients and physicians in reference to elements such as the use of intensive care, whether resuscitation should be considered, whether nutrition/hydration should be initiated, and similar elements. The disparities were due to various differences between patients and doctors, including education, age, social class and race (over 50 percent of the patients were African Americans, whereas the doctors were almost entirely white). What surprised the researchers was that "there was a substantial correlation between the preference of individual physicians and those of their patients" (1997: 349). This fact would make sense if patients were able to choose physicians with similar views to their own. But patients in the study had no choice, and so the researchers surmised that physicians, who control the clinical encounter, were the ones influencing the views of their patients.

Establishing the patient's choice of place where to die, albeit scarcely studied, is recognized as very important. The philosophy of end-of-life care aims at providing the patient with a dignified death, a "good death." The Institute of Medicine (2003) recognizes the wishes of the patient and the family concerning the place to die as a crucial component of a "good death" (see also Tang, 2003). This is what hospice cancer patients themselves consider to be a good death:

> Just go to sleep and not wake up anymore.
>
> Quietly, in my sleep. I do pray sometimes that I would go, when I'm in pain, you know, and then I think how awful it's going to be for my family, you know, 'cause we are very close.
>
> Without pain. Yes, what more can I say, I don't know. Like the guy opposite and went to sleep one night and forgot to wake up.
>
> (Payne et al., 1996: 1791–2)

While it is generally accepted that Americans overwhelmingly favor dying at home, there are other factors that supersede or modify this choice: freedom from pain, the quality of end-of-life healthcare, fear of being a burden to the family, availability of caregivers, and finances (Tang, 2003).

Actual places of death

Many Americans do not get to die where they wish. Consider the following:

> Mrs. Morgan . . . begged to stay home. He [the doctor] had her moved to the hospital 'for tests' . . . She dreaded the hospital, partly because

the misery her husband had endured there. She said she was prepared
to die at home with her souvenirs, her dog, her favorite phonograph
records, and the memories that lingered around favorite possessions.
Her tears were bitter when she was taken off in an ambulance against
her will. (Rossman, 1977: 27)

There are many factors that transcend individual wishes and decide
where Americans die; some are structural while others are related
to social class and race. A study that examined all death certificates
in America from 1980 to 1998 found some interesting demographic
changes (Flory et al., 2004). In 1980, 54 percent of Americans died in a
hospital; that figure had gone down to 41 percent in 1998. The most
dramatic change was in cancer patients, with a hospital rate decrease
from 70 percent in 1980 to 37 percent in 1998. This astounding drop
can be explained by the growing popularity of hospice programs in
America and the fact that in 1983 Medicare introduced hospice benefits with the Medicare Prospective Payment System (Weitzen, 2003).
Correspondingly, deaths at home increased from 17 to 23 percent and
those in chronic care facilities from 16 to 22 percent during the same
period. Another significant change was that in 1980 the numbers of
both whites and blacks dying in hospitals were about equal. While
the rate for both had gone down by 1998, there was a marked difference between the races – 40 percent for whites and 48 percent for
blacks – and even more for women – 30 percent for white women and
50 percent for black women (see Flory et al., 2004: 198, exhibit 4). The
authors speculate on the reasons for the growing racial gap and find
mixed evidence, some of it pointing to different level of social class.
Black patients seem to have less support from potential family caregivers but also less access to hospice programs and home care services.

Two other studies used the National Mortality Followback Survey
that examined the death certificates of a nationally representative
sample of 22,658 people for the year 1993. The first one, by Iwashyna
and Chang (2002), adds to the study of Flory and his colleagues by
including Mexican Americans. The study found that 43 percent
of white patients, 50 percent of black patients, and 56 percent of
Mexican Americans died in a hospital, although it provided no
rationale for these differences. The second study, by Weitzen and his
colleagues (2003), gives some additional information. Men are more
likely to die in a hospital than women (64 percent versus 52 percent).
Uninsured patients die in hospitals in greater numbers than Medicare
recipients (70 percent to 55 percent). Black patients die more often
in a hospital than at home or in a chronic care facility. One explanation is that terminal black patients are more likely to seek aggressive
medical care, but another is that "poverty and social deprivation may
make the hospital the preferred setting in which to die and that being

black in the United States is a surrogate measure for relative deprivation" (2003: 332).

Geographical location affects one's chances to die in a hospital. Westerners are more likely to die at home than those in other parts of the country, on account of the lower availability of acute care hospital beds (Tolle et al., 1999). Another factor dealing with availability affects cancer patients. If hospice programs are available in the region, patients are more likely to die at home (ibid.). A study of 28,828 cancer sufferers found that those being treated in a hospice were 2.8 times more likely to die at home than non-hospice patients (Moinpour et al., 1989). Another study, looking at older persons with dementia, found that, for that specific cohort, states with fewer chronic care facility beds have a larger number of hospital deaths. It summarized nicely the distribution of death in America: "the majority of dementia-related deaths in the United States occurred in nursing homes (66.9 percent). In contrast, most older persons with cancer died at home (37.8 percent) or in hospitals (35.4 percent). The hospital was the most common site of death for all other conditions (52.2 percent)" (Mitchell et al., 2005: 299).

It is clear that, while individual preferences concerning where to die are important, there are other factors beyond the patient's control that override their wishes. The availability of healthcare services, the presence of caregivers, the plethora of factors associated with social class – education, finances, understanding of options – and the type of illness one contracts all help determine where one dies, despite one's actual desires.

The hospice movement

In the rest of this chapter we will discuss the hospice movement and its profound repercussion on where and how people die in America. We follow the hospice from its inception in ancient times to its waning in the sixteenth century and its resurgence in the nineteenth century, and we discuss the modern-day hospice, which began in the British Isles in the middle of the twentieth century. We then turn to the United States, where the first hospice program, the Connecticut Hospice, did not came into being until 1974, only to see the number of hospices mushroom, to 4,500 in 2006 (NHPCO, 2007).

The hospice through history

The Latin word *hospes*, meaning both host and guest, is the root of a variety of names referring to many institutions based on the notion of hospitality (Stoddard, 1978) – hotel, hostel, hospice, and hospital – all of which provide shelter for various kinds of needy individuals. Historically the terms were often used interchangeably (Siebold, 1992).

Ancient civilizations, such as those of Egypt, Greece, Rome and the Islamic world, made use of their churches and temples to care for pilgrims and the sick. In ancient Rome, as far back as 1,500 years ago, there were hospitals that were primarily concerned with curing their wounded soldiers. Yet a Roman matron, Fabiola, became instrumental in founding a different type of place of refuge, a hospice, in Ostia, near Rome, in AD 475 (Siebold, 1992). The hospice was a place of rest for travelers, pilgrims, and the destitute and the sick (Rosen, 1963). Thus, from the Roman days, we can see the main difference between a hospital, a place of *cure*, and a hospice, a place of *care*.

Both hospitals and hospices found great impetus to their development with the advent of Christianity. Christian theology upheld care for the sick and the dying as a sacred duty. The aim was to care for the bodies to save the souls, so not only the sick but also the poor, the downtrodden, and anyone in search of refuge was welcomed in Christian hospitals and hospices. As early as AD 325 the Council of Nicaea directed bishops to establish hospitals in every city with a cathedral. Shortly afterwards, in AD 398, another church council, that of Carthage, instructed bishops to maintain hospices near churches. The basic theme of caring for the body to save the soul was evident in the staffing of religious hospitals, which were usually administered by a priest, aided by nuns, with lay people to do housekeeping chores, and a doctor, who lived on the premises. Also, monks provided shelter in their monasteries for travelers and the poor. Especially famous was the monastery in the Swiss Alps (AD 962) run by Augustinian monks that used St Bernard dogs to rescue the travelers stranded in the mountain passes.

The Crusades, for a few centuries from the eleventh century, led to a tremendous growth in hospices. Both travelers and the crusaders on their way back from fighting the infidels could rest in the numerous hospices that had been established along the way. McNulty and Holderby (1983) report that by the thirteenth century there were 750 hospices in England, thirty in Florence and forty in Paris; despite their simplicity, even austerity, the hospices were oases of rest.

The sixteenth and seventeenth centuries saw a decline in hospices as the Catholic Church took a stance against them, feeling that too much time was spent physically caring for patients by clergymen and that this detracted from the Church's spiritual goals; very few new hospices were built while many were shut down. The governments in England and other European countries built almshouses and workhouses for the poor, the sick, and the dying, but these institutions were primitive and overcrowded. The Catholic Church's interest in maintaining hospices continued to decline until, in the eighteenth century, the Reformation caused a change, removing control of healthcare from the monasteries and allowing the secular influence of scientists to take over (Siebold, 1992).

Medicine and the hospice in the nineteenth century

The nineteenth century saw a major shift in the social structure of Western societies with the coming of the Industrial Revolution. This phenomenon caused the movement of people away from the country-side and into the cities, where they hoped to find work in the newly developed factories. Thus, cities grew at a very fast pace and their streets became filled with a great number of strangers, many of them poor and sick, who had no place to turn to. These conditions made the healthcare of the poor and the sick a pressing issue and, beginning in England, infirmaries (primitive hospitals) for the poor were estab-lished (Abel-Smith, 1964).

Changes

Cities

Doctors were leaving behind the days in which their principal cure was that of leaching and purging the patients and were availing themselves of new scientific discoveries. New technological equip-ment, such as X-ray machines and various medical scopes for ears and eyes, the reduction of infection through asepsis, the identification of bacteria, and the development of vaccination enhanced the scientific control over healthcare matters (Ackerkecht, 1955). Medical schools in Europe increasingly associated themselves with hospitals, which became centers of learning and research for students and doctors. The tremendous improvement in hospitals brought about a significant change. Traditionally, the middle and upper classes had been cared for in their homes by physicians. Now they increasingly sought cure in hospitals, to the point that hospital authorities were left in a quan-dary as to whether to call their clients "paupers," as was traditionally the case, or refer to them as "patients" (Abel-Smith, 1964).

The high quality of hospitals and the rising expectations of patients gradually increased the emphasis of the hospital from care to cure. Hospitals began specializing in acute illness, refusing admission to chronic or hopeless patients. The acutely ill found a new breath of hope – but what of the old, the chronically ill, and the hopeless cases? The old were sent to newly developed nursing homes and convales-cent centers, and the chronically ill were placed in special homes. These institutions, however, held little resemblance to the new hos-pitals. The quality of care in these places was very uneven and went largely unchecked (Abel-Smith, 1964).

In ancient days the hospice had provided care for both the body and the soul of the patient. In the aseptic, scientific setting of the

modern-day hospital the patient lost his or her wholeness as an individual and came to seen as a physical specimen; few, if any, cared for
his or her soul. The modern-day hospice aimed at restoring the wholeness of the person, and thus it became its hallmark to care for every
aspect of a patient. It is with this idea in mind that in the middle of
the nineteenth century Mary Aickenhead, the founder of the Irish
Sisters of Charity, opened a hospice for the dying in Dublin.

While America followed the European pattern of treatment of the
sick and the poor, and also in the increasing power of doctors, the
changes occurred fifty years later (Starr, 1982). A small number of hospices were opened in the US in the 1890s, but these institutions differed
from the hospices that came into being in the second part of the twentieth century in the following ways. Hospices today involve the family
in the process, while in the early centers it was felt that the family had
suffered enough and now the hospice staff should relieve them of the
duty of caring for the patient. Today's hospices, besides cancer patients,
admit those diagnosed with a variety of illnesses, such as heart disease,
dementia, and strokes; in fact non-cancer diagnoses account for 53.6
percent of all admissions, versus 46.4 percent for cancer patients
(NHPCO, 2007). Early American hospices took in only cancer patients.
Today's hospices rely on Medicare and Medicaid programs for financial
reimbursement, while early American hospices were free.

The Dominican Sisters of Hawthorne (led by the daughter of the
famous American novelist Nathaniel Hawthorne) began providing
hospice home care in the 1890s and then founded St Rose's Hospice
in Manhattan, followed by six more hospices in other American
cities. Another famous early hospice, founded in 1899 by Catherine
McPardan, was Calvary Hospital in New York. Calvary combined traditional hospital treatment with hospice care and for a long time was
staffed by Catholic nuns (Siebold, 1992).

The conditions that led to the twentieth-century hospice

1960s-1970s
Changes

In the 1960s the modern hospice movement took off, primarily under
the guidance and leadership of Cicely Saunders. Although America
was already following the example of Europe, social conditions
helped promote the hospice movement and aided its development in
the 1970s. During this period, various social movements such as feminism, gay rights, and civil rights challenged the established order.
Even the powerful medical establishment and the healthcare system
came under attack. A heightened concern with quality of life, the
exorbitant cost of healthcare, and the belief that individual life had
come under too much control from the medical establishment all led
to challenges to the system. Both birthing and dying in the twentieth

century had come under medical aegis; Americans were being born and were dying in hospitals. A movement that valued the expertise of midwives and placed an emphasis on home delivery and in alternative birthing clinics sprang up (Robinson and Fontana, 1989). At the other end of the life course, the hospice movement saw the light as people recognized that hospitals and chronic care facilities did not care adequately for the dying.

A number of scholars wrote extensively about the problems encountered by dying patients, especially poor ones, in American hospitals. They argued that the medical emphasis on curing acute illness implied to doctors and hospitals that death itself was a failure of the physician and the hospital. This view of death as medical failure encouraged the medical establishment to deny the fact of death and caused doctors and other medical staff to distance themselves from their dying patients (Glaser and Strauss, 1965). Additionally, the financial imperatives and capitalist model of healthcare and of the American hospital led to differential treatment for patients of different social status and favored white, wealthy patients (Fox, 1979). The hospital environment, with its impersonal and bureaucratic work pattern, also tended to isolate dying patients and routinize the dying process in dehumanizing ways (ibid.; Sudnow, 1967). For example, the following was observed by Strauss and Glaser during their research in a hospital:

> The most vital force shaping the end of Mrs. Abel's dying trajectory was the growing *intolerance* of the staff to her complaints of pain, her ritualistic demands during baths, meals, pain medication, and so forth, and her abiding need for companionship and attention which were further stimulated by the staff's avoidance of her. (1970a, p.165)

The barrage of criticism of the mechanics of death in hospitals led to a growing concern by academicians and proponents of the hospice movement with "quality of life" and "death with dignity." The United States Senate heard testimony on "death with dignity" in August 1972 (Rinaldi and Kearl, 1990). In 1974, the Hospital National Advisory Council was formed, comprised of a large number of academicians, physicians, and community leaders, with Elisabeth Kübler-Ross as its first chair (Siebold, 1992).

In their classic study, Glaser and Strauss (1965) analyzed individuals' awareness of dying and the different interactions that result between staff and patient in different situations. The authors consider four types of awareness: closed, suspicion, mutual pretense, and open. *Closed awareness* occurs when the staff knows that the patient is dying but the patient does not know it; this leads staff to control information about the patient's condition closely so as not accidentally to let the patient know about their impending death. *Suspicion awareness* is when the staff knows about the impending death and the patient suspects that he or she is dying; this type leads to evasive tactics by the staff and inquisitive ones by the patient, who is trying to find out information about his or her fate. The third type suggests *mutual pretense*, whereby the dying person and the medical staff know that death is forthcoming but do not discuss it and continue acting as if nothing has happened or is about to happen. Finally, *open awareness* is when both staff and the patient know that death is imminent and acknowledge the situation.

The literature on this topic is filled with reports of physicians' hesitancy to inform terminally ill patients about their situation (see chapter 8 for a detailed discussion of this point). Doctors traditionally have been expected to balance positive news with bad news (Leydon, 2008). For example (Rodriquez et al., 2008, quoted in Leydon, 2008: 1085): "I think the reality is we can rarely cure this type of problem [*bad*]. What we can do . . . is . . . um, increase . . . quality of life [*relative good*]." At times, this hesitancy spills over into outright lying to the patient and the family. In one example, a widow explained how she was kept in the dark about her husband's impending death from cancer of the tongue (Seale, 1991, quoted in Maynard, 2003: 46):

> I knew he was losing weight rapidly so I felt there was something the matter. I was not told anything. *The doctor said it was trapped wind and I believed him.* I wish someone had told me what was wrong. No-one gave me any help. They seemed to skip over things and never told anything.

Examples such as these, coupled with the growing understanding of the problems with death in hospitals and physicians' avoidance of death, helped fuel the hospice movement in America. It was becoming clear that a different, more humane model was necessary, one that puts patients and families at the center and prioritizes death with dignity and comfort. Before looking at the modern hospice we briefly outline the hospice philosophy and its methods of care.

The hospice philosophy

As we have seen, the modern hospice came into being as a reaction to the shortcomings of acute care hospitals in dealing with dying patients. The hospice philosophy is to provide physical, spiritual, and emotional care for the dying patient, and the goal of the program is to allow the patient to live as meaningfully as possible the last period of her or his life. In this context, the hospice staff functions as an interdisciplinary team made up of physicians, nurses, social workers, and clergy, who all work together, providing a supportive environment for the patient and the family.

A notable difference between British and American hospices is the role of volunteers. In the United Kingdom hospice volunteers are given important work roles while in America they tend to be placed in subordinate positions and allowed little authority. To wit, "in England, having volunteers provide direct services is an accepted practice. In America, volunteers are more likely to stuff envelopes or conduct bake sales; they are rarely allowed to provide direct services" (Osterweiss and Champagne, 1979, quoted in Siebold, 1992: 71). In 2006 there were 400,000 hospice volunteers in the United States, and only 0.2 percent of them were in direct patient care (NHPCO, 2007).

American hospice volunteers do have occasion to work with dying patients, although they do not provide actual medical care. They must undergo training prior to and supervision during their interactions with patients. In some cases, volunteers may do seemingly simple tasks such as sitting with or reading to patients or interacting with their family members. For many people who volunteer to do this kind of work it is their first encounter with the realities of death, and they themselves may need emotional or spiritual support. Still, many find it very rewarding to assist a stranger on their journey and find that the experience changes their own views of life and death.

One of the main concerns of the staff is to find a balance between pain-killing medications and maintaining the patient's consciousness. Severe pain is not always present in terminal cases; however, there tends to be some kind of physical discomfort, such as nausea, vomiting, muscle spasms, headaches, and difficulties with bladder and bowel movements (Stoddard, 1978). In the hospice, whenever possible, the staff attempts to control pain before it mounts in the hopes of bringing it under control while also striving to maintain the lucidity of the patient.

Family members are an important part of the hospice model and are included in the caring process, since they are also affected by the dying of their loved one. Death is viewed as an experience for the patient and the family, rather than a medical condition, and the hospice staff tries to humanize the experience, for example by answering the multitude of unanswered questions that the family has or simply by listening to them. After the death, bereavement therapy for the family is often part of the care provided.

In hospices, patients are not passive vessels as they are in hospitals but are encouraged to be aware of and take part in decisions about their own treatment, such as deciding which medical procedures will be necessary or keeping their own pain chart. The environment is home-like: patients wear their own clothing rather than hospital gowns and are surrounded by familiar objects and people. Guest

rooms are often available right next to the patient's room to allow a
family member to spend nights within reach.

Recently, beginning at Dartmouth Medical School, a new movement called "slow medicine" has emerged (Gross, 2008). Physicians
are encouraged to focus more on comforting, palliative medicine
than on aggressive procedures such as biopsies, surgery, or medications. This of course reduces the cost of the medical care provided
to the patients. At times, it also may avoid a quicker demise brought
about by too many invasive medical measures, also called "death by
intensive care" (ibid.: 1). Modern-day hospices emerged with these
priorities at their center.

The twentieth-century hospice

In the United Kingdom the Irish Sisters of Charity opened St Joseph's
Hospice in London in the 1950s (Lamerton, 1975). At St Joseph's worked
one of the most prominent figures in the hospice movement, Dr
Cicely Saunders, a doctor trained also as a nurse and a social worker.
Years later Saunders left St Joseph's to open in 1967 St Christopher's
Hospice, also in London.

St Christopher's became a model for those interested in hospices
and many American notables visited it. It incorporated many notions
of the ancient hospice, such as caring for the whole person. However,
there are differences between the old and the new hospices. In the old
days, anyone in need of care – the sick, the weary, and the destitute
– could find asylum in hospices. Today, the hospice restricts entry to
those suffering from a terminal illness and who are dying. In the 1970s
most of the patients admitted were diagnosed with cancer. Today, the
majority of patients have non-cancer diagnoses, primarily chronic
conditions. Those in need of palliative (maintenance) rather than
intensive care are admitted.

Seven years after the inception of St Christopher's, in 1974, the
first American hospice, Hospice, Inc., was founded by the Yale Study
Group in Branford, Connecticut, to serve the Greater New Haven
region, a community of about twenty towns with a population
of about 500,000 (Craven and Wald, 1975). It followed closely the
British model as many of its leaders had gone to London to observe St
Christopher's. Indeed, its first medical director was Sylvia Lack, who
had been a physician at St Christopher's, alongside Cicely Saunders
(Kastenbaum, 1997).

The architect commissioned to build the hospice, Lo-Yi-Chan, had
never designed a hospital, and was thus able to approach the project
without bias. Lo-Yi-Chan's problem, as that of other hospice designers,
was to avoid creating a building that would be labeled "the house of

death." To produce a setting for the dying that is aimed at fostering living is a hard task. Lo-Yi-Chan said: "Buildings speak to people on many levels . . . They convey efficiency, coldness or impersonality. Or they convey the opposite – warmth, relaxation and attention to individuals" (Kohn, 1976: 56). The building was designed to communicate openness and warmth by including large glass windows, skylights, brick fireplaces, live plants, and even a children's sandbox. There are many common rooms to avoid isolation and increase contact among people, and a lounge room includes a bar for the patients, a piano, and a library.[1]

Given the high cost and the limited financial support of hospices (remember that the United Kingdom has a national healthcare program and the United States does not) other types of hospice have been made available. There are <u>six</u> different types, the first being the one we have discussed, the hospice as a freestanding facility built especially for that purpose (although in Great Britain homes have been refurbished and used as hospices) (Lamerton, 1975).

The second alternative is the home healthcare hospice program. Often, this second type is integrated with the first one; St Christopher's and Hospice, Inc., offer both facilities. Terminal patients who need palliative care and who have help are kept in their homes under the auspices of the hospice program. The immediate advantage of staying home is a reduction in medical expenses. The patient receives expert care and support by the hospice personnel, varying from doctors to nurses to clergy, while remaining in a familiar setting among relatives and friends.

Caring for a terminally ill patient at home may become very strenuous for family members. During these times the patient may be moved to the hospice building for a while, a week or so, just enough time to provide respite for the caregivers and allow them to recharge their emotional batteries.

Another important option for a combination of the purpose-built and the home types of hospice is that they provide the patient with an option of where to die. Some patients may prefer to go home while others may wish to die in the hospice to spare further anguish to their families. In 2006, only 8.8 percent of hospice patients died in a hospital, with 17.0 percent dying in a hospice facility and a combined 74.1 percent in a place they called "home" (private residence 47.1 percent, nursing home 22.5 percent, and 4.6 percent residential facility) (NHPCO, 2007).

The first hospice home care program in America was the Hospice of Marin, now called Hospice by the Bay, just north of San Francisco. It was founded by the psychiatrist William Lamers, who apparently was convinced to do so by Elisabeth Kübler-Ross (Siebold, 1992). Initially it relied entirely on volunteers to provide in-home support care. Lamers abandoned plans to build a freestanding hospice for financial reasons and instead incorporated it as a non-profit organization and sought funding as a home healthcare agency (Stoddard, 1978).

The Hospice of Marin was credited as the third hospice program in America. St Luke's Hospice was the second. St Luke's Hospital in New York is a cure-oriented cancer-treatment facility. In the early 1970s, under the guidance of the hospital senior chaplain, the Reverend Carlton Sweetser, a hospice board was formed and a staff was assembled. The hospital administrators had no intention of securing or building a separate facility for the hospice so the team went to the patients wherever their beds were within the hospital. Those designated as hospice patients were given special privileges, such as longer visiting hours, but they remained among the rest of the patients. The nature of this hospice program led to its name: the scattered-bed approach (Siebold, 1992). St Luke's hospice program closed its doors in 1991 due to financial difficulties.

The fourth type of hospice actually began in Canada at the Royal Victoria Hospital in Montreal in 1975 and was later copied by a number of United States hospice groups. The administrators simply designated a wing of the hospital as the palliative care unit, which was served by a specially trained staff.

Hospices of the third and fourth types are not quite as successful as the first two. The patients are still a part of the acute care hospital and exposed to the problems of routinization and depersonalization that led the hospice movement to seek an alternative. It has been reported that it is a practice in some hospitals to recall staff from the palliative care unit when other wards need more staff (Lamerton, 1975).

The fifth type of hospice is community-based. It relies on volunteers that visit patients and families in their homes and discuss with them the dying process and help them cope with their grief. Community-based hospices tend to be small, run by non-profit organizations, and are often beset by financial problems.

The last type of hospice is a rural hospice program. This program tends to be small, with few staff members and patients, yet usually covers a large geographical area. It tends to lack resources and cannot easily find professionals based in the area. Rural hospices generally rely almost entirely on volunteers.

While we have provided a typology of hospices, it is also noteworthy that some deviate from these models. Hybrid hospices combine elements from two or more of the above types. Although hospices and hospice services are more common in the US than before, patients usually do not have a choice among the various models but are typically geographically limited to those available in their vicinity.

Next, let us see more recent changes in the American hospice programs.

Hospices today

A growing interest in the hospice program began in America in the 1980s. Under President Ronald Reagan the Health Care Finance Administration started a demonstration project to observe the functioning of the hospice program. The hospice was expected to provide better healthcare but, in keeping with Reagan's conservative financial policies, it was also expected to cut costs (Kastenbaum, 1997). The project found that the hospice program did not reduce healthcare costs because what money it saved on medications was spent on increasing the caregiver-to-patient ratio. However, the pilot program was viewed favorably and the notion that hospices were cheaper, whether warranted or not, persisted. In 1982, the hospice program was incorporated in the Medicare reimbursement system.[2]

Not everyone involved in hospices was anxious for hospice organizations to become a part of the American healthcare system. The hospice had begun as a reaction to the flaws of the impersonal, costly, and highly bureaucratic health system, and some saw that becoming incorporated into the system negated the program's basic values and ideas and was a selling-out to the medical industrial complex. Nevertheless the hospice did join mainstream American medicine, and initially the favored model was that of a separate building. Yet, given building costs, the hospital model became the most popular form of hospice, despite the reluctance of those who felt it would compromise its goals to the exigencies of the bureaucratic and cost-conscious medical system.

After becoming part of the Medicare program, hospices shifted toward the home healthcare model. Yet, despite the impetus there were some obstacles to its expansion (Siebold, 1992). The cost of a new hospice program was an obstacle to its development, but so was also the initial reluctance of physicians to embrace the team concept, the major role of nurses in the system, and the new ideas. Eventually physicians came to see the worth of the hospice program and their opposition to it waned. Also, some scholars scoffed at the popularity of the hospice concept, with its emphasis on dying rather than saving lives. For example, Lyn Lofland (1978) sarcastically referred to the hospice program as the happy death movement.

In the 1980s and 1990s an increasing number of US states approved hospice licensing, more hospice organizations were formed, and numerous conferences on hospices took place. However, as AIDS became a public health problem in America, hospices were faced with a new group of patients, whose stigma could slow down and damage their positive public image. Initially some hospices denied access to AIDS patients on the grounds that they required aggressive medications rather than mere palliative maintenance. Eventually, but slowly, AIDS sufferers were incorporated into hospices (Siebold, 1992).

The hospice program had begun and continued primarily as a not-for-profit enterprise but, given its growth, in the mid-1980s a number of large corporations began for-profit franchises on a national scale, emphasizing the home healthcare concept and leasing room from hospitals to create hospice wings. These hospices charged for their services (Siebold, 1992). However, the primary source of payment for hospices today is Medicare: 83.7 percent of patients are covered by the Medicare Hospice Benefit versus other sources (NHPCO, 2007).

The hospice program has kept growing, benefiting about 1,300,000 patients in 2006, a 162 percent increase in ten years (NHPCO, 2007). It serves primarily the elders, 81.7 percent of patients (four out of five) in 2006 being over the age of sixty-five (ibid.). Yet it remains by and large a white middle-class phenomenon; in 2006 hospice patients were 80.9 percent white. While the figure was down from 82.2 percent in 2005, the integration of minorities is slow. Hospice conferences are attended primarily by white women (Neubauer and Hamilton, 1990) and the ethos of hospice is generated by the growing awareness and attention of the middle class to issues such as death with dignity, euthanasia, and quality of terminal care. African-American patients, for instance, tend to die in acute care hospitals more often, since poor people with little education or financial support end up in public hospitals and because they seem to wish to forestall death at any cost, regardless of circumstances (ibid.).

Other recent evidence shows that hospice care is not equally distributed throughout society. In the context of the American capitalist economy we also have evidence of how the medicalization of death and dying affects its distribution. A 2003 study indicated that, between 1988 and 1999, cancer patients who were enrolled in Medicare-managed care plans were more likely to receive hospice care (32.4 percent) than patients who were enrolled in Medicare's fee-for-service insurance (19.8 percent) (McCarthy et al., 2003).

It is also worth noting how family members interpret and evaluate the actions of doctors and nurses in caring for dying patients. In a large study of the quality of end-of-life care in institutional settings, researchers surveyed family members of 1,578 decedents about the patient's experience at the last place of care at which the patient spent more than forty-eight hours. They were interested in determining the extent to which healthcare workers "(1) provided the desired physical comfort and emotional support to the dying person,

(2) supported shared decision making, (3) treated the dying person with respect, (4) attended to the emotional needs of the family, and (5) provided coordinated care," and whether there were differences across institutional settings (e.g., hospitals, nursing homes, home) (Teno et al., 2004: 88). The study found significant shortcomings in end-of-life care. For example, according to surviving family members, 25 percent of dying patients did not get enough pain medication, and sometimes received none at all. One in three family members reported that hospital and nursing home staff didn't offer enough emotional support and 25 percent felt the doctor's communication was poor. Only 15 percent of respondents stated that they felt that their institutional healthcare providers had enough knowledge of the patient to provide the best care possible. Overall the study that found family members whose loved one died at home with hospice services were more likely to report that the death was a favorable experience than those who died in other settings.

The hospice and the individual

After examining the impact of the hospice on the American health-care system we will briefly examine its influence at the micro-level. At the individual level the hospice program brought profound changes. The ancient hospice, run in Europe by the clergy, had employed a monastic approach. It cared for the individual's physical well-being, but its principal aim was to save the soul of the patient. It, therefore, dealt with the whole person. The advent of the modern-day hospital and the increasingly scientific outlook and nature of medicine removed concerns with the soul of the patients, focusing entirely on their physical condition.

Individuals went from dying in their homes, in a familiar environment, surrounded by their family and friends and familiar items such as their own clothing, to dying in a foreign environment – the hospital. In the modern-day hospital Americans are cared for by strangers in white robes, at times wearing masks, in a sterile, sanitized environment that is not consumer-friendly. Familiar items of clothing are considered "unclean" and are replaced by ill-fitting robes that barely cover the body. Family and friends can only visit at given hours and children not at all. To use the metaphor of the theatre, the dying patient who once was the leading actor in the drama of her or his death is now relegated to the role of supporting cast, while the physician controls the situation and acts as the protagonist.

The hospice aims at returning the soul to the patient; it looks beyond the merely physical attributes at the whole person. The setting returns to the familiar one of the home or one that is "home-like." Visitors come and go at will, and can stay overnight if they so wish. There are no "unclean" items. The patient can provide input on her or his treatment and medications. The dying patient is once again center stage and in control of her or his death.

 Finally, it is worth noting that thousands of patients who enter hospices do not die. To be admitted to a hospice a patient must have less than six months to live, according to their physician's prognosis, and two-thirds of them die within thirty days, yet it is estimated that between 5,000 and 20,000 hospice patients live on satisfactorily for a while (Greve, 2006). A recent famous case is that of the American Pulitzer-prize winning humor columnist Art Buchwald, who checked himself into a hospice after refusing to continue dialysis for his failing kidneys. Buchwald continued to live and spent a summer on Martha's Vineyard in order to write a book about his near-death experience. He was witty to the end: "Buchwald likens surviving hospice to booking a seat on a plane, having the flight canceled and ending up on a standby indefinitely" (ibid.: 24A). Buchwald died in Washington, DC, at his son's house. The next day the *New York Times* (2006) presented an obituary video in which he told the audience: "Hi, I'm Art Buchwald and I just died."

Conclusion

In this chapter we have examined Americans' preferences about the location of their death. Overwhelmingly people report that they would like to die at home. We then presented evidence that most often people do not die in their preferred locations. There are many variables that influence the place of death and unfortunately, even in the face of death, ethnicity, race, and affluence make a big difference. Mexican-American and African-American terminal patients have far less chance of having their wishes met than their white, middle-class counterparts.

The rest of the chapter examined the importance and the various types of hospice programs and the difference they have made on quality and place of death for Americans. The ancient hospice was open to all – poor, destitute, sick, and elderly. Yet its modern counterpart is largely a white, middle-class phenomenon. Again, race, education, and affluence weigh very heavily on where people die.

In conclusion, we briefly examined the changes on the individual person brought about by the hospice program. The hospice restores a sense of wholeness to the patient, allowing death to take place, if not actually always at home, at least in a home-like setting.

CHAPTER

Dying

04

Introduction

A<small>CCORDING</small> to the US Census we are growing older as a nation, not only as individuals; in 2002 life expectancy at birth was 77.3 years for all Americans, up from 75.4 in 1990, 70.8 in 1970, and 68.2 in 1950 (NCHS, 2002). Additionally, the median age in the United States was 36.2, meaning that half of the population was below and half of the population above this age, which is an increase of 1.4 years from 1990. As we grow older we seem to be more willing to face the long-avoided issue of death. Over two-thirds of married people (69 percent) have discussed end-of-life care with their spouse and three in ten people (29 percent) have a living will, which explains their instructions for determining their final medical treatment. Over 70 percent of Americans feel that, under certain circumstances, some patients should be allowed to die (all figures are derived from the Pew Research Center, 2006). Table 4.1 shows some of the widespread concern and increasing support for clarity in people's end-of-life decisions (results are based on a nationwide sample of 1,500 adults aged over eighteen).

Some of the figures in table 4.1 show a degree of public confidence in physicians and end-of-life issues, yet, ironically, physicians' developing ability to control and at times eliminate some terminal illnesses has resulted in an increased fear of death in contemporary society (Illich, 1976; Spiro et al., 1996). Despite this newly found openness toward dying, we still fear death. We speak of prolonging life, but we are prolonging the dying process. This may seem like a subtle difference, but the important point is that the emphasis is on life, not death (Henig, 2005). We no longer believe that we have stoically to accept a fate we cannot change; instead we always hold out the hope that a cure is at hand or just around the corner. The door of life is cracked open, and we are terrified that it will shut on us. We use all our means to cure illnesses and postpone death, and those of us with more resources tend to have a better chance to do so.

Table 4.1 American public support for the right to die (percentages in agreement)		
	1990	2005
Support right to die	79	84
Have a living will	12	29
Have discussed end-of-life treatment with spouse	30	37
Always try to save a patient's life	–	70
A terminal patient (in pain) has the right to suicide	–	60
Doctors should attend to terminal patients' wishes	20	30

Source: Derived from Pew Research Center (2006).

The social stratification of death

Just like all of our other social institutions, death and dying are structured by social inequality. Not only do wealthier people live longer and healthier lives than people with fewer resources and opportunities, medical professionals also make judgments about whose lives are most worth saving. For scholars, the ability of medicine to forestall or save us from death has accentuated the fact that we are not all equal in the face of death. In ancient times, doctors tampered with the dying process only in exceptional circumstances. The following account is from a doctor who was attending to an ill pharaoh in ancient Egypt:

> Great Pharaoh lay beneath a golden canopy; . . . his swollen body was naked, stripped of all symbols of sovereignty. He was unconscious, his aged head hung sideways, and he breathed stertorously, saliva running from the corner of his mouth . . . since throughout the ages the skull of the Pharaoh has been opened as a last resort . . . it must be opened now, and we set about our task. (Waltari, 1949: 53–4)

This illustrates the fact that, even among bygone civilizations, doctors engaged in heroic measures when faced with the death of a high-status person. Remains of pharaohs' mummies indicate that doctors practiced trepaning (perforating the skull) as a last resort. Doctors at that time believed that evil spirits were responsible for the Pharaoh's illness and bored a hole in his skull to release them.

In a classic study of the social and organizational aspects of death in America, Sudnow (1967) conducted an ethnography of two different hospitals. He found that physicians and other medical personnel pass judgment on patients arriving in their emergency rooms and rely on their own societal upbringing and expectations as they determine whether or not to resuscitate patients and what kind of treatments to offer. He found that both age and physical grooming elicited different responses from medical workers; the lives of children and well-dressed persons were judged to be worth more than the lives of old people, winos, and unseemly looking characters.

On a related note, Strauss and Glaser identified three elements that are important factors in determining who shall live: "(1) the likeli- hood that, if saved, the patient will be able to live a normal life . . .; (2) if the case is medically interesting; and (3) the patient is of such high social value that his loss must be averted at all cost" (1970b, p. 135). An example of the interplay between potential recovery, medical challenges, and social status for determining a patient's worth was in 1968, when Robert Kennedy was shot. Doctors feverishly worked on him for over eight hours, even though his EEG (electroencephalogram, which is a test that records the level of electrical activity in the brain) indicated no activity.

Social stratification also pertains to the distribution of human organs for transplants. The Uniform Anatomical Gift Act (UAGA) and the National Organ Transplant Act (NOTA) were designed to ensure equity in access to organs. Indeed, the NOTA specifically prohibits assigning monetary value to organs so that they cannot be commer- cialized and, in theory at least, patients have equal access to both organs and organ transplants (Simmerling, 2007). Furthermore, the NOTA prohibits discrimination based on the socioeconomic status of the transplant candidate. Nonetheless, larger patterns of social ine- quality still impact the availability and distribution of organs, even if only indirectly. For example, many people felt that the famous base- ball player Mickey Mantle, one of the greatest Yankees of all times, was favored because of his superstar status when he received a new liver in 1995. At the time Mantle was aged sixty-three and had to wait only one day, while in that year the average wait time for a new liver was three to four months (Munson, 2002).

The problematic nature of death

It was not too long ago that the determination of death was an unproblematic event. If the individual experienced irreversible ces- sation of circulatory and respiratory functions, he or she would be pronounced dead (Capron, 2001). Visual observations of respiration along with feeling for the pulse were common measures used to verify the presence of death. Death was a clearly definable event and little could be done to forestall it.

Beginning in the middle of the twentieth century increasingly more sophisticated techniques and equipment to provide life support were developed, such as the use of mechanical ventilators to keep the patient breathing (Wijdicks, 2001). As a consequence vital functions could be maintained after the cessation of brain activity, leading to the inclusion of the status of the brain as a part of the diagnosis of death. Mollaret and Goulon (1959) in France were the first to introduce the term "irreversible coma." In 1968, in the United States, the concept of "brain death" was described by an ad hoc committee of Harvard Medical School. In order to be clear and specific, the committee did not provide a blanket definition but limited itself to comatose patients who show no central nervous system activity (Ad Hoc Committee, 1968).

It was considered that the definition was needed because of two elements: (1) to spare any burden to those involved with a comatose patient; and (2) to clarify the controversy surrounding the timing of organ removal and transplant. The committee's definition was based on four points: (1) total unreceptivity and unresponsiveness to stimuli; (2) complete absence of movement and breathing; (3) absence of any reflexes of the central nervous system; and (4) whenever feasible, the use of an electroencephalogram (EEG) to monitor the neocortical responses of the brain (in the form of waves). If the EEG monitor displays a flat line it indicates that the neocortex has ceased to function. Thus, the committee suggested brain death as a confirmatory check. Tests were to be repeated after an interval of twenty-four hours to account for cases of hypothermia and/or to allow the brain to metabolize certain drugs.

The Harvard definition was widely accepted in the United States, though further developments have modified it to some degree. In the United Kingdom, the Conference of the Medical Royal Colleges (1976) included brain-stem functions in the definition of brain death, while, according to the Quality Standards Subcommittee of the American Academy of Neurology, "brain death is defined as the irreversible loss of function of the brain, including the brainstem . . . [there is] . . . need for standardization of the neurological examination criteria for the diagnosis of brain death" (1995: 1012). Today, in America, all fifty states and the District of Columbia accept brain death as the legal definition of death (Angell, 1994: 1524).

Despite the numerous attempts to define it clearly, several controversies surround brain death. Pinpointing death in an organ, the brain, in a way removes it from the "death of the whole person." It is as if the brain dies first, and that allows medical personnel to remove life support from the rest of the person, causing "complete" death. Capron (2001: 1244) suggests that a more precise definition, such as "brain-based determination of death," would help clear any remaining confusion, but it is unlikely to replace the current terminology.

Hans Jonas, a philosopher (1974), noted that defining brain death is not to define death at all, but rather the conditions that allow doctors to turn off the respirator. He pointed out that the crux of the matter is not whether a brainless body is alive (after all, he stated, a vegetable is a form of life), but whether life in a brainless body ought to be pre-served or discontinued. If Jonas is right, the question of life and death moves from the medical realm to the moral and ethical one, and therefore beyond the exclusive competency of physicians.

Who dies?

The ugly underside of the decision-making process about life and death concerns "who dies." In some societies, the decision of selective death was rather unproblematic, as it was forced by the fact that resources were scarce and there was no such a thing as retirement. In his study of aging in pre-industrial societies, Simmons (1960) found that in many cases there existed a clearly established set of expectations about who should die. The young and the old shared a perspective that life was a useful, productive period. During old age, when individuals entered the "useless stage" of life and were universally considered to be of no further value to the tribe, they were left to die.

Simmons (1960) reported that the actual disposal of those defined as the "useless" old varied across societies. Among nomadic native North American, the common practice was to neglect or abandon the person designated to die, who could be left on the prairie with a couple of days' supply of food and water. In some societies, death was hastened in a rather brutal form. Among the Samoans, for example, old people of high social status and who were considered important were burned alive. When the old person felt very sick and thought he was about to die, he warned his children, who prepared the final ceremony: "It was even considered a disgrace to the family of an aged chief if he were not so honored" (ibid.: 63). In an end-of-life ceremony, the chief was lowered in a pit alongside wild pigs to accompany him in the here-after, and the ensuing barbecue freed the chief's soul toward heaven while his screams were masked by the screeching of the pigs. In a more recent example, in modern-day Japan, a society more oriented toward shame than guilt, an increasing number of elderly, when confronted with their inability to be useful to the family, will commit suicide to end what they consider a life of dependence that would shame both them and their families (Takahashi, 1995).

 Old Age Death Practices

Another classic example of the relationship between social status and the value judgments that people make about whose lives are considered worthy of saving is when the *Titanic* sank. The rate of sur-vival was 60 percent in first class, 44 percent in second class, and only 25 percent in third class, almost the same as that of the crew, at 24 percent (Padfield, 1966). The official inquiry into the tragedy attributed the differential survivorship to the fact that the disaster occurred at night, with most passengers in their cabins, and that the less expensive accommodation was further below on the ship. Yet some accounts reported that lower-class passengers were actually held at gunpoint until the wealthier ones had a chance to board the scarce life boats.

The ways of euthanasia

Although scholars continue to address healthcare inequality and how it relates to death and dying, today the controversy about who lives and who dies is often centered around the issue of euthanasia. Euthanasia translates literally from the Greek as "good death," which is a diametrically different concept from "dysthanasia," bad death. Euthanasia is also known as mercy killing or, crudely stated, pulling the plug. The idealized notion of a good death evokes a quiet, easy, and merciful death that ends someone's suffering or terminates a qualitatively inadequate life. With this term, the concept of death is redefined in a positive light around the notion of death with dignity; death becomes a friend (Veatch, 1976). With this idea we no longer envision the sinister, skeletal 'grim reaper' but a friendly figure ready to welcome the dying person in a warm embrace.

The concept of euthanasia also helps to redefine the dying individual, who ceases to be viewed merely as a medical case and reassumes the wholeness of a total person. Euthanasia as a practice emphasizes the quality of the end of life, pain management, and the patient's right to dignity, as well as his or her return to becoming the protagonist in the tragedy of death. Thus, euthanasia is commonly understood as practices that allow a person to shorten his or her miseries.

Euthanasia is a particularly contentious issue in American culture because it involves issues of mental health, informed consent, and, of course, death. There are very few instances in which the American government grants any individual or group the right to kill another. Wartime is such an instance, perhaps the only one viewed positively by many. Other types of state-sanctioned death are highly controversial, such as capital punishment, abortion, suicide, self-defense, and killing as a form of law enforcement.

Recall that at the beginning of this chapter we mentioned that most Americans feel that patients should have the right to decide whether or not to be kept alive through medical treatment. The public support for right to die laws increased from 79 percent in 1990 to 84 percent in 2005. The public also feels that a person in great pain with no chance of improving has a right to end life, up from 55 percent in 1990 to 60 percent in 2005, according to a recent poll (Pew Research Center, 2006). Indeed, various groups have initiated social movements in support of the individual's right to die (Fox et al., 1999). Nonetheless, euthanasia remains a highly controversial topic in America and across the globe. There is no general agreement in the literature on whether there is a difference among the various types, such as, for example, actively killing a patient versus removing life support, since the end result is the same in both cases.

Involuntary "euthanasia"

Involuntary "euthanasia" can be on a large scale when a group decides to annihilate another group for political, religious or other reasons. In this case the term "euthanasia" is clearly misused. What we really have is genocide. Involuntary euthanasia can also take place on an individual level when a doctor or other individual takes upon himself or herself to kill a patient who is not competent to express his or her wishes in the matter.

Genocide – Involuntary "euthanasia," in which the person does not give consent (or, if they are unable to communicate, their proxy does not give consent), equates to murder (the active killing of a person) and is not legal in the United States. History provides many examples of such killing that was racially and ethnically motivated but also sometimes carried out under the guise of mercy. Nazi Germany, the former Yugoslavia, Albania, and present-day Darfur, in the western region of Sudan in Africa, all provide examples of genocide.

Perhaps the best-known example of state-sanctioned genocide, and certainly one of the most horrifying, was the mass extermination of Jews that was carried out in Nazi Germany by Adolf Hitler's regime. Not everyone is aware that, in addition to Jews, the Nazis singled out other groups whom they considered to be less than human and persecuted and murdered them as well, including political prisoners, gypsies, and homosexuals (Yahil, 1987). Scholars of the Holocaust have also studied the fate of disabled people during Hitler's reign and have documented how relatively easy it was for those in power to define those with disabilities as "useless, subhuman, of no economic value, and incapable of anything resembling a decent quality of life" (Mostert, 2002: 168). Once these different groups were viewed as subhuman, and therefore unworthy of living (*lebensunwertes*), the Nazis were able to justify their mass extermination as a "merciful" act that, in their view, would benefit society as a whole as well as the condemned (Alexander, 1949; Mitscherlich and Mielke, 1949). The Nazis used the term "mercy killing," but of course this is misapplying a thin veneer to disguise and justify the brutal extermination of innocent people. At first, those killed were specific groups of the mentally ill,

then the practice was expanded to the aged, the disabled, and criminals (Alexander, 1949). Having successfully perfected their methods of
genocide, the Nazis expanded their program to include physically and
mentally 'normal' individuals who were deemed to be undesirable to
the Reich, such as Jews, Poles, and gypsies (it may perhaps eventually
have been brought to bear on all non-Aryans (Aryan was the term for
Hitler's German super race).

In American society, the issue of mercy killing recalls neither the
primitive brutality of the early Samoans nor the chilling duplicity and
amorality of Nazi Germany. Yet, not all is well. Today mercy killing is
couched in medical, scientific terms, but an outsider may view the US
situation as not too different from those of other times and cultures.
Death in green robes, while plugged into machines, may seem brutal
and primitive to some. And, while society does not overtly extermi-
nate groups of people it considers to be less valuable or desirable, the
medical community has nonetheless conducted experiments on low-
status groups that would never be practiced on high-status groups.
Consider, for example, how the US military exposed its personnel to
nuclear radiation without their knowledge during the atomic age and
the Cold War, or how American soldiers in Vietnam were provided
with LSD without their knowledge. Another example is the now infamous Tuskegee experiment, in which 399 poor black men in Alabama
went untreated for syphilis so that doctors could watch the progression of the disease and eventually conduct autopsies on the bodies.

Direct killing – There have been a number of cases in which doctors
have engaged in the direct killing of dying patients who were legally
incompetent and unable to express their wishes. Of course, active
euthanasia is particularly contentious because it specifically hastens
the death of the dying person, which appears to be against the
Hippocratic oath, the ethical oath taken by doctors in which they
swear not to harm their patients.

The direct killing of dying patients is considered murder in America.
It is not reported often and is highly publicized when it occurs. Two
landmark cases involved Dr Herman Sander (Veatch, 1976) and
Dr Vincent Montemarano (Baughman et al., 1973), both of whom
injected intravenously a lethal substance (air and potassium chloride,
respectively) into suffering patients who were about to die of cancer.
Both doctors were charged with murder but walked away free when
lawyers called on the testimony of physicians as expert witnesses, who
were able to cast doubt on the actual cause of death of the patients in
both cases.

Another highly sensational and controversial case involved the pub-
lication of an anonymous letter, attributed to a gynecology resident,

entitled, "It's Over, Debbie," published in the *Journal of the American Medical Association*. Debbie was a twenty-year-old woman who was dying of ovarian cancer and in extreme pain. The author, who was called in the middle of the night to assist her, was moved by Debbie's suffering. Knowing that she could not be cured, but that she could be "given her rest," the doctor injected her with a large dose of morphine. The effect of the morphine was to suppress and eventually stop her breathing. A deluge of letters to the editor was overwhelmingly against the resident, most feeling that the doctor, who had not seen the patient before, had acted hurriedly and without enough knowledge or search for evidence (Was there a living will? What did the patient's primary physician think? Why wasn't the family consulted?). The following is from a letter from two faculty members at Boston University:

> "It's Over, Debbie" constitutes a textbook example of medical arrogance, and criminal conduct. We plan to use it as a teaching vehicle in courses at our medical school, law school, and school of public health. Truth can indeed be more frightening than fiction. Thank you, Debbie, for reminding us. (Miller and Annas, 1988: 2095)

A more recent example of alleged direct killing occurred in the wake of Hurricane Katrina in New Orleans, Louisiana. A doctor and two nurses were arrested for "putting patients out of their miseries" by injecting them with a lethal combination of morphine and a powerful sedative; they were charged with the second degree murder of four patients (Nossiter and Hauser, 2006). The doctor, Anna Pou, and the nurses did not seek permission from anyone before their actions. They were responding to being confronted with rising water, the uncertainty of whether they could eventually move the patients (and whether the patients could survive the move), and being without any electrical power or air conditioning (which meant manually operating ventilators to help some of the patients breathe and fanning others for days at a time). Twenty-three months after they were indicted, Dr Pou and the two nurses were cleared of all charges by a Louisiana grand jury (WDSU, 2007).[1]

Voluntary euthanasia

Voluntary euthanasia takes place when a competent patient repeatedly asks for assistance in dying. The aid may come from medical personnel who kill the patient, usually in the form of an injection of a lethal substance such as potassium chloride, or from a layperson, usually a relative. A famous case was reported by Veatch, in which a young man remained permanently paralyzed from the neck down due to a motorcycle accident. He begged to be put out of his misery and his brother intervened. "On Wednesday evening, Lester Zygmaniak brought a sawed-off shotgun to the hospital, said to his brother, 'Close your eyes now, I'm going to shoot you,' and fired the gun" (Veatch, 1976: 79).

One type of voluntary euthanasia that is particularly controversial is the practice of physician-assisted suicide (PAS). PAS is when the doctor makes lethal drugs available to the dying patient (usually through a prescription) but does not administer them him- or herself. PAS is illegal in the US, with the exception of Oregon and, recently, Washington and Montana. Many bills have been submitted for passage in the US, and many other nations, such as New Zealand, Western Australia, England, Canada and Japan, are attempting to pass legislation allowing either PAS or voluntary euthanasia (Youngner et al., 1999; Humphry, 2001).

Dr Jack Kevorkian, who actually engaged in assisted suicide, raised the controversy in the United States over PAS to a new level. "Dr Death," as he came to be known, created a machine that would help patients terminate their lives by self-injecting a lethal substance. The key in assisted suicide is that one can make the means available and instruct the patient on the method of termination but may not actively intervene. Kevorkian assisted about 130 people, yet fewer than 30 percent of them were considered terminal. Eventually, he was convicted of second degree murder for his highly publicized, televised, killing of Thomas Youk, on April 13, 1999. Although Kevorkian had the full support of the patient's family (Youk was suffering from amyotrophic lateral sclerosis, also known as Lou Gehrig's disease), he crossed the legal line between "assisting" and "actively helping" someone to die. He was a pioneer of euthanasia and openly flaunted the legal system, helping patients rather hurriedly, without following the protocol the medical community considers to be required for the delicate situation. According to his own standards, Kevorkian's patients should have undergone psychiatric counsel, consultation with a pain specialist, and waited twenty-four hours after their final request. The suicide should have been postponed if there was any ambivalence expressed (Kaplan, 1998). In his zeal, Kevorkian cut corners and violated state laws, and for those infractions he was convicted to serve ten to twenty-five years in a US prison. He was imprisoned in 1999 and released on June 1, 2007, possibly on account of his failing health.

Passive euthanasia

Passive euthanasia involves the omission of treatment or removal of life-support equipment already being used on the patient.

Withholding treatment

Despite the legal taboo against euthanasia, a number of medical practitioners and other groups across the United States engage daily, if silently, in its use. In fact, the most common type of euthanasia requires no action at all. In passive euthanasia the physician can simply omit to start a new medical procedure aimed at saving the patient's life. Examples of passive euthanasia include withholding a respirator for a patient showing no activity on an EEG, refraining from defibrillating a patient who has obviously expired, or prescribing nothing for the pneumonia that is slowly drowning the lungs of an old, confused patient in a chronic care facility.

The medical community generally regards passive euthanasia as an ethical practice as long as the patient (or guardian) is competent to make an informed decision about refusing any life-saving treatments. In the majority of these cases the goal is to avoid prolonging pain, suffering, or ineffective medical treatments and to allow the patient to die in peace. In contrast to active euthanasia, passive euthanasia can be practiced safely, most of the time, since it would be very difficult to prosecute a physician for "having done nothing." The doctor, the patient, and/or family members may define the situation as a "wait and see," letting nature take its course without intervening.

Withdrawing treatment

Withdrawing treatment entails the removal of medical therapy or equipment that is keeping the patient's body functioning. We have seen that the Harvard committee discussed comatose patients (Veatch, 1976). The committee was focused on patients in irreversible coma, "flat liners," with absolutely no vertical oscillation on their brain graph. Other patients have minimal vertical spikes of brain activity and they are considered to be in a persistent vegetative state. While this minimal brain activity can be attributed to the autonomic (rather than the central) nervous system, it results in patient activities that may be confused for sentient behavior. So the patient may seem to be listening or looking at the visitor while in fact those actions are actually the result of autonomic reflexes. There have been three landmark cases dealing with "stopping treatment" in the United States and we now examine them briefly.

Karen Quinlan – This was the first case in the United States to allow removal of a ventilator. In 1975, Karen Quinlan had just moved out of her parents' home. She was about to go to a party and felt somewhat apprehensive, so she took some Valium to calm herself (some say there

Table 4.2 Summary of types of euthanasia

Involuntary

Genocide: when a dominant group annihilates a subordinate group for political, religious or other reasons

Direct killing: when a medical practitioner or a lay person kills an incompetent patient, unable to express his or her will in the matter

Voluntary

Direct killing: when a medical practitioner or a lay person kills a competent patient who makes persistent requests for help in dying

Physician's Assisted Suicide (PAS): when a doctor makes the means of death available, such as lethal medication

Passive

Witholding treatment: when no potentially life-saving medical procedure is attempted on the patient

Withdrawing treatment: when life support e.g., of feeding tubes, is removed from the patient

---

were more drugs involved). At the party she had a few (allegedly two) gin and tonics, and it is believed that this chemical mix caused her to lapse into coma. The diagnosis was never clear, but the oxygen starvation that ensued caused Karen to go into coma – a persistent vegetative state.

The young woman's body quickly withered away as she was kept alive with the aid of a ventilator and intravenous feeding and hydration. Karen's deeply religious parents held hope for almost six months, then decided that that shriveled body curled in a fetal position was no longer their daughter and asked the physicians to remove her ventilator. The physicians adamantly refused, and a lengthy and costly court battle followed. Fourteen months from Karen's collapse, the supreme court of the state of New Jersey ruled in the parents' favor. Devoid of help from a ventilator, Karen did not die. Her body kept breathing, digesting intravenous food, sweating, evacuating, and reacting to autonomous stimuli for ten more years. Eventually, an infection overcame her weakened immune system and she died of pneumonia (Quinlan, 2005).

Nancy Cruzan – This was the first American case to allow removal of a feeding tube. In 1983, Nancy Cruzan rolled her car at night and lay in a ditch, during which time she suffered oxygen deprivation. The 26-year-old woman was taken to the hospital; although she was in a vegetative state, she could breathe without the aid of a ventilator, but she needed to be fed intravenously. The state of Missouri paid for her care as her father, Lester Cruzan, was a sheet-metal worker and had little money.

Her parents visited Nancy assiduously, but it became clear to them that the swollen body with glazed eyes was never going to be their vivacious, beautiful Nancy again. Since, unlike the Quinlan case, there was no ventilator to turn off, the parents asked the hospital staff to remove the feeding tube. Withdrawing a ventilator usually results in the patient stopping breathing within a few minutes (although not in Quinlan's case), yet taking away nutrition and liquids results in the slow dehydration of the patient. Once their food source is removed it takes several days for patients to die.

The American Civil Liberties Union (ACLU) facilitated pro-bono counsel for the Cruzans as they pursued legal ways to have the feeding tube removed from their daughter. The case moved from court to court for four years and ended up at the United States Supreme Court, the first such case to reach the high court. In a ninety-page majority ruling by Justice Antonin Scalia, the court decided that "hearsay is no evidence" and rejected the parents' request to remove the feeding tube. It determined that there was no document written by Nancy herself addressing the specific situation of removal of care and that the general talk about it with her family did not constitute evidence. Shortly after the ruling, three former co-workers of Nancy, who knew her under her married name of Davies, stepped forward and testified that she had clearly indicated to them her preferences in such a case. Thus, the Cruzans' wish was granted and, against a wave of protesters, Nancy's feeding tube was removed. The young woman expired quietly eleven days later (Colby, 2002).

Nancy Cruzan's case received a tremendous amount of press attention and helped individual people talk about their own wishes about end-of-life care and the circumstances under which they would have life support withdrawn. Particularly because the court case emphasized the degree to which other people could attest to Nancy's wishes, a large number of Americans decided to write a living will (see below) expressing their demands in the face of death, should they be unable to give consent. Two large national patients' rights organizations concerned with death and end-of-life care, the Society for the Right to Die and Concern for Dying, mailed over 400,000 living wills forms after Nancy's death. The sad coda of the story is that Nancy's father was unable to live with the heavy burden of his decision and the public pressure. On August 17, 1996, he hanged himself in the carport of his home (Annin and Peyser, 1996: 54).

Terri Schiavo – The case of Theresa Marie Schiavo, who was in a persistent vegetative state, was the first in which the family did not agree on how to address the patient's care. Terri was a young woman struggling with bulimia who suffered a cardiac arrest in 1990 because of a potassium imbalance. After eight years, in 1998, Michael Schiavo, her husband, petitioned the Florida courts to remove her gastric feeding tube. Terri's parents, Robert and Mary Schindler, who were deeply religious people, objected strenuously.

The case was in the courts for years and the press and numerous groups became acutely interested in it. Terri's feeding tube was removed twice but had to be reinserted both times on account of legal rulings; the second one, the so-called Terri's Law of 2003, enabled Florida's governor, Jeb Bush, to intervene in the case. He immediately had Terri removed from the hospice facility where she was dying to a hospital, where the feeding tube was reinserted. Terri became somewhat of a symbol for religious, civil, and political groups, with the mass media fanning the fire. It should be noted that every court challenged by her parents eventually was overturned, and "Terri's Law" was ruled unconstitutional in the state. Eventually, the tube was removed for good for a third time on March 18, 2005. Terri died on March 31, at the age of forty-one (Fuhrman, 2005).

Terri Schiavo's situation was another instance where one person's tragedy raised awareness about patients' rights in their end-of-life care. Indeed, researchers have documented that these cases have helped identify the feelings of most Americans that medical cases should not be decided by politicians but that patients have the right to refuse or terminate life-sustaining medical interventions. Further, scholars attribute the increased awareness from Terri Schiavo's case to a growth in the number of people who complete living wills (Hampson and Emanuel, 2005).

Legal euthanasia and assisted suicide

Currently, PAS is legal in the Netherlands and Belgium, which followed its neighbor's example in 2002 (*Ethical Perspectives*, 2002). Both countries have very small populations (the Netherlands, for example, has about 16 million people) and both have national healthcare, thus allowing close control over their limited number of patients. These two European countries are the only ones where the doctor actually injects the patient, usually with barbiturates first, to induce sleep, and then with a lethal injection of curare (Angell, 1996). In addition, both Switzerland and the states of Oregon, Washington and Montana in America permit PAS whereby the physician make the means available and assists in the procedure but does not inject the patient.

The Netherlands and Belgium

For many years before the legalization of euthanasia, physicians in the Netherlands illegally helped some patients to terminate their lives while the Dutch legal system traditionally turned its head the other way (Gomez, 1991). The Netherlands parliament finally legalized euthanasia in 1993. The legislation outlined four conditions that must be met in order for patients to be eligible:

- the patient must be a mentally competent adult
- the patient must request euthanasia voluntarily, consistently, and repeatedly over a reasonable period of time, and the requests must be documented
- the patient must be suffering intolerably, with no prospect of relief, although the disease need not be terminal
- the doctor must consult with another physician not involved in the case.

The number of people who availed themselves of the euthanasia option was minuscule; only 1.8 percent of all deaths in the Netherlands in 1990 were the result of euthanasia, and "87% of the patients were expected to die within a week" (Angell, 1996: 1676). The Netherlands are now moving toward the other end of the spectrum, addressing a more controversial issue – that of allowing euthanasia for severely ill newborns (Verhagen and Sauer, 2005).

Switzerland

Switzerland established its assisted suicide program in 1942, the only place to do so until the Netherlands and the states of Oregon, Washington and Montana (Humphry, 1991). In order to be eligible, patients have to meet several criteria. They must decide for themselves to commit assisted suicide. While a doctor or a nurse must be present to witness the event (along with two more witnesses), they cannot provide any actual help in bringing the death about – the patients must do it themselves. There is, however, a major difference between the Swiss system and those in other countries, as in Switzerland there is no residency requirement.

This lack of a residency requirement is an important feature, because non-Swiss patients have gone to Switzerland specifically to die. In 1998 in Zurich a former journalist, Ludwig Minelli, founded Dignitas, which accepts international patients and aspires to help people "to live with dignity and to die with dignity" (Minelli, 2006: 18). It provides people whose quality of life is compromised with living wills and assistance in achieving a risk- and pain-free suicide. Dignitas subscribes to the Swiss requirements, but it is rather liberal in accepting patients: "A Dutchman afflicted with advanced Alzheimer's disease wasn't permitted assisted suicide in the Netherlands because Alzheimer's isn't deemed to be a terminal disease in that country. But Mr. Minelli took him on, and the man did kill himself. In another Dignitas case, a 33-year-old Frenchman and his 29-year-old sister, both suffering from schizophrenia, chose to end their lives simultaneously and side by side" (Naik, 2002:2). People have traveled from as close as Germany and as far as the United States to avail themselves of the services of Dignitas; from its inception in 1998 through 2006, it had helped 619 members end their lives (Minelli, 2006).

Besides Dignitas, there are three other organizations assisting in suicide in Switzerland. The first, EXIT, is the largest such organization and it helps about 120 patients per year to commit suicide. Also located in Zurich, it is German-speaking and does not help foreigners. The second, EXIT-International, is a splinter group from EXIT, and is located in Bern. Its leader, Rolf Sigg, PhD, often travels to Germany to assist German patients commit suicide. Assisted suicide has been legal in Germany since the 1930s, but after the Nazi atrocities almost no German doctor will have anything to do with it. Dr Sigg has had some trouble with German authorities for bringing in pentobarbital and was convicted several times, but the charges have, thus far, always been dismissed on appeal. The third organization is a much smaller French-speaking group, Exit/ADMD/Suisse Romande, which operates out of Geneva and limits itself to advising people about how to obtain a physician-assisted suicide but provides no physical or organizational assistance in the act (Humphry, 2001).

Swiss leaders are not pleased by the fact that Switzerland, and Zurich in particular, is gaining the reputation as the place where people go to die. Nonetheless, the number of people who employ physician-assisted suicide remains a very small percentage of the total deaths. In German-speaking Switzerland, 0.4 percent of deaths are through assisted suicide, versus 0.2 in the Netherlands and 0.01 in Belgium (Swissinfo, 2003).

Oregon

In America, the controversies around physician-assisted suicide are many, and only Oregon and, recently, Washington and Montana have legalized the practice. However, its decision to legalize PAS was tied to other decisions it made about the delivery of healthcare in the state. During the 1990s, Oregon decided to move to a more fiscally dependable approach to healthcare in order to contain costs and improve access. Part of the plan was for administrators to make value judgments about what medical conditions and what type of patients qualify for state coverage. For example, under the plan a young person would obtain a liver transplant while a chronic alcoholic would not. Another major change was passed on October 27, 1997, which legalized physician-assisted suicide in the state.

The Death with Dignity Act (DWDA) is only available to residents of Oregon. In order to apply for PAS, the patient must be able to communicate his or her own decisions about their healthcare and make one written and two oral requests over a given span of time. The act covers only terminally ill adults, and it allows them to obtain and use lethal prescriptions to self-administer. Other restrictions also apply, but once the patient has successfully met all requirements he or she will be given a prescription for a lethal medication.

The DWDA is highly controversial and relatively few people have taken advantage of it. From when the law was passed until 2006, 292 patients had died under its terms. In 2006, the year for which the most recent statistics exist, doctors wrote sixty-five prescriptions for lethal medication. Of these, "35 patients took the medications, 19 died of their underlying disease, and 11 were alive at the end of 2006. In addition, 11 patients with earlier prescriptions died from taking the medications, resulting in a total of 46 DWDA deaths during 2006. This corresponds to an estimated 14.7 DWDA deaths per 10,000 total deaths" (Oregon Department of Human Services, 2007: 1). Not surprisingly, the trend in Oregon since 1997 has been that the majority of people who used the DWDA had cancer and were better educated than other Oregonians who died during this time. Further, the majority of patients died at home and were enrolled in hospice care at the time of their death.

However, the DWDA remains highly controversial. Indeed, under George W. Bush's conservative and evangelical presidency the executive branch of the US government attempted to stymie the Oregon initiative. Since it was unable to take away the licenses to practice of the Oregon doctors who had prescribed the lethal medications for terminally ill patients under the act (because licensure belongs to the states), the federal government threatened to remove their licenses to prescribe drugs, which is a federal license under the Controlled Substance Act (CSA). The case made it all the way to the US Supreme Court, but the ruling upheld the physicians' case, arguing that the federal government had overstepped its authority. The argument was as follows: "The CSA does not allow the Attorney General to prohibit doctors from prescribing regulated drugs for use in physician-assisted suicide under state law permitting the procedure" (Legal Information Institute, 2006: 2).

Living wills and power of attorney

In the cases of Quinlan, Cruzan, and Schiavo that we discussed previously in this chapter, many of the legal battles were caused by the lack of written documentation by the patients about their wishes.

The US Supreme Court ruling in Cruzan's case would very likely have been different if a legal document indicating Nancy's wishes had been produced at hearings. Similarly, the family fight over Terri Schiavo would have been seen in a different light if she had left a living will. The living will must be signed by two witnesses (not blood related) and notarized. It is a very simple document that could potentially avoid a lot of trouble. Today American hospitals must ask, mandated by federal law, incoming patients if they have a living will and where it can be found. If the patient does not have one they must sign a statement as to whether he or she wishes that extraordinary measures be performed in order to keep them alive. However, because

---

Figure 4.1

Living Will for the State of Nevada

DECLARATION

If I should have an incurable and irreversible condition that, without the administration of life-sustaining treatment, will, in the opinion of my attending physician, cause my death within a relatively short time, and I am no longer able to make decisions regarding my medical treatment, I direct my attending physician, pursuant to NRS 449.535 to 449.690, inclusive, to withhold or withdraw treatment that only prolongs the process of dying and is not necessary for my comfort or to alleviate pain.

If you wish to include this statement in this declaration, you must INITIAL the statement in the box provided:

Withholding or withdrawal of artificial nutrition and hydration may result in death by starvation or dehydration. Initial this box if you want to receive or continue receiving artificial nutrition and hydration by way of gastrointestinal tract after all other treatment is with held pursuant to this declaration.

[_____]

Signed this _____day of _____, _____

Signature _____

Address _____

The declarant voluntarily signed this writing in my presence.

Witness _____   Witness _____

Address _____

many people arrive at the hospital unconscious and cannot indicate their wishes or sign a document about them, a living will can provide those instructions. In addition to discussing end-of-life treatment and quality of life issues with family and friends, it is also advisable to give a copy of one's living will to one's primary care physician (US Living Will Registry, 2007).

Figure 4.1 is an example of the many different ways of expressing a living will, which may differ in language and content across various states in America. A living will is an important first step for people as they think about their own end-of-life care and the circumstances under which they wish to die or the attempts to postpone death. However, at times, physicians have ignored living wills, since the latter were not readily available (for example, people may keep such documents in a secure location such as locked in a safe deposit box in a bank vault), the doctor felt that there was a chance to 'save' the patient, or there was no one around to speak for the patient. Medicine often is not as cut and dried as people would have it, and opinion on prognoses may differ widely.[2]

A durable power of attorney for medical reasons is a more compelling way to have one's wishes heard by the medical community. It reads very much like the living will but it appoints a principal (a relative, friend, attorney, or anyone else) to make decisions on behalf of the patient if he or she is incapable of doing so. This statement has more legal weight than a simple living will, partly because it is actually drawn up by an attorney-at-law as a legal document rather than merely being notarized. Given both the fact that there is a spokesperson to represent the patient and the tremendously litigious nature of American society, the medical community is more likely to listen to the wishes of the patient under these circumstances.

Conclusion

In this chapter, we have examined the issues surrounding the dying process. We pointed out that the dying process and the ceremonies surrounding death are socially stratified, with some being given preferential treatment or having more resources. The definition of death has changed over time and has become more complex, going from examinations of vital signs to include the whole brain in the diagnosis. Choices have to be made on who lives and who dies, and we have seen that different cultures address the issue in diverse ways.

We discussed euthanasia in its various forms – voluntary passive, and legal. The case of Dr Kevorkian was presented as an example of assisted suicide. Three landmark cases regarding stopping treatment were summarized – those of Karen Quinlan, Nancy Cruzan, and Terri Schiavo. The controversial killing of "Debbie" was presented as an example of direct killing.

Active euthanasia is illegal in forty-seven of the fifty US states albeit, as we have mentioned, gaining increasing public favor, but it is legal in the Netherlands and in Belgium. We outlined the eligibility requirements in the Netherlands. We then looked at assisted suicide in Oregon and Switzerland, where only support is provided to the prospective dying patient rather than actual help in the process. Finally, we discussed living wills and powers of attorney for medical reasons.

CHAPTER

Funeral Practices

05

Introduction

Almost two and a half million people die in the United States every year (Hoyert et al., 2006). Two and a half million people are a lot of loved ones to lose, say farewell to, and grieve for, and they also comprise lot of bodies to dispose of. Tables 5.1 and 5.2 provide some ideas of rates and methods of disposal of the body, both internationally and in America. We can readily see the great discrepancy in people's chosen method of burial, both between nations and between American states. While individuals' preference for cremation is increasing, in certain areas of America, especially in the more socially conservative states, we still find traditional burial the overwhelming choice. In this chapter we examine how we dispose of the body, why we follow certain customs and procedures, and why we choose specific ways to be buried.

Durkheim once stated that "men do not weep for their dead because they fear them; they fear them because they weep for them" (1965: 447). In other words, people's feelings are a reflection of their customs,

Table 5.1 International trends in cremation, 2001

Country	Number of cremations	Number of crematoria	Cremations as a percentage of total deaths
Argentina	14,652	42	7.5
China	3,737,000	1,420	47.3
France	93,412	98	18.9
Great Britain	437,609	243	70.7
Italy	29,783	36	6.6
Japan	999,255	1,630	98.0
Switzerland	45,104	27	75.5
United States	630,800	1,711	26.9

Source: Derived from *Pharos International* magazine (winter 2002).

Table 5.2 American trends in cremation, 1999 and 2004		
	Percentage of dead who were cremated	
	1999	2004
United States	24.8	29.61
Alabama	4.55	9.11
Mississippi	5.32	8.82
Hawaii	59.53	67.5
Nevada	56	67.12

Source: Derived from Cremation Association of North America, http://www.cremationassociation.org/htmlstatistics.html (accessed April 17, 2006).

rather than vice versa. Durkheim was not denying the unique place of individual expressions of feeling but focusing instead on the cultural relevance of death. Both the types of ceremonies and the types of grief expressed mirror the society in which the death occurs. We wear black and look somber at American funerals regardless of our knowledge of the deceased, in the same way that Melanesians used to blacken their bodies with charcoal when an important person died, regardless of their personal feelings for that person (Seligman, 1910) (see chapter 9 for the differences between grief, mourning, and bereavement).

The dead are usually either buried or cremated, with some cultures, such as modern-day America, using both methods. Another, less common, way is that of burial at sea, used by the US Navy, and sometimes ashes are scattered at sea. Since John Kennedy Jr. was a Catholic his ashes could not be scattered (because this practice would go against the Catholic belief about the resurrection of the body); instead the sealed urn was dropped to the depths of the sea (Rosen, 2004). The Inuit used to leave bodies exposed to the elements for natural disintegration (Weyer, 1932).

In this transition from life to death, the cadaver is treated for the last time as a "person" before becoming a decaying body. Ceremonies that govern this transition from person to body can be elaborate, simple, or nonexistent, depending on the status of the deceased. The following report shows how elaborate a funeral can be when a very important person dies. It describes the funeral of Pope John Paul II on April 8, 2005 (popes are buried inside St Peter's Basilica in Vatican City, Rome):

> VATICAN CITY – Presidents, prime ministers and kings joined pilgrims and prelates in St. Peter's Square on Friday to bid an emotional farewell to Pope *John Paul II* at a funeral that drew millions to Rome . . . After the Mass ended, bells tolled and pallbearers with white gloves, white ties and tails presented the coffin to the crowd one last time, and then carried it on their shoulders back inside the basilica for burial – again to the sustained applause from the hundreds of thousands in the square, including dignitaries from 138 countries. (Associated Press, 2005: 1)

In contrast, Simone de Beauvoir describes a simple funeral, that of her mother:

> There were cars waiting at the gates of the cemetery: the family. They followed us as far as the chapel. Everybody got out . . . We went in, making a procession: the chapel was full of people. No flowers on the catafalque: the undertakers had left them in the hearse – it did not matter.
>
>   A young priest, wearing trousers under his chasuble, celebrated the Mass and gave a short, strangely sad sermon. . .Two kneeling chairs had been placed for the communion. (Beauvoir 1965: 100)

George Orwell describes dying for the very poor, whom he calls the "down and out," as he witnesses the following scene as a non-paying patient in a public ward of a hospital in Paris in the year 1929:

> I could see old Numero 57 lying crumpled up on his side, his face sticking out over the side of the bed, and toward me. He had died some time during the night, nobody knew when . . . it struck me that this disgusting piece of refuse, waiting to be carted away and dumped on a slab in the dissecting room, was an example of 'natural' death . . . that is how the lucky ones die, the one who lives to be old. (1956: 90)

Early burials in Europe

The practice of burying the dead has been the norm in some cultures for thousands of years. They have been buried in the ground and above ground in mausoleums, churches, and caves (Jesus was buried in a cave), outside the cities, in the suburbs, and in pyramids. The dead have been buried facing up, facing down, facing East, with feet and hands tied together, with animals such as snakes and roosters inside the grave, or with sacrificed slaves or live maidens to accompany them to the great beyond; they have been given clothing, gifts, gold, food, and drinks inside their burial vessel. The dead have been buried whole or with their bones separated from the flesh. In their best Sunday suit or in their armor. They have been placed in cloth and leather shrouds, sheets, paper, and coffins made from every imaginable substance, including metal, marble, wood, and gold. In 1993, "a Swedish candy salesman was buried . . . in a coffin made entirely of chocolate" (Quigley, 1996: 84).

   Ariès (see chapter 2) wrote that in pagan times and in the early Christian days the dead were buried outside the city walls, going back to the ancient Roman law of the Twelve Tables (*c.* 450 BC) (Ariès, 1974, 1981), which was the cornerstone of the Roman Republic. As European cities expanded and the distance to travel to the outskirts of the city became too long, burials began to take place in the suburbs around the sixth and seventh centuries. Christians broke with tradition and began to bury the dead adjacent to the church rather than in cemeteries as early as 540 AD (Ariès, 1981), while high-ranking church dignitaries and officials were entombed within the church itself. Again we see the difference that status makes, as the poor were unceremoniously dumped in common graves, sewn in their death shrouds. Once the common grave was filled, it was reopened and the old bones taken to an ossuary (also called a charnel house – a repository for bones) (Ariès, 1974). The modern idea that every body must have its own "death house" did not apply to the poor, who accepted this as long as their remains were entrusted to the care of the church.

Class

While burial ceremonies themselves applied to individuals, we can also see macro-level implications of these rituals and norms about how to dispose of dead bodies. Particularly in times of plague and mass disease, how communities dealt with human remains had societal-level consequences. Thus, societies established acceptable burial practices to ensure the health of survivors. For example, burial was viewed as a sanitary way to insulate the living from the dead, such that "English law once required a burial depth of 6 feet to ensure the corpse didn't spread the plague [London, June 1665] to the living" (Defoe, 2001). Traditional burials fueled a great deal of debate among the pro-cremation advocates in the 1800s on both sides of the Atlantic, since they held that burials created sanitary problems, from miasma (a poisonous atmosphere) to the spread of germs.

Burials in America

Beginning in the 1600s, early puritan funerals in America were very simple. In the rugged environment of the New World, death was familiar and the settlers dealt with it on a daily basis. In fact, the most common symbol on announcements and gravestones was the skull and crossbones (Dethlefsen and Deetz, 1977). Funeral rituals included a sermon given in the church, after which a procession moved on foot to the gravesite, with pallbearers carrying the coffin. Once there, mourners remained silent as the casket was covered with dirt. If gravediggers were not available, friends and neighbors did the necessary work. Afterwards there was a party with great quantities of food and liquor (Habenstein and Lamers, 1955).

Despite the simplicity of the funerals, paradoxically the displays of mourning were often elaborate – as with other aspects of rituals and practices surrounding death, the higher the status of the deceased, the more elaborate the expressions of mourning. Mourning became a vehicle to allow wealthy people to show off their riches. Often presents, such as scarves and rings, were given to friends and relatives. In Virginia during the puritan era it was common to shoot guns at funerals, regardless of laws regulating the use of firearms. In New York, in the 1600s and 1700s, the pattern of a Dutch funeral was a common model (Earle, 1977). The Dutch ceremony proceeded as follows: as the bell tolled, the *aanspreecker* (funeral inviter), dressed in black, announced the death and the time and place of the funeral to all friends and relatives. Usually people did not attend the funeral unless they had been invited. It was not uncommon for someone to have their coffin and death shroud made while they were still alive. The family of the deceased would cover all the mirrors in the house until after the funeral. Only men would take the coffin to the grave, while the women stayed behind. The coffin was wooden, often covered with a black cloth. After the funeral the attendees were served "dead cakes" (*doed-koecks*) at the house of the deceased. In the 1700s the dead were interred in churches, for a fee of four pounds per adult (in Flatbush, Brooklyn): "a church attendant could be buried under the seat in which he was wont to sit during his lifetime" (ibid.: 38). Extravagance was common among the wealthy, as guests were provided with copious quantities of food, alcoholic beverages, and gifts.

This tendency to "show off" became magnified in America during the 1800s. Both the separation from England and the industrialization of the cities created an increased status consciousness. The rise of industrialization and the growth of the cities led to greater social inequality as well as greater conspicuous consumption (Jackson, 1977). In keeping with these macro-level changes in society at large, funeral rituals and beliefs about how to honor the dead also changed. In contrast to the simplicity of early American rites, funerals themselves now turned into a status-seeking display as they became increasingly elaborate, and great attempts were made to make them beautiful, with colors, ornaments, music, and elaborate caskets. For example, "The epitome of extravagance was reached at the funeral of Andrew Fanueil in 1738 when three thousand pairs of gloves were given away and over eleven hundred people accompanied the funeral cortege" (Habenstein and Lamers, 1955: 206). Andrew Faneuil was an extremely wealthy merchant; at the time of his death he was the richest man in Boston.

A symbol of the changing relation to death in America can be seen in the modifications in the design of the headstone, from skeleton's head (symbolizing the finality of death) in the sixteenth century to jubilant cherubs (symbolizing the hope for an afterlife) in the nineteenth (Dethlefsen and Deetz, 1977). Inscriptions on headstones also changed drastically, from crudely plain in the sixteenth century:

> Soon ripe
> Soon rotten
> Soon gone
> But not forgotten.
> (Wallis, 1954: 181)

to being filled with hope for a future life afterlife in the eighteenth
century:

> Tis but the casket that lies here
> The gem that fills it sparkles yet.
> (ibid.: 185)

In the nineteenth century, Romanticism was a predominant artistic
and intellectual movement in both Europe and America. Romanticism
stressed strong emotions in relation to aesthetic experience; it also
influenced sensibilities toward dying, and to the funeral as something
expressive and beautiful to be remembered. In America:

> By 1880 the enterprising town or city undertaker could present a
> customer with at least a hundred different choices of casket styles,
> embracing such materials as wood, wood–cloth combination, metal,
> wood and metal, and metal and glass combinations. Colors ranged
> from the conventional black to varieties of silver, bronze, aniline blue
> and lavender, in many variations. (Habenstein and Lamers, 1955: 417)

However, the expensive burials were reserved for Caucasian people.
If you were African American, you could not be buried in a "white"
cemetery; it was not until 1958 that the famous chain of mortuaries
in California, Forest Lawn, loosened its "white only" policy (Quigley,
1996). Cemeteries were also transformed into beautiful parks (see
Cemeteries, p. 80).

In twentieth-century America, tremendous advances in technology
and the increasing wealth of the nation saw Romanticism being partially replaced by an aura of practicality and commercialism. These
trends led to a paradoxical bifurcation in the country (Ariès, 1974).
On the one hand, Americans continued to favor traditional funerals,
complete with embalming, open casket viewing, elaborate casket,
and the rest. The traditional respect for the dead continued, as exemplified in Washington, DC, with the creation of Arlington National
Cemetery for fallen soldiers, the Vietnam Wall (dedicated in 1982),
and the memorials to past presidents.

On the other hand, technology demanded more modern cemeteries and a move to practicality (for instance, low-marker gravestones
to facilitate mowing the lawn). This led to treating the dead in a different manner. Today in some parts of England it is only necessary
to cover the coffin with 30 inches rather than 6 feet of soil, while
in California only 18 inches of dirt and turf are required (Videojug,

2008). The dead are buried alone, or up to three deep on the same plot (NYS Department of State, 2006), depending on the state and the cemetery; they are buried side by side (or above) their loved one; they even can be buried with their pet (Gordon, 2002).

Commodification also increased greatly in the US. For example, in Las Vegas, the commodification of the dead has lead to a whole entertainment genre, in which famous deceased stars, such as Elvis Presley, are imitated by impersonators. Jessica Mitford shocked the nation with her bestseller *The American Way of Death*, in which she attacked, with dry British irony, the overt consumeristic tendencies of the American funeral, which she felt were but a gimmick to sell wares to be exhibited in a final display of poor taste: "Also for the ladies is the 'new Braform, Post Mortem Form Restoration,' offered by Courtesy Products at the demonstrably low price of $11 for a package of fifty – 'they accomplish so much for so little'" (1963: 46).

Today, as we discuss later in this chapter, consumerism has reached a new plateau, all the way to turning the cadaver (carbon-based) into an expensive diamond (also carbon-based), giving a new facet to disposing of the body and grieving for the deceased. Clearly, funeral practices are in line with the rest of American practices – a display of wealth to indicate one's success and social standing.

Embalming

In colonial America, funerals were centered in and around the home of the deceased person. During this time, undertaking was slowly developing as an occupation and was gradually replacing the services previously provided by friends and neighbors, but it was not until the first half of the nineteenth century that there was widespread acceptance and use of the services of undertakers (Habenstein and Lamers, 1955). A major reason for this shift lies with the development of embalming techniques.

In the mid-1880s embalming fluids and the requisite equipment were developed (although some forms of embalming go back as far the ancient Egyptians). Private classes in embalming initially were offered by the companies that developed the fluids. These were soon followed by more rigorous state-run courses, along with increased control over the procedure itself (Habenstein and Lamers, 1955). Embalmers used to say that the procedure could keep the body intact forever, but legal suits soon disputed this (leading to a ruling in 1982 by the Federal Trade Commission specifically forbidding such a claim). In fact, embalming keeps the body "fresh" for only a few days, for the viewing and the funeral. The customary (and expensive) addition of an airtight vault around the casket does little to retard decomposition (Roach, 2003).

In the modern practice of embalming, the blood is pumped out of the body via the carotid or other convenient artery and replaced with embalming fluids, which differ in color depending on the skin complexion of the deceased. Various methods and devices are used to keep the eyes and mouth closed, and at times aspirators are used to remove gaseous matter from the body. Embalming fluid does improve the appearance of the deceased: "Within minutes, the man's face looks rejuvenated. The embalming fluid has rehydrated his tissues, filling out his sunken cheeks, his lined skin. His skin is pink now (the embalming fluid contains red coloring), no longer slack and papery. He looks healthy and surprisingly alive" (Roach, 2003: 80). Given the nature of the procedure, euphemisms are used to maintain the "dignity" of the situation. Embalmers take great pride in their profession and, not surprisingly, act as professionals. For example, they do not refer to the deceased as a "stiff," a corpse, or other derogatory terms but address the body as Mr or Mrs or, more generally, as the "decedent."

As we have previously illustrated, social status greatly influenced the customs and practices associated with deaths and funerals. Since antiquity, "important people" lay in state for about a week after their death so that people could see and pay their respects before the burial. The practice of embalming made this possible, since it slowed down the decomposition process.

In early America, views about burials began to change as, in line with the democratic views of Americans, people agreed that, in contrast to the use of mass graves, everyone should have a decent burial (Hammond, 2000). This was part of the trend toward industrialization and commercialization. However, along with industrialization came great inequality and poverty in the growing cities, which meant that not everyone could afford the expense of a decent and dignified funeral. This is how embalming became even more important. Bodies were embalmed in order to preserve them while family members raised money to pay for the funeral expenses. Thus we see the interconnectedness of societal views about death and death practices and social class as the embalming process was extended to lower status people.

Embalming was also important for practical reasons. For example, it was necessary if a person died away from home and the body had to be shipped across the country to be buried. Crude attempts at preservation have been around for centuries, such as soaking the body in alcohol or using ice coolers. Often, when people died far away from home, they were either buried near where they died or, if they were prominent enough to warrant such a measure, preserved in a barrel of alcohol and shipped back home. Wealthy European traders were routinely transported this way. Legends circulated about sailors imbibing some of the preservative fluid. The most popular story is about the famous English admiral Horatio Nelson. After his death at the Battle of Trafalgar in 1805, he was taken home in a barrel of brandy (not rum, as the legend has it). The brandy was replaced with wine at Gibraltar. Allegedly, when the body arrived in London the level of the wine had decreased considerably, giving birth to the saying "tapping the admiral." This saying was later used to indicate the sailors' surreptitious drinking of rum from a cask, by inserting a straw through a small hole (Brunvand, 1984).

During the Civil War, many soldiers were buried close to where they died. However, the sheer number of dead necessitated temporary preservation by embalming in order to allow some extra time so the necessary arrangements for their disposal could be made. Embalming soldiers during the Civil War helped facilitate the shift toward a general societal acceptance of the practice (Bowman, 1977). In modern days the American practice of viewing the body also necessitates embalming. In fact, currently in America, embalmers are trained not only in embalming itself but also in cosmetology, and must pass, among others, an exam on what are called the restorative arts, aimed at creating an acceptable physical appearance for the deceased (Habenstein and Lamars, 1955). In an effort to re-create the living image of the dead person as closely as possible, it is not uncommon for relatives to supply photographs.

Body snatching

During the eighteenth and nineteenth centuries in Europe, bodies were sometimes illegally removed after burial. For a long time, the Christian Church had been opposed to the dissection of human bodies by physiologists, doctors, and medical students. Determined to learn about human anatomy, physicians turned to the unsanctioned practice of body snatching. Indeed, a number of anatomists were known to pay money for delivered bodies, no questions asked (Roach, 2003). Since medicine was expanding as a profession the market for fresh bodies escalated, and cadavers had a limited shelf life. In fact, "It is said that in Scotland anatomy students could pay for their tuition with corpses rather than coin" (Richardson, 1987: 54). In response to greater awareness of the phenomenon of grave-robbing, the wealthy began to have their loved ones' graves guarded or enclosed by elaborate iron railings. In an effort to guard against body snatching, churches in Scotland would incorporate "deadhouses" within the churchyard where bodies would be allowed to decompose until they were of no use to anatomists. Similarly, in America, there was inequality, even in death, as the bodies of the poor and African Americans remained easy prey: "It is estimated that by 1850, 600 or 700 bodies were snatched annually from the burial grounds of New York City" (Quigley, 1996: 296).

The most nefarious practitioners of this trade were William Burke and William Hare, who, in the 1820s, suffocated a number of lodgers at Hare's lodging house in Edinburgh and sold them to an anatomist, Dr Robert Knox. The notoriety of these two men was so widespread that the term "burking" became synonymous with smothering (Quigley, 1996; Roach 2003).

Eventually the Church relented to the pressure from medical schools that needed cadavers to train their students, and allowed a small number of executed prisoners and stillborn infants to be used for anatomical training purposes. In Massachusetts in the late eighteenth century, the bodies of executed criminals and slain duelists were made available (Quigley, 1996).

Today body snatching is no longer a common practice since there seem to be plenty of cadavers, furnished by donors, available for medical research and training. However, advancement in surgical techniques has heightened the demands for body parts to be used in organ transplantations. Since there are not enough organs available, a brisk, illegal market in body parts has developed, especially kidneys. Just as with the body snatching, it is the poor that become the targets for this illegal trade, while those who can afford to pay the high contraband price reap the benefits by receiving a much needed organ (Davidson, 1993).

Cremation

Cremation[1] was widely practiced by ancient civilizations such as the Greeks and Romans. Many leaders, among them Julius Caesar, were cremated. The Jews and early Christians preferred interment, and when the Roman emperor Constantine spread Christianity throughout his empire (c. 400 AD) cremation all but disappeared for many centuries. It resurfaced in England in 1658, when Sir Thomas Browne wrote the first modern-day book on cremation. The real breakthrough, however, came later, when the Italian Professor Brunelli, at the Vienna Exposition in 1873, presented 4 pounds of cremated human ashes in a glass container. Sir Henry Thompson, Queen Victoria's personal physician, was also strong supporter of cremation.

In America, the move toward cremation and away from burial occurred in the nineteenth century, and was prompted by the over-crowding of cemeteries, sanitation threats of decaying bodies, and fears about the possibility of being buried alive. In rural Pennsylvania, Dr LeMoyne built the first crematorium, in which Baron De Palm was the first American to be cremated.

Initial opposition to cremation came from the spiritual movement called the Resurrectionists, who held firm that it would not allow for resurrection of the body, despite those who believed that God would have no problem resurrecting a cremated body. Many religions were and still are against cremation, including Orthodox and Conservative Jews and Muslims. Germans are reluctant to accept it for the memory of cremation ovens in Nazi Germany, where millions of murdered Jews and others were burned (Final Exit, 2005).

The Catholic Church officially ruled against cremation in 1886. However, the turning point for cremation came in 1963 when Pope Paul VI overturned the earlier ruling and allowed his priests to conduct mass over cremains (this was the same year in which Mitford published the highly controversial *The American Way of Death*, which was widely read in America). As a result, the numbers of bodies which were cremated increased from 67,330 (3.71 percent) in 1963 to 708,671 (29.61 percent) in 2004 (National Funeral Directors Association, 2006).

Cremation has since become increasingly popular in America due in no small part to the fact that many famous people (such as John Lennon) chose this method of disposal. But even as celebrities helped popularize it as an option, cremation was still not the norm for most Americans and was viewed as somewhat countercultural. In the 1990s it became even more popular as the advice columnist Dear Abby began instructing people on how to address cremation and the evangelical minister Billy Graham admitted that it was "no hindrance to resur-rection" (Prothero, 2001: 189). Cremation offers versatility on how to dispose of the cremains; they can be buried, placed in an urn, mixed with the ashes of loved ones, divided among relatives, planted with a new tree (as a symbol of life), or scattered over land or water.

The role of the funeral director

Funeral directors are the group of professionals whose job it is to handle various types of burial. Their role is central to the way that many people grieve, since, for example, following the loss of a loved one, the surviving partner's world is in a state of confusion. Remember that, in the wake of such a loss, nothing seems the same, there are no certainties; one's role in the world is suddenly changed – from spouse to widow or widower, and perhaps from homemaker to breadwinner. Funeral directors deal with death, loss, and mourning on a daily basis and therefore have the skills necessary to help survivors cope with the situation. The funeral has been shown to be an event that provides some stability in this time of turmoil (Pine, 1975). For the funeral to be a stabilizing and comforting the arrangements must be made with tact and skill and the ceremony must be performed well; there is nothing more nightmarish than having something go wrong which can haunt a survivor for years to come. Reputable and experienced funeral directors can ensure that things go smoothly.

The open-casket ceremony is still the preferred type in America (see table 5.2, which indicates that only 29.61 percent of Americans chose cremation in 2004, leaving over 70 percent choosing a traditional burial.) Quite often the casket is open before the actual service but closed and brought to the front of the assembly when the service begins. A traditional funeral will often also have viewing of the body at the mortuary. Funeral directors work to ensure that this viewing is satisfactory to mourners, and will carefully offer them the full range of services available, as well as various options for the service, casket, flowers, and more. In addition, funeral directors have the role of coun-selor, as they not only orchestrate the arrangements but also provide survivors with emotional support. Their constant exposure to death and bereavement situates them to be able to provide practical as well as emotional support. In fact a number of funeral directors often refer to themselves as "grief therapists."

The viewing ceremony is composed of elements that Durkheim (1965) referred to as a combination of "sacred" and "profane." It rests on a delicate balance between the cold elements of everyday life (profane) and the spiritual, ritualistic elements needed to convey a last tribute to a dead person. The body presents a sacred image, the last image of a loved one to whom one is bidding farewell. The fact that the mouth is shut close by a wire, that the body has been filled with chemicals, and that this beloved body is quickly decaying are among the profane elements of everyday life.

In order to conduct a successful funeral, the director and support staff, composed of embalmers, ushers, cosmeticians, pallbearers, lim-ousine drivers, and others, must give painstaking attention to every detail. The mood must be set, the appropriate music must be played, the tone of voice must convey the seriousness and the clothing under-score the importance of the event, and the flowers must speak of somber homage.

In keeping with social norms and expectations, everyone present both at the viewing at the mortuary and/or at the funeral service must behave appropriately and bond together to maintain the fitting balance between sacred and profane. Durkheim, (1965) called this bond 'collective consciousness', that is, the rituals reinforce the collective societal values and bring the living closer together as they offer a proper farewell to the departed. Unsuitable behavior endangers the invisible bond between those present at the service. The "profane" must not be allowed to dominate either the funeral service or the visitation ceremony at the mortuary; for instance, accidentally putting too much rouge on the deceased's face, making him or her look grotesque rather than "natural," or allowing children to laugh, cry, yell or run about, places an undue stress on the funeral service and mourners.

For the open-casket ceremony the body must be prepared and made to look as natural as possible. This requires considerable skills on the part of the embalmers since, by this time, the deceased has been dead at least two or three days, and his or her blood has been replaced with formaldehyde. Those who come to the viewing wish to remember the deceased as he or she was; cosmetologists prepare the body so that it may look like a living person for a last time:

> The undertaker closes the staring eyes, the gaping mouth, strengthens the sagging muscles, and with the aid of cosmetics and the help of soft silks and satins in the coffin's interior provides the central character of the tragic ritual with the proper appearance. Some of the favorite expressions of those who pass by "to pay their last tribute" are "He looked very well" – "He looked just like he did when he was well" or "You would think he was taking a nap or was resting his eyes for a minute." (Warner, 1959: 315–16)

Finally, at the service the deceased is paid formal tribute in the form of a eulogy, which must be, and always is, a positive, although at times not easily so:

> [At times the eulogy] makes for considerable juggling of the available facts of a person's life, especially when dealing with those whose lives have been less than sterling. When mentioned at all, such elements will always be placed in contexts that were not used while he was alive: recalcitrance being redefined as "independence," or purposelessness as a "restless spirit." (Turner and Edgley, 1976: 388)

The funeral director must carry out the ceremony without a hitch, supervising the change of status of the deceased while also reconciling those who are left behind with the loss of a loved one. In a service economy, in which we rely upon strangers to do a multiplicity of personal services for a fee, funeral directors have become grief merchants who direct the final ceremony.

Currently, profound changes are taking places in the American funeral industry. The rapid increase in the number of cremations and the wide cultural differences across the US have altered both the nature of the ceremony and the role of the funeral director. In some cases this has meant that the nature of the ceremony has been simplified and families have chosen to eliminate the viewing altogether. These changes have the overall effect of reducing the ritual complexity of the traditional funeral. In this context, the role of the director and staff is further reduced by the rise in the number of cremations, which eliminates the need for embalming. Thus, Americans are relying less on the funeral director and making more choice themselves. Also, the funeral industry is becoming increasingly corporate: Service Corporation International (SCI), the largest funeral company in North America owns more than 1,400 funeral homes. While the business use to be run largely by family operations, funerals are now big business. With this new corporate model come changes in the nature of the relationship between directors and mourners. Funeral directors become employees in a large company and thus do not merit the kind of trust that came with a more personalized service. The popularity of cremations hurts the industry as well, by removing the need for high-priced caskets.

Cemeteries

We have seen that burial sites gradually moved from the countryside (c. 350 BC) to the suburbs and then within the city, next to or inside churches.[2] In the past, cemeteries were not the sole domain of the dead but were arenas for numerous activities of the living. They were used as meeting places, as locations to conduct business, as rendezvous points for lovers, and as settings for gambling, playing, and even dancing, as documented by paintings from the Middle Ages of town folk dancing on tombs (Ariès, 1974, 1981).

Cemeteries were often the site of artistic endeavors such as statues, mausoleums, tombstones, and monuments. Artists were commissioned to create works that would leave an imprint reflective of the greatness of the deceased. For example, Michelangelo was hired by Pope Julius II to sculpt a series of statues for the pope's tomb, a project that occupied him from 1505 to 1545, ending in the masterpiece that is the statues of Moses.[3] At times, the bones and skulls of the dead were used to create intricate works of art; in Rome, the crypt underneath Santa Maria della Concezione dei Cappuccini, near Piazza Barberini, contains the bones of dead friars arranged along its walls, reminding us of the nexus between the living and the dead.

In America, cemeteries were once commonly called graveyards. The Protestant influence in America (Stannard, 1973) led to a fear of death, and this fear translated into how people thought about cemeteries.

Indeed, cemeteries were not inviting places but were instead sites to be avoided. This had the effect of leaving many neglected and unkempt until around 1830 (Harris, 1977). With the coming of Romanticism in the nineteenth century, the general ethos of romantic beauty was extended to burial places. Mt Auburn Cemetery, which was established in the Boston area in 1831, became a pacesetter, artistically decorated and luxuriant with vegetation.

The most famous Western cemetery is Père Lachaise Cemetery, in Paris. Adorned with over 12,000 trees, Père Lachaise is the resting place of who's who in France: Frédéric Chopin, Oscar Wilde, Edith Piaf, Isadora Duncan, Sarah Bernhardt, Gertrude Stein, Alice B. Toklas, Marcel Proust, Georges Bizet, Auguste Rodin, Amedeo Modigliani, and Jim Morrison, to name only a few. Père Lachaise has historically been a place for the living as well as for the dead. Young lovers meet there, old folks come to feed the over 400 cats that populate the cemetery, some Parisians come to pick *escargots* after rain, scores of tourists wander about admiring the statues and mausoleums, and local mourners bury their dead and then cross the street to drown their sorrows at a tavern aptly named Mieux Ici Qu'en Face (Better here than across the way) (Wallace, 1978).

In America views about cemeteries are in a flux. Most tend to be relegated out of sight and in their stark simplicity have come to reflect the nation's ethos: they have become increasingly practical, functional, and removed from the living. Bodies are buried or ashes are placed in urns, live flowers are slowly giving way to plastic bouquets, and even perpetual torches (burning to keep the memory alive) are being replaced by battery-operated facsimiles. On the other hand, there is a tendency to seek new, alternative ways to dispose of the body (discussed later in this chapter), from ecologically minded to very commercial. Finally, others are attempting to re-establish the medieval connection between the living and the dead by expanding cemeteries into places where people can also be married or hold other functions, and by attempting to beautify the surroundings, as in the 1900s. Burials are, as other important events in people's lives, a cultural and social expression, and many elements, such as education, religious beliefs, wealth, personal experiences and family pressure, influence decisions regarding final disposition.

Romantic burial

Americans have created their own version of Père Lachaise, a marvel for the living and the dead. Forest Lawn, which began in Los Angeles in 1906, now has a number of locations across the US where one can be baptized, married, or buried, in an attempt to mingle the living with the dead. To draw visitors and re-create the European tradition, Forest Lawn includes artistic attractions. The Los Angeles Forest Lawn has a marble replica of the David, a stained-glass window reproducing Leonardo's Last Supper, and some of the coins mentioned in the Bible, and much more. Among its monuments, mosaics, and chapels, it offers different burial sections, bearing names such as Whispering Pines, Triumphant Faith, Everlasting Love, Haven of Peace, and Babyland. The famous Americans buried here possess an unmistakable Hollywood flavor: Humphrey Bogart, Errol Flynn, Lucille Ball, Lou Rawls, Rod Steiger, and Brad Davis. Forest Lawn in Buffalo has a mausoleum designed by Frank Lloyd Wright, "The Blue Sky," with only twenty-four crypts, ranging in price from $125,000 to $300,000 (Brown, 2007), clearly a very exclusive and elitist choice for one's final resting place.

Forest Lawn's mixture of pseudo-romanticism and commercialism has been criticized and ridiculed since its founding, the classic spoof being the 1948 novel by Evelyn Waugh, *The Loved One*. The following excerpt provides the flavor of Waugh's caustic attack:

> He drew the sheet back and revealed the body of Sir Francis lying naked save for a new pair of white linen underwear. It was white and slightly translucent, like weathered marble.
>
> "Oh, Mr. Joyboy, he's beautiful."
>
> "Yes, I fancy he has come up nicely"; he gave a little poulterer's pinch to the thigh. "Supple," he raised an arm and gently bent the wrist . . .
>
> "But, Mr. Joyboy, you've given him the Radiant Childhood smile."
>
> "Yes, don't you like it?"
>
> "Oh, I like it, of course, but his waiting One did not ask for it."
>
> "Miss Thanatogenos, for you the Loved Ones just naturally smile."
>
> (Waugh, 1948: 68-9)

Perhaps Forest Lawn is guilty of dubious taste, but it must be credited with providing the first major attempt in America to reunite the dead and the living in a place of replicated classical beauty.

Modern-day cemeteries

Forest Lawn's chain of cemeteries, initiated in 1917 by Dr Hubert Heaton[4] became the model for memorial parks across America, which became the main type of burial location in the second half of the twentieth century. Memorial parks are typically laid out in grids and often encompass some high-rise building where burial takes place at different levels, from eye level to "heaven level"; they also are filled with statuary. The tombs become mirrors of the social class and ethnic background of the deceased. For instance, remembering the deceased through pictorial memorials is very characteristic of American culture. In cemeteries in general the dead are remembered through photographic images, while in the more upscale memorial parks they are remembered through sculpted busts and full-length statues.

Ethnic sections of cemeteries are also very different, as they reflect the traditions, the saints, and the symbolism of the country of origin. Italian-American sections of cemeteries are adorned with life-size statues, often depicting the Virgin Mary or angels, whereas "a profound sense of sadness and loss distinguishes German monuments and markers from those of other ethnic groups. The predominantly classical imagery consists of lamenting female figures, inverted torches, wreaths, urns, and perfect spheres" (Jackson and Vergara, 1989: 52). Irish-Americans sections, not surprisingly, are filled with Celtic crosses, those of Jewish Americans sport the emblem of the Star of David, while the Hispanic-American sections are overflowing with flowers and candles.

Consumerism and burial

As mentioned above, Jessica Mitford's (1963) classic work *The American Way of Death* launched a scathing and sarcastic attack on the whole American funeral industry. Mitford claimed that the American burial is orchestrated by the funeral directors, who skillfully channel people's unresolved guilt and fear of death into a buying spree. As a result, families spend more than intended and, to make matters worse, purchase grotesque, useless paraphernalia such as coordinated satin sheets and easy-rest mattresses. According to Mitford, the practice of having an open casket at a funeral and the predilection to show the body, hopefully made to look natural, are related to American consumerism and the desire to show through costly displays one's social status and wealth. In America even the dead become an object of consumption and social stratification.

Another famous American cemetery is Woodlawn Cemetery in the Bronx, New York, in which over 300,000 people are buried. Woodlawn was established in 1863 and is home to some extremely famous names of the past, such as Duke Ellington, Miles Davis, Herman Melville, F. W. Woolworth, Fiorello LaGuardia, "Bat" Masterson, and Joseph Pulitzer (Mirsky, 2008). It also has over 1,300 mausoleums, which are above-ground stand-alone structures. A tour through Woodlawn provides a view of American consumerism and the inequality that persists into the afterlife. The "landscape-lawn plan" layout promotes open spaces, and plots often include a centerpiece memorial and matching footstones. This scheme helped encourage the construction of major central monuments and grand private mausoleums that showcased the most affluent families (Woodlawn Cemetery, 2008; Mirsky, 2008). The cemetery was designed with great aesthetic care and patrons paid more for the most coveted plots.

This emphasis on consumerism continues today. The rebuilt Cathedral of Our Lady of the Angels in Los Angeles, consecrated in 2002, has a mausoleum in its lower levels with 6,000 crypts and niches for sale, with a starting price of $50,000. The head of the Los Angeles archdiocese has the final say on who may be buried there. To date, the most famous person is the actor Gregory Peck (Lassel, 2005).

In keeping with the American penchant for mass consumption, even funeral accessories have become more pricey and available to the public at large. For example, one of the largest warehouse-style stores in America, Costco, sells caskets online, its twenty different models ranging from $1,299 to $2,999. This trend toward mass commercial funeral accessories was begun in the 1990s in France by Michel Leclerc, who opened a chain of funeral-service "supermarkets," complete with piped music, and some items actually featuring a "sale" sign. While this method of selling reduces costs, ordering a casket online or buying it on sale in a superstore is symptomatic of the business ethos surrounding the funeral business.

It would seem that Durkheim was right: the way we bury our dead is a reflection of the social values of the living. Yet, Durkheim did not say enough. Not only do death rituals reflect positive societal values aimed at strengthening the moral fiber of society, they also reflect negative values. Americans are great consumers, and throughout their lives many tend to spend more than they can afford: public ceremonies such as weddings are a way to show one's financial success as much as a celebration; it follows that many would want to bid farewell to their loved ones in the same conspicuous manner.

Alternatives to traditional burial

The quest to find new ways of disposing of the body can be found in both America and Europe. Scattering cremains at sea is a popular means of disposal. Family and friends can do this as long as state-legislated rules are followed. In some cases professionals are available for such a service. For example, the yacht *Determination* is available for hire in order to scatter ashes off the coast of Long Island, New York, and in San Diego, California, the boat *Ashes of the Sea* provides a similar service (Rosen, 2004). Scattering ashes over mountains is also gaining popularity in France. The Association Française d'Information Funéraire states that it "will scatter the ashes over three different sites in the French Alps: Mt. Blanc's summit, Vallée Blanche, and Mer de Glace. For the content of one urn scattered across all three peaks, the cost is approximately 1,410 Eurodollars, or $1,627. The ashes are carried out by helicopter" (ibid.: 133).

Traditional burials require a large amount of construction material that, many would argue, are simply wasted. Furthermore, the use of embalming fluid and toxic substances to preserve the dead means that those chemicals also go into the ground. For example, every year the commercial funeral industry in the US uses 827,060 gallons of embalming fluid; 180,544 pounds of steel for caskets; 5,400,000 pounds of copper for lining caskets; 30,000,000 board feet of hard woods, including tropical woods, for caskets; 3,272,000,000 pounds of reinforced concrete for burial vaults; and 28,000,000 pounds of steel for vaults (Woodson, 2003: 1). In part to address this issue, Americans have begun to move toward green burials to offset the wasteful use of material and the damage caused by toxic material.

In Sweden, an organization called Promessa, led by the ecologist Susanne Wiigh-Masak, is pioneering an environmentally friendly method of burial that does not involve the use of harmful embalming fluid (Worldchanging, 2004). The new process involves using liquid nitrogen to remove water from the body, which turns it to dust, at which point it is essentially ready for burial (Promessa Organic, 2008). The recycled body is then used as fertilizer. In Brussels, *Arteus Europa* offers coffins made from cellulose fiber (Worldchanging, 2004). In South Carolina, the 32-acre Ramsey Creek Preserve, which was founded in 1998, offers caskets that are made from biodegradable wood and only non-toxic embalming fluids are used. The casket costs about $ 2,300, while for a conventional funeral the average cost of a casket is about $6,500 (Basler, 2004). This is an example of a green cemetery (Osgood File, 1999). Another famous green cemetery is Fernwood in Northern California. The ecological idea is to protect rather than consume green space while also providing a cheaper burial.

Americans have always found creative ways to save the cremains, and the increasing commercialism of the funeral industry has encouraged the proliferation of ever more methods. In San Diego, the company Celebrate Life will mix cremains with gunpowder and launch them in firework displays (Rosen, 2004). Another alternative, by Eternal Reefs, is to mix the ashes with wet cement and manufacture a boulder to be lowered under water with others to create a new "coral" reef. The cost varies with the size of the boulder (for a lesser fee, it is also available for pets). Canuck's Sportsman's Memorial, Inc., in Des Moines, Iowa, will preserve cremains in hourglasses, basketballs, duck decoys, and urns shaped as golf bags. Reportedly, the owner, Mr Knudsen, plans to have a portion of his ashes loaded into rifle shells, so that his son will be able use them when he goes hunting (Graham, 2001).

Perhaps the most esoteric and expensive way to preserve cremains is by turning them into a diamond. Dean and Rusty VandenBiesen developed a carbon collection kit that can be used to recover carbon from the tissue of the deceased (Rosen, 2004). Along with other investors, the brothers formed a company called LifeGem, which has outlets in the US, Canada, and Europe, which trains crematoria to use their carbon recovery kit. LifeGem can produce a rough diamond in about twelve weeks; the diamond is then cut into the desired shape and polished. The finished product is expensive, blue diamonds more so than yellow ones. The cheapest blue diamond choice, between 0.20 and 0.29 of a carat, costs $3,499, while the most expensive, between 0.90 and 0.99 of a carat, is $19,999 (www.lifegem.com/). The newest marketing technique of LifeGem is in cooperation with John Reznikoff, who owns University Archives:

> Reznikoff holds the Guinness World Record for the largest and most valuable collection of celebrity hair. Reznikoff's collection also includes such figures as Napoleon, Albert Einstein, Abraham Lincoln and John F. Kennedy. In total, the collection is valued at over $5 million dollars. (www.lifegem.com/secondary/BeethovenLifeGem.aspx)

Body and organ donation

Some people hope their death may help bring life to others, and one way to ensure this is by donating their remains to medical science or to donate their organs to people in need. Organ donations have the potential to save many individuals who would otherwise die. The total number of deceased donors increased by 35 percent over the period from 1992 to 2001 (Nathan et al., 2003). In greater New York, in 2005, 778 organs were recovered from deceased donors, 406 of which were kidneys (Donate Life, 2005).

Additionally, donated cadavers allow medical students and physicians to practice before applying their skills on living patients: "Transplant of kidneys, livers, lungs, hearts, corneas, pancreas, and some glands has been done successfully" (Quigley, 1996: 197). Medical, osteopathic, and dental schools as well as teaching medical institutes require every year more donations of bodies than are available. Selling body parts is illegal in the US, but some countries sanction it, which has led to a booming and highly profitable illegal market. The horror stories in regard to this practice are numerous. Consider the following:

> In March 2004 . . . UCLA director of the Willed Body Program, Henry Reid, was arrested and a criminal investigation launched into the activities of others at the University of California for the illegal sales of

body parts. That series of events focused attention on the fact that one
cadaver could be dismembered and sold in parts for over $200,000 to
the pharmaceutical and medical industries. (DiJoseph, 2006: 1)

Many Americans, when asked, agree that they should donate their
bodies and organs, though only a limited number actually do. They
are allowed to do so by the Uniform Anatomical Act, adopted in some
form by all fifty states. A signed organ donor card or, in some states, a
driver's license indicates whether a person is an organ donor. By the
end of 2005 there had been 13,335 organ donors in America, of which
6,997 were deceased (Donate Life, 2005).

Besides the use of organs for transplants, various tissues and other
substances can be harvested from the body; blood, heart valves, skin,
veins, cartilage, and disks can help restore a number of needy patients.
In 1974, Dr Willard Gaylin, then the president of the Institute of
Society, Ethics and the Life Sciences, published an article that shocked
the medical community (Gaylin, 1974). He suggested that "neomorts,"
brain-dead individuals, should be kept functioning in large "bioempo-
riums" and used for a number of purposes, from training to harvesting
of human byproducts. Yet, over thirty years later, America has hardly
embraced such an idea. While Gaylin's suggestion was hypothetical,
in the real world bodies are used for procedures donors may not have
thought of. Heads are often used for sharpening the skills of plastic
surgeons, and bodies may be crashed in tests to better determine the
safety of cars (Roach, 2003).

A more esoteric use of the body is found at the "body farm," at the
University of Tennessee's Forensic Anthropology Center (Bass and
Jefferson, 2003). Founded in the 1970s by Dr Bill Bass, the research
facility uses unidentified or unclaimed bodies donated by the medical
examiners' office. The bodies (thirty to forty per year) are allowed
to decompose while lying in an open field – some are dressed, some
are naked, some are buried in shallow graves, some are wrapped in
plastic, all to better understand forensic details about death, and
the causes and time of death. Basically, the bacteria in the gut, after
death, finding no more sustenance, begin to consume and gradually break down the body's tissue in a process called putrefaction.
According to Roach (2003), what happens to our bodies is similar to
the fate of the wicked witch of the West, in *The Wizard of Oz*, who lique-
fied into a brown puddle on the ground.

There are many other bizarre (if not so new) ways of using cadavers. Both French and American militaries have shot bullets into dead
bodies, both to understand the effect of being shot and to provide protective measures against it. When the guillotine was being developed,
the necks of cadavers provided testing guidance for the force of the

impact and the height from which the blade should be dropped. The list of experimentation goes as far as scholars attempting to explain Christ's crucifixion by nailing cadavers to a wooden cross (Quigley, 1996; Roach, 2003).

The latest use of cadavers comes from Germany. Dr Gunther von Hagens invented a process called plastination, which involves freezing the body, removing the blood, and replacing it with liquid plastic. The preserved bodies can then be sliced into thin sections, or stripped so only the muscles or the blood vessels, or any other part of the body, are shown in action. The effect is dramatic and highly valuable for teaching purposes. The exhibit has traveled from country to country using the donated bodies of over two hundred plastinated humans and has attracted 20 million people across the world in the last ten years, while grossing over $200 million (Bodyworlds2, 2005).

Ethicists and others have been upset by the showmanship associated with the use of the bodies (for instance, one of the exhibits depicts a plastinated rider on a horse extending his hand forward, upon which rests his brain). To add to the controversy, another show, Bodies, the Exhibition, modeled itself after von Hagens's exhibit while using bodies obtained from China. Human rights groups have raised questions about the voluntary status of the bodies used for the display, given the alleged disregard for human rights in China. The *New York Times* reported that "at least ten . . . Chinese body factories have opened in the last few years. These companies are regularly filling exhibition orders, shipping preserved cadavers to Japan, South Korea and the United States" (Barboza, 2006).

Conclusion

We began the chapter by viewing the choice of rituals associated with death in America. Cremation is an increasingly popular option but it is still overshadowed by conventional burials. We discussed early burials and the ways in which bodies were disposed of. The chapter followed by surveying death in America, from the simple ways of the sixteenth century to the diverse trends in burials and the preservation of remains used today.

We discussed the process of embalming, followed by the problems of body snatching in days when cadavers were not widely available for scientific inquiry, and then cremation. Next we turned to the role of funeral directors and the changing nature of the funeral industry and of cemeteries and their appearance and meaning. Specifically, romantic cemeteries and the commercialism of the burial were addressed. Finally, new ways of disposing of the body, from ecological to commercial, were enumerated. Body donation and its nuances were discussed.

There is a strong theme of favoritism toward the wealthy and power-ful throughout the social history of funeral practices. It was the kings, the rich, and the high priests who were given expensive, elaborate funerals, while the poor shared a common grave with other unfor-tunates or were fitted in a simple wooden coffin. Later, it was again the wealthy who were able to protect their burial sites from grave robbers. Today it is the wealthy who can buy organs for transplanta-tion or avail themselves of the best clinics and medical practitioners. In fact, one of the latest alternative modes of burial, that of turning the cremated body into a diamond, is a perfect symbol for death in America – a display of wealth forever.

PART III

INDIVIDUAL AND COLLECTIVE DEATH

CHAPTER

Children and Death

06

Age and death

ALTHOUGH we mourn the loss of any loved one, we can *understand* and even rationalize death among older people much more readily than we can among children. While we recognize that old age itself does not cause death, we associate death with being old and accept it as a normal end to a long life. The link between old age and death has not always been the dominant view. It used to be the case that death was commonly associated with youth. In puritan America, for example, where families had an average of about nine children, parents could expect that more than one in four of their children would not live to see their tenth birthday (Stannard, 1974). With the dramatic advances in public health and the resulting increases in life expectancy since the Industrial Revolution in both Europe and the United States, we no longer routinely expect early deaths in developed countries. Now, death has come to be viewed as a timely event, the completion of the normal life course in old age. In this context, since the young are not *supposed* to die, the loss of a child is particularly devastating for society, and even more so for parents and family.

In this chapter we focus on the unfortunate topic of children and death. In keeping with the emphases of the book, we will explore death and dying from both macro- and micro-levels and also address our theme of social inequality. From a macro-sociological perspective, the incidence of infant and child deaths in a population is an important indicator of the health of a society. Infant and child mortality rates both tell us about privilege and poverty as we compare across different societies and allow us to compare across various groups *within* a particular society to examine how income and health inequality predict the rate at which children die. At the micro-level, the reality of children's death and the resulting parental bereavement and changes within the family are important to consider as we study grief and mourning for specific types of losses. Although the majority of research about the consequences of the death of a child focuses on parents' experiences, we also examine death from the siblings' perspective and from the perspective of children themselves. Scholars now recognize that children have their own thoughts and fears about death. We end this chapter by examining the main theories about how children think about death and how their notions of death and dying relate to their feelings about mortality and their own experience of loss and grief.

Changing conceptions of childhood

How we deal with and understand child mortality at both the individual and the group level is linked to how we as a society think about children and childhood more generally. In contemporary society, children are seen as prized possessions whom we recognize as dependent on adults for their well-being and protection. At both societal and individual levels, we value children for their innocence, for their optimism, and for what they represent about the possible future. For privileged people in the United States, the death of a child is a relative rarity and as such it is a particularly great loss, unlike any other crisis or trial that we may experience. This has not always been the case, since views about children and childhood have changed radically over time: in previous eras, how people dealt with the death of a child was also influenced by adults' expectations and understanding of children's core attributes and roles in society.

Historians have debated about children's changing social status over time, usually with a historical focus on Europe and America. The French philosopher and historian Philippe Ariès, who wrote extensively about death and dying (as we discussed in previous chapters), also wrote about changing conceptions of childhood. Ariès argued that in the pre-industrial period the modern concept of childhood as a special time in which children were to be protected from the harsh realities of adult life was nonexistent. Instead, they were considered to be "miniature adults" who were expected to grow up quickly in order to survive in their dangerous and harsh social and physical environments (Ariès, 1962; Prescott, 2004). Ariès wrote,

> In medieval society the idea of childhood did not exist; this is not to suggest the children were neglected, forsaken, or despised. The idea of childhood is not to be confused with affection for children: it corresponds to an awareness of the particular nature of childhood, that particular nature which distinguishes the child from the adult, even the young adult. In medieval society this awareness was lacking. (Ariès, 1962: 128; quoted in Corsaro, 2005: 61)

Although some of Ariès' claims have more recently been challenged or debunked, the core of his contribution to the sociological understanding of childhood was that he showed how both the concept and the experience of childhood are socially constructed and historically specific (Corsaro, 2005: 62).[1] Many historians as well as family and childhood scholars have since built on his work. Clearly, Ariès' description of the absence of a distinct phase of childhood in medieval times is in stark contrast to how we think about children and childhood in contemporary society.

Other historians have emphasized that, although pre-industrial parents were faced with the realities of frequent childhood deaths, they focused specifically on their religious education out of love and concern for the child's soul (Prescott, 2004). In puritan America, for example, settlers' strong religious beliefs meant that, although parents loved their offspring deeply, they also viewed them as afflicted by original sin. Thus, they encouraged children to "recognize their depravity and pray for salvation" from a very young age (Stannard, 1974: 462). Colonial parents felt that they should not shield their children from the realities of everyday death but should instead spiritually prepare them for their dealings with their own and others' death (Prescott, 2004). The challenge for us today is to remember how the dominance of religious ideology and the lack of basic public health measures and advanced medical technologies combined directly to shape the ways in which early Americans thought about, raised, and loved their children, and also how they understood the relationship between children and death.

In the eighteenth century, as the age of Enlightenment spread across Europe and began to influence American thinkers, views about children and childhood evolved. The new emphasis on reason and science gradually weakened the strong religious ethic during the late eighteenth and early nineteenth century. New philosophies about children and childhood emerged during this time that explained how children were not innately depraved, as the puritans thought, but were naturally innocent and pure (Prescott, 2004). One influential work that challenged the religious view of children as naturally sinful was *Emile* ([1762] 1979) by Jean-Jacques Rousseau, which is a semi-fictional account of a boy's education. Its central theme, and Rousseau's intended message, was that humans (and specifically children) are born naturally good and that it was society that corrupted them as they grew into adulthood. These new ideas coincided with other American social trends, gaining popularity as they entered the cultural milieu and influenced parenting beliefs and practices (Mintz and Kellogg, 1988; Prescott, 2004). The notion that children are innocent and should be shielded from the corruptive influences of society is still with us today.

Thus far our discussion of the changing understanding of children and childhood serves as a backdrop for the next section on infant and child mortality. We now turn to an overview of macro-level changes in the frequency of infant and child deaths in America since colonial days, followed by current trends in contemporary American society, and also a discussion of how the US compares with other countries.

Infant and child mortality

Early America

In early America children died with great regularity. In the New World, the physical environment was harsh, epidemics were frequent, work was dangerous, sanitation was poor, medicine was rudimentary, and parents were not always able to protect their children from threats. Puritan settlers had very large families partly because the rates of infant and child deaths were so high.

In colonial times, the famous and prolific Boston minister Cotton Mather was intimately acquainted with child death, as he saw nine of his fifteen children die before their fifth birthday (and maternal mortality was so high that he outlived several of his wives as well) (Prescott, 2004). Mather wrote in his sermon *Right Thoughts in Sad Hours* (1689), "a dead child is a sight no more surprising than a broken pitcher, or a blasted flower" (quoted ibid.: 25). While this might seem to be an insensitive view of children's death, there is also plenty of historical evidence that suggests that puritan and early American parents had deep affection for their children and valued them greatly. Although Cotton Mather wrote about the regularity of childhood death, he also acknowledged the intense pain that came with it, comparing it to losing a limb (Avery, 1994; Prescott, 2004). Some historians have argued that puritan parents kept children at an emotional distance partly because they expected them to die, and it helped them insulate themselves from the pain of their loss (Stannard, 1974).

From a sociohistorical perspective we would be remiss if we did not also consider the frequency with which children died within the institution of American slavery. As we have shown thus far, infant mortality was a standard part of life in early America and if the harsh environment and living conditions were challenging and perilous for free (white) children they were exponentially more difficult for slave children and infants born into slavery.[2] Estimates of infant mortality among slave children on American plantations range dramatically, "from 152.6 to 350 per thousand – compared with 179 for the infant mortality rate of the American population as a whole – with some estimates of total losses (stillbirths plus infant deaths) before the end of the first year of life of almost 50 percent" (Campbell, 2006: 266; Steckel, 1986). These estimates vary widely in part because of changing historical definitions of infant mortality and because of a lack of comparable demographic records across plantations and cities throughout the colonies. However, it was also the case that living and working conditions varied throughout the colonies and from plantation to plantation.

Historians have also investigated the leading causes of death among slave children. Slave owners widely believed that the primary cause of infant death among slaves was mothers' negligence. However, another likely explanation of infant mortality was what is now recognized as sudden infant death syndrome (SIDS), which we discuss in more detail later in this chapter. Nonetheless, there is also some historical evidence to suggest that some slave women did in fact commit infanticide in order to spare the child a life of slavery and toil (Campbell, 2006; Yanuck, 1953). In one example, during a harsh winter in New York City in 1741, a slave woman named Diana, "driven to desperation by the ferocity of the cold and by the hopelessness of bondage, 'took her own young Child from her Breast, and laid it in the Cold, that it froze to Death'" (Lepore, 2006: 15). Although it is a horrific image, in reality, in North America these cases accounted for a small minority of deaths. A more likely explanation for the high infant mortality among slaves was the harsh and demanding physical work that pregnant mothers had to perform, even up to the moment that their labor began, as well as lack of prenatal care, deficient diets, and unsanitary, unsafe deliveries (Campbell, 2006).

Beloved

Contemporary America

Like other scientific measures, infant and child mortality rates have been socially constructed and negotiated, and have evolved over time. The current definition of the infant mortality rate (IMR) is the number of deaths before one year of age per 1,000 live births, and this has been the standard definition in the US since the 1880s (Brosco, 1999). To calculate the rate for a given year we divide the number of infant deaths by the total number of live births for the same year and then express it as deaths per 1,000 births (WHO, 2006a). The child mortality rate (CMR) is the number of deaths before the age of five per 1,000 live births (WHO, 2006b) and is calculated the same way as the IMR. For both measures, social demographers and other researchers often calculate separate rates for males and females, since there are distinct gender differences in mortality rates among children (as there are among adults). The clarity of the definition and the ease with which the public can understand it has meant that, at various points during the twentieth century, "politicians and public health officials viewed the IMR as a measure of community health, economic efficiency, collective moral wellbeing, and future military strength" (Brosco, 1999: 479).

At the beginning of the twentieth century, for every 1,000 live births that occurred in the United States, approximately 100 infants died before they reached their first birthday. In 1900, in some US cities, 30 percent of children died during their first year of life (CDC, 1999; Meckel, 1990). Through various improvements in public health, social welfare, and medical technology, the IMR declined precipitously such that, "from 1915 through 1997, the infant mortality rate declined greater than 90% to 7.2 per 1,000 live births" (CDC, 1999: 849; Hoyert et al., 1999).

White the trajectory of the IMR has been consistently downward, at different points in history the decline has been more or less dramatic, and these starts and stops have coincided with other social trends. Beginning in the 1960s, with the creation of Medicaid (government-sponsored health insurance for the poor) and widespread improvements in neo-natal medical technology, the IMR fell sharply and then in the mid-1980s leveled off (Kleinman, 1990; Pharoah and Morris, 1979). However, it began to drop again in the late 1980s and through the late 1990s. During this time part of the reduction was a result of decreases in the occurrence of sudden infant death syndrome (CDC, 1999; Schoendorf and Kiely, 1997), a topic on which we elaborate further later in this chapter.

The most recent data available show that, in 2004, the US IMR was 6.78, which was down slightly from 6.84 in 2003 (CDC, 2007). From a sociological perspective it is especially important to consider how the IMR varies across different groups in this country. Sociologists are not surprised to find that the well-documented link between socioeconomic status (in terms of education as well as income and wealth, for example) and race/ethnicity correlates with different levels of infant death across various groups. In 2004, the IMR "ranged from 4.67 per 1,000 live births for Asian and Pacific Island mothers to 13.60 for non-Hispanic Black mothers" (ibid.: 1). Even within specific ethnic groups, we find variation in the rates of infant deaths. For example, among Hispanic mothers in 2004, the IMR for Cubans was 4.55 and for Puerto Ricans it was 7.82. These differences are partly explained by socioeconomic status but also by other sociocultural factors, such as nativity and marital status. Indeed, "infant mortality rates were higher for those infants whose mothers were born in the 50 states and the District of Columbia, were unmarried, or were born in multiple births" (ibid.). One of the central points to take away from this discussion is that, although we tend to focus on aggregate IMR for particular countries, it is important to explore these macro-level trends more deeply to uncover within- and between-group differences in societies.

What are the main causes of infant mortality in the US in the 2000s? According to the Centers for Disease Control, babies who are born prematurely and at the lowest birth weights account for a large pro-portion (CDC, 2007). Full-term births are defined as those that reach 40 gestational weeks, although pregnancies that last between 38 and 42 weeks are considered to be within the normal range. Fetuses born before the thirty-seventh week are considered to be premature. Of all of the infant deaths in 2004, 55 percent occurred among the very small group (2 percent) who were born before the thirty-second week of gestation. Premature births aside, 45 percent of the infant deaths in 2004 were caused by the three leading causes of infant death in the US: congenital defects, low birth weight, and sudden infant death syndrome (ibid.).

Recently, changes in the IMR in parts of the US have provided clear evidence of the link between infant mortality and poverty, inequality, and race. In the South, IMRs had been dropping since the 1960s, but in recent years they have begun to increase in some of the country's poorest states, including Mississippi, Louisiana, Alabama, North Carolina, South Carolina, and Tennessee (Eckholm, 2007). The trends in Mississippi are particular alarming. Recall that, in 2004, the national average IMR was 6.78. In contrast, in that same year Mississippi's IMR was 9.7, and in 2005 it actually increased to 11.4 (ibid.). Scholars, public health officials, doctors, and social workers have argued that the increase in infant deaths in Mississippi is partly on account of reductions in spending on welfare and Medicaid in the 2000s, combined with poor rural women's lack of access to doctors. The social conservative political climate of the 2000s has increased spending on military efforts abroad while simultaneously cutting back domestic expenditures on social welfare programs that benefit the poorest citizens. Furthermore, some cite education, health, and lifestyle factors related to what many doctors call "the growing epidemics of obesity, diabetes and hypertension among potential mothers" (ibid.). And underlying these trends are striking racial differences:

> In Mississippi, infant deaths among Blacks rose to 17 per thousand births in 2005 from 14.2 per thousand in 2004, while those among whites rose to 6.6 per thousand from 6.1. (The national average in 2003 was 5.7 for whites and 14.0 for Blacks.) The overall jump in Mississippi meant that 65 more babies died in 2005 than in the previous year, for a total of 481. (Eckholm, 2007)

It should be disturbing to Americans to find, that in some parts of the United States, infant mortality is actually increasing. With the dramatic changes in health and medicine over the past century, the country's overall prosperity, and the relative infrequency of infant deaths in general, many Americans take for granted that infant mortality is not a real problem here, and certainly not one that is getting worse in the 2000s. Rather, we expect to find these high, and steadily increasing, rates of infant and child death in poor, underdeveloped countries. These trends, then, should be particularly alarming for those of us interested in eradicating inequality and health disparities in the US. As the developments in Mississippi illustrate with distinct clarity, from a sociological perspective, the macro-level trends in infant mortality tell us a lot about which people in our society have access to material and social resources such as education, employment, and healthcare, and how these differ by geography. How do we fare in comparison with other countries? In the next section we briefly look at infant mortality in the US and across the globe in order to locate our country's health within the larger context and examine relative inequality across countries.

Infant mortality in global context

The IMR is an important macro-level indicator of the health of a society and is commonly employed as a yardstick by which to judge how well particular societies are taking care of their citizens. According to the US Central Intelligence Agency's *World Factbook* (CIA, 2007), as of 2007, the country with the highest IMR is Angola in Africa, with a rate of 184.44, followed by Sierra Leone (158.27), Afghanistan (157.43), Liberia (149.73), and Niger (116.83). The United States ranks 180th with an IMR of 6.37, and the United Kingdom ranks 193rd with an IMR of 5.01. The top five countries with the lowest measures begin with Iceland, which is ranked 217th and has an IMR of 3.27, followed by Hong Kong (2.94), Japan (2.80), Sweden (2.76), and Singapore (2.30).

The United Nations Children's Fund (UNICEF) also ranks countries according to various measures of health and literacy, including the IMR and the CMR. It has documented that, in 2002, the country with the highest CMR was Sierra Leone, with a measure of 284 (meaning that 28 percent of all children born die before they turn five years old), followed by Niger (265), Angola (260), Afghanistan (257), and Liberia (235) (UNICEF, 2003). The United States ranks 158th with a CMR of 8, while the United Kingdom ranks 161st with a CMR of 7. Among the countries with the lowest CMRs are Sweden (3), Singapore (4), Norway (4), Iceland (4), and Denmark (4) (ibid.).

The UNICEF report also provides evidence that, globally speaking, the IMR has declined significantly since the 1960s for both less developed and more developed countries. In 1960 the world IMR was 126, and by 2002 it had declined to 56. Similarly, the mortality rate for children under five years old was 196 in 1960 and 82 in 2002. However, upon closer inspection we do find dramatic differences between countries according to their level of development. Furthermore, although the IMR and CMR have declined for less developed countries over the past forty years, on average, their declines have been less steep than those found in the more developed countries (UNICEF, 2003). Nonetheless, these changes are positive indicators of worldwide improvements in education and public health, including a significant decrease in the number of measles deaths due to the spread of vaccination, increases in breastfeeding, the use of mosquito nets, and an upturn in the number of babies and children who are taking vitamin A drops (McNeil, 2007).

The point of this discussion so far is to demonstrate that, according to either measure of child mortality, the United States is not leading the world at the top of the list. Rather while the US does not have the worst child mortality rates (that end of the list is dominated by less-developed African countries), based on these indicators, we also are not as healthy as our Nordic or Asian counterparts. It should also be clear that the IMR is linked to the level of a country's development and the organization of its state.

We now turn to the topic of sudden infant death syndrome (SIDS), which has been relevant to several of the subjects we have discussed so far. SIDS is one of the leading causes of death of very young children, and the ways in which it has been tackled as a public health problem provide a sociological example of issues related to the healthcare inequality that directly affects children's lives and deaths.

SIDS

Sudden infant death syndrome, sometimes referred to as crib death (in the US) or cot death (in the UK) is a syndrome (a group of symptoms that together indicate a particular disorder or disease) that is characterized by the sudden and unexplained death of an otherwise apparently healthy infant aged one month to one year. The apparent health of the infant means that a SIDS diagnosis is necessarily based on exclusion – that is, it may only be pronounced as the cause of death after discounting any and all other possible causes.

The syndrome is least likely to occur in an infant's first month of life, but most SIDS deaths occur in babies that are less than six months old (AAP, 2005). The actual causes remain unclear, although doctors and healthcare practitioners have identified some risk factors; the most frequently cited cause is putting babies to sleep on their stomachs. Researchers have identified patterns which suggest that the risk is related to the infant's sex and the age, ethnicity, education, and socioeconomic status of the parents. The American Academy of Pediatrics has identified the following risk factors associated with SIDS and has listed them in their policy statement on the issue:

> Prone sleep position, sleeping on a soft surface, maternal smoking during pregnancy, overheating, late or no prenatal care, young maternal age, preterm birth and/or low birth weight, and male gender. Consistently higher rates are found in Black and American Indian/ Alaska Native children – 2 to 3 times the national average. (AAP, 2005: 1245)

Other recent medical research has found some evidence that children who have brainstem abnormalities that interfere with the delivery of the neurotransmitter serotonin may be more prone to SIDS (Paterson et al., 2006; Weese-Mayer, 2006).

In 1994, in response to recommendations put forth by the American Academy of Pediatrics, the federal Back to Sleep public health campaign began. Back to Sleep was designed and launched in order to raise awareness about SIDS and first and foremost to teach parents to put their infants to sleep on their backs. Although it remains the leading cause of death in the US for infants under age one, "during the 1990s, a greater than 50 percent decline in SIDS rates (attributed to the recommendation that infants be placed to sleep on their backs) has helped to reduce the overall infant mortality rate" (CDC, 1999: 852; Willinger et al., 1998).

As we mentioned above, reductions in the infant mortality rate and in the incidence of SIDS have not been the same across groups. White infants have benefited the most from the Back to Sleep campaign (meaning that their IMRs declined the most) and African-American children's survival has been the least affected, a point to which we return below. An additional ethnoracial difference is that, although African Americans have higher rates of SIDS than non-Hispanic whites, Hispanic and Latino infants have lower rates than white infants (Mathews et al., 2000). Adherence to the Back to Sleep recommendations vary according to parents' education as well as to race/ ethnicity (Willinger et al., 2000). In response to these ethnoracial differences, by 2000, the Back to Sleep campaign was reoriented to target minority parents and to increase awareness of SIDS and sleeping positions particularly. Recent research has found that the ethnoracial inequalities in SIDS rates that existed in the 1980s and 1990s have not been reduced by the Back to Sleep campaign, but that class and race disparities have actually widened (Pickett et al., 2005).

More recently, sociologists and even some medical scientists have begun to emphasize the relevance of cultural differences that contribute to the differences in SIDS rates across racial and ethnic groups (Hackett, 2006; Weese-Mayer, 2006). Some sociologists have studied the ways that racial stereotypes have been invoked in the Back to Sleep campaign materials in order to place the blame for SIDS on black parents themselves, who are seen as intransigent and culturally incompetent (Hackett, 2006).

SIDS is an example of a specific cause of infant mortality that has clear patterns related to socioeconomic and cultural differences within American society. As such it is crucial for our sociological examination of children and death. However, regardless of how an infant dies or the socioeconomic status of the family, parents, family members, and other survivors are left to cope and mourn the loss of that child. As we explained at the outset of this chapter, because we associate death with old age and not youth, the loss of a child may be among the most difficult for people to endure. We now turn to a discussion of how parents and family members grieve and deal with the death of a child.

Parental bereavement

Bereavement outcomes

The loss of a child can be one of the most stressful and enduring life events and has been linked to various types of problematic psychological outcomes for parents, siblings, family, and friends. The majority of research and theory in this area focuses on how parents deal with the loss of a child, although it is clear that others are also affected. For our purposes we first discuss the research about parental grief and later in the chapter turn to some of the other research on how siblings deal with the loss of a brother or sister.

Parental grief can be especially difficult to understand and treat because it involves symptoms that are cognitive, affective, behavioral, somatic, and social in nature (Stroebe and Stroebe, 1987). It can be particularly severe when compared with grief experienced as the result of other types of losses (Hazzard et al., 1992; Rando, 1985). Research in this area has found evidence of various consequences of the death of a child for the health and well-being of the parents. One study found that parents of boys or children who died suddenly experienced higher levels of despair, anger, guilt, and depersonalization than parents of girls or parents of children who died after a prolonged illness (Hazzard et al., 1992). Furthermore, the amount of social support that they had, as well as their perceived level of stress after the death, mattered for how parents grieved their lost child.

Parental identity

Why is the loss of a child such a painful event for parents? The answer to this question might seem obvious; however, articulating the reasons why a child's death is so difficult is more complex than it appears. Some research on parental bereavement has focused on how such a loss changes a parent's identity and sense of self. Not only is the death of a young person considered to be an untimely event, but the loss "robs them [parents] of their parental status and identity" (Hastings, 2000; Riches and Dawson, 1996a, 1996b; Toller, 2005: 46). As Klass explains,

> Parenting is a permanent change in the individual. A person never gets over being a parent. Parental bereavement is also a permanent condition. The bereaved parent, after a time, will cease showing the medical symptoms of grief, but the parent does not "get over" the death of the child. (Klass, 1988: 178)

Parents must mourn the loss of the child itself but also parts of themselves and their identity as parents. Researchers have suggested that those who lose a child take on a liminal (in-between) status as they continue to feel parental responsibilities to a child who is no longer physically there (Romanoff and Terenzio, 1998; Toller, 2005). That is, they may no longer technically or logistically be a parent to the deceased child but they still *feel* as if they are, and thus they are simultaneously both a parent and no longer a parent to that child. From a micro-sociological perspective, the way that a parent feels about their identity and role is extremely important and possibly more important than the fact that they may no longer actually be a parent to a living child.

Because parents are *supposed* to die before their children, the death of a child may also topple their understanding of the order of the universe, causing them to question their own understanding of the world (Hazzard et al., 1992). Drawing on the work of Giddens (1991), Riches and Dawson (1996b) assert that part of parents' confusion centers on the fact that they take great responsibility for shielding their children from harm, as well as teaching them not to be afraid of the world and to trust that they will be protected. In this context, a child's death calls into question all of these promises and underscores parents' inability to carry out their protective role – indeed it "starkly demonstrates the fragility of this cocoon and the fallibility of existential inoculations" (Riches and Dawson, 1996b: 3). Parents also often express a strong sense of survival guilt, as they wish that they themselves had died rather than their child. This sense of survival guilt is linked to whether parents blame "fate" or themselves for the death of the child and also impacts the ways in which they manage their own bereavement (Hazzard et al., 1992).

Parents' social roles

From a sociological perspective it is also important to consider the *social* consequences for the parents of the death of a child. In chapter 9, we will explore how the loss of a spouse changes widows' social relationships, but here we must address how bereaved parents experience dramatic changes in their social lives and relationships (Rando, 1986a).

While most bereaved parents report that they feel the need to talk about their deceased child and the experience of the death (Attig, 1996; Murphy, 1996), family and friends often feel uncomfortable and unsure about what to say or do in response, and therefore they do not usually find ways to enable bereaved parents to talk (Rando, 1986a). As one parent laments, "a lot of people will keep their distance . . . they are frightened . . . they are frightened of catching it" (quoted in Riches and Dawson, 1996b: 5). This lack of connection with bereaved parents' usual social network of family and friends may encourage them to seek out new and alternative relationships with other bereaved parents in which they feel that the significance of their loss is recognized and validated, and where they may explore the meanings associated with their loss with others who have lived through the experience – possibly the only people who can truly understand (Riches and Dawson 1996a, 1998, 2000). Researchers and practitioners have found that support groups for bereaved parents and families can be effective in offering resources and helpful information as well as comfort, because "those involved in these family support groups know what the death of a child is like, including what it is like when weeks pass and the active support and concern of many friends, neighbors, classmates, and coworkers diminishes" (Field and Behrman, 2003).

In keeping with the notion that bereaved parents may feel the need to continue to talk about and remain connected to their deceased children, another strain of ethnographic research has emphasized the importance of "continuing bonds" (Klass 1993a, 1993b; Rosenblatt, 2000; Talbot, 2002). Based on a ten-year study of support groups for bereaved parents, Klass (1993a, 1993b) emphasized the ways in which parents maintained their relationships with their deceased children and how talking about and sharing their memories with others who had lost a child allowed them to construct continuing relationships with those children, find meaning in their loss, and help heal their pain. This line of research is in stark contrast to previous models of "healthy" or "normal" bereavement (mostly from a psychoanalytic perspective), in which those left behind were expected to sever ties with the deceased and move on with their lives (Davies, 2004).

Support groups also exist for "parents in waiting" whose child was stillborn or miscarried. In the US "more than 25,000 pregnancies a year end in stillbirth, generally defined as a naturally occurring, unintentional intrauterine death after more than 20 weeks of gestation. A cause for the death is usually not determined" (Lewin 2007: 1). The experience of a miscarriage or stillbirth has long been ignored in our culture and shrouded in mystery. Parents who experience a pregnancy loss typically do not have the public recognition or support that other types of child loss evoke. Over the last twenty years support groups have emerged that actively seek to redefine perinatal loss as a legitimate source of grief (Layne 1990). Even more recently, since 2001, nineteen US states have enacted laws in response to pressure from parental support groups and organizations that allow parents of stillborn babies to receive birth certificates (Lewin 2007). For the parents who have experienced stillbirth, receiving a birth certificate is extremely important and symbolic of their child's existence and their experience of the pregnancy and labor, and provides a sense of validation. In this case, support groups have not only acted as a source of emotional support but have also been mobilized to change public policy.

The effect on marriage

We know that the loss of a child usually has a dramatic impact on parents' relationships with people in their close and extended social networks. It is logical, then, to assume that the death of a child would also affect the much more intimate relationship between that child's parents. Much of the research on the impact of the death of a child emphasizes the effect on marital relationships and examines how spouses communicate (or fail to communicate) about their loss as well as long-term changes in the relationship. While married parents share a common relationship with their children, they also have relationships with their children that are independent of their spouse. These independent relationships mean that, although the parents may mourn the loss together, they also lose their own individual relationships and therefore must mourn those as well – and sometimes this is not something that a couple can do together but that each person must work through independently. Some research suggests that, through talking about their child's death, marital partners can come closer together (Riches and Dawson, 1996b), while others find patterns of marital dissolution and divorce (Lauer et al., 1983).

For several decades it was considered "common knowledge" within this field that most marriages break up after the death of a child (Schiff, 1977). However, some scholars have called this assumption into question (Rando, 1986b), and a review of the large body of research on this topic found more variation in marital outcomes than has been assumed. In his review, Schwab found that marital relationships are indeed strained by a child's death but that divorce is not an inevitable outcome of the loss. Instead, most marriages survive the death over the long run, but how long and in what form the marital recovery takes depends on several factors, including the status of the marital relationship before the death of the child, the cause of the death, and the circumstances surrounding the death (Schwab, 1998). Therefore, while the majority of evidence shows that divorce is not unavoidable, the trajectory that marriages follow after the death of a child is highly dependent on the specific characteristics of the marriage itself as well as the circumstances of the child's death.

Circumstances of the child's death

Clearly, the death of a child is never an easy experience to endure. However, the circumstances of the death also matter for how parents experience the loss and the duration of their grief, as well as for how healthcare professionals and social workers respond to the dying child and the family's needs (Institute of Medicine, 2003). If the death is preceded by an extended illness and the child is given a terminal diagnosis by a doctor, it is possible that family members have time to begin to come to terms with the impending loss and begin to grieve the death before the child actually passes. Bereavement scholars have termed this process "anticipatory grief" or "anticipatory bereavement" (Lopata, 1986; Rando, 2000), which is characterized by the same feelings that we expect to find in post-death bereavement, including sadness, anger, regret, loss, and even guilt (Institute of Medicine, 2003).[3] When the diagnosis is not terminal but is instead *potentially* fatal, parents may also engage in anticipatory bereavement as they try to prepare themselves for worst possible outcome while hoping for the best.

Having forewarning about a child's possible or imminent death may allow the family to begin to prepare in various ways, including by talking with their child about death and letting the child express their fears and concerns. Some research suggests that talking with a dying child about her or his own death can be beneficial for the parents' bereavement. One study of Swedish parents who had lost a child to cancer found that, although a minority of the adults in their sample talked with their children about their impending death, none of them regretted it. Those parents who sensed that their child was aware of their own imminent death, but who did not discuss it with the child, were more likely to regret not having done so than those who did not feel that their child was aware that they would soon die (Kreicbergs et al., 2004).

In the face of an extended illness, parents may not only begin to think about coping with the impending death of a child but may also make practical arrangements. For example, the family might arrange for the child to die at home or prepare to help him or her die at peace in the hospital or hospice setting (Institute of Medicine, 2003). It also allows family and medical staff (and potentially the child him- or herself) to discuss at length their end-of-life preferences, what kinds of medical interventions they are willing to accept, and their plans for pain management (called palliative care). These types of plan require that medical staff be extremely involved in the care of the family as well as the dying child. Parents who have time to anticipate the loss may also arrange for religious and/or cultural rituals and practices that may be emotionally or spiritually important to them and that may provide some sense of comfort.

When the death is from SIDS, accident, suicide, murder, or otherwise without warning, parents and family tend to have the most difficult time dealing with the loss.[4] Some evidence suggests that grief and bereavement after the sudden death of a child is even longer-lasting and more complicated than if the parents and family have time to consider and prepare (Institute of Medicine, 2003). A study of parents who lost an infant to SIDS in the preceding twelve to fifteen years used in-depth qualitative interviews to study the long-term consequences. The authors found that, even after such an extended period of time, when most people who assume that they are over their loss, "most parents still viewed the death of their child as affecting their daily life in important ways" (Dyregrov and Dyregrov 1999: 635). Consider also that many of the circumstances surrounding a child's sudden death (such as SIDS, or when the death is due to abuse or neglect) require the involvement of a medical examiner's office and include an autopsy and potentially other procedures that may add to the parents' stress and grief (Institute of Medicine, 2003).

In the case of a sudden, traumatic accident the relationship between family members and medical practitioners is particularly intense and crucial for the family's well-being. One case study of an eighteen-month-old girl who was accidentally hit by a car and arrived at the hospital with severe head trauma is particularly illustrative of the significance of an integrated plan for caring for both the patient and the family members. In this case, the toddler's prognosis was unclear when she was admitted, but over the course of several hours she was diagnosed as brain dead and the family made the decision to donate her organs. Imagine for a moment what this family went through as they were initially uncertain about how the toddler would fare and within hours found themselves discussing whether or not to donate the child's organs to others. Within this context, the doctors and nurses had quickly to establish a trusting relationship with the family and help them emotionally, while simultaneously providing them with honest medical information about the fate of the child and broaching the subject of donating her organs (Truog et al., 2006). None of these are simple or easy conversations. And just as they are difficult for families to endure, talking about an impending death can be hard for healthcare professionals too.

When parents whose children experienced life-threatening conditions recall what was important to them while their child was under medical care, they often focus on healthcare professionals' kindness as well as their sincerity and empathy, and they also stress the value of having clear and honest communication (Meyer et al., 2002). In this same case study, the medical team demonstrated great care for the toddler's parents in addition to the child herself. Once the child was pronounced brain dead, Dr W, the director of pediatrics at the trauma center, talked with the parents about how they wanted to say goodbye:

> We gave them as much time as they needed. It's important to give parents access to the child. Because of the intensive care unit and everything about it, there's a loss of control and a lack of feeling close. Many parents would like to lie in bed with their child, and that's fine. Anything that can make parents, for at least a time, able to cry, to touch and talk to the child, to lie with and hold the child, I think that's very important. We try to set things up so that's possible. We often will cut a lock of hair from the child and take handprints and footprints of their child. Many parents have found that to be a very positive memory. (Truog et al., 2006)

At the individual level all of these considerations and decisions have implications for how parents experience the death of the child. Doctors are rarely well trained in end-of-life care or in talking with their patients about death (Groopman, 2002), and working with dying children and their families can be both logistically and emotionally challenging for healthcare providers. While it might be simpler if there were a standard guide for medical professionals to follow in these situations, it is clear that providers must be ready and willing to attend to the individual needs and desires of particular families. In these situations there is no one-size-fits-all practice.

Coping with the death of an adult child

Unlike most other social relationships, the specific relationship between parent and child is not one that we choose and it is also one that lasts a lifetime. For parents, losing a child of any age is difficult. Among all of the various research studies about parental bereavement, a subset focuses on parents who have lost adult children. A recent study of a small group of bereaved parents whose adult children were either fallen soldiers or victims of terrorism describes how they dealt with their grief, their anger, and their attempts at forgiveness. Their findings showed that anger was one of the most prominent emotions that parents experienced after the loss and that it had three sources: the circumstance of the death, the institutionalized response to the loss, and a certain political policy and its makers. Regarding this last source, parents often talked about "the enemy" as the target for the majority of their anger, but the enemy was never the person who actually killed their child; rather, they named a political leader whose policy decisions they felt were responsible (Ronel and Lebel, 2006). In other words, for the parents the cause of death became something much larger than a bullet or a particular enemy soldier; it was the wider social and political forces that put the child in harm's way to begin with.

Another study, of bereaved parents who lost an adult child during military service in the Israeli defense forces, found four main types of grief responses: absence, delayed, prolonged, and resolved (Ginzburg et al., 2002). The majority of their sample of parents displayed prolonged or delayed grief reactions. Furthermore, the authors found that parents' level of education and religious attitudes and the circumstances under which the child died all affected what type of reaction they experienced. Three-quarters of their respondents who were classified with low levels of education demonstrated an absence of grief, compared with just 14 percent of the respondents who had higher education. Regarding prolonged grief reactions, the authors found that just over half of respondents with the highest levels of education experienced this type compared with only 6 percent of those with a high-school education. Findings concerning religiosity showed that over half of respondents who identified themselves as "traditional" Jews experienced an absence of grief compared with only 7 percent of "orthodox" subjects. Finally, parents whose child died as the result of an accident were much more likely to demonstrate an absence of grief (compared with those whose child died by suicide or during military service), and those who lost a child from suicide or military service were much more likely than the first group to show a prolonged reaction (Ginzberg et al., 2002).

Parents' gender and ways of coping

Just as individual people deal with death and loss differently, we can also expect that bereaved parents do not all cope with their children's death in the same way. Researchers have problematized the role of gender and gender differences in bereavement responses among parents who have experienced the death of a child (Cook, 1988; Murphy et al., 2002; Sanders, 1993; Schwab, 1996). Some scholars have suggested that, because much of the research on parental grief has focused on mothers' experiences, we know less about how men respond to child loss (Cook, 1988). In this light we must be careful not to judge, devalue, or ignore fathers' typical experience of grief by comparing it with those of mothers. From a sociological perspective we should note that the way in which mothers and fathers grieve as individuals is related to socially constructed expectations about women's and men's appropriate behavior more generally. Our social relationships and realities are constantly shaped and affected by gender norms (rules and expectations) about how women and men *should* be, without much regard to how individual women and men actually *are*. Furthermore, sociologists acknowledge that focusing on groups of people and group differences can often obscure the ways in which individuals within groups differ from each other. Indeed, it may be the case that, although fathers and mothers grieve differently, there are even more differences among mothers and among fathers than there are between mothers and fathers.

Some research suggests that mothers grieve more deeply than fathers do (which is attributed to the bonding that usually takes place between an infant and mother) and that mothers' grief tends to be longer lasting than fathers' (Fish, 1986; Sanders, 1993). Theories of gender socialization suggest that, during bereavement, women will focus on emotional strategies for coping while men will focus on problem-oriented strategies. In support of this gender difference perspective, there is evidence that fathers are more likely both to return to work sooner than mothers and to engage in "distractive" activities as part of their coping (Rando, 1991; Riches and Dawson, 1996b). While some gender differences exist, women and men may not be as different as we think. A recent study of bereaved parents whose child died as a result of an accident, suicide, or homicide found that women did in fact focus on emotional-based strategies in addition to other coping methods. However, men did not use only problem-based strategies but employed various coping methods (Murphy et al., 2002).

One study of fathers who had experienced the death of a child from cancer in the previous ten months to five years found that their responses to the loss were something that they experienced internally and alone, since they felt that showing their grief outwardly was unhealthy for themselves and for the people around them. They expressed how they were caught in a double bind that was the result of two cultural expectations – "the societal expectation that men should comfort their wives and . . . the cultural ideal that healthy grieving cannot be accomplished without the sharing of feelings" (Cook, 1988: 285). The fathers in this study described how they tried to resolve these conflicts within themselves while processing their own grief. Other research has found support for the notion that men feel the need to be strong for their families, and in doing so they tend not to discuss their feelings about the loss or grieve openly (Riches and Dawson, 1996b).

Siblings

The effect of the death of a sibling has not until recently been a major focus in the research literature. This omission is partly due to the ways in which scholars and clinicians have theorized about children's experiences of grief and loss in general, which we will discuss in the next section. Recently, however, we have begun to acknowledge and study how the loss of a sibling affects children as well as the implications of the loss for the dynamics between family members.

The sibling relationship is unique because it is usually lifelong and because siblings have a shared history within a family. Indeed, "the death of a sibling marks an end to what is expected to be one of the longest and most intimate relationships of a lifetime" (Robinson and Mahon, 1997). Not only does the child lose a brother or sister, but their understanding of themselves may be affected and change as well. Sibling relationships play a role in identity development through the ways in which brothers and sisters interact and define each other (Bank and Kahn, 1982), and thus the death of a sibling can actually mean the death of part of the identity of the surviving child (Devita-Raeburn, 2004).

Within the family, the loss of a child can change the relationship between surviving children and parents. For example, if the death follows a prolonged illness, the organization of family life may already have changed as the sick child became the center of everyone's attention. Often in these cases healthy siblings may be sent to stay with other family members or friends in an effort to shield them from the reality of their brother or sister's illness and death, even though some research suggests that this can hamper their bereavement process (Giovanola, 2005).

Just as with other types of losses and relationships, siblings react to the death of a brother or sister in a large variety of ways,[5] although some trends are discernible. First, several studies have noted that siblings sometimes feel the need to suppress or hide their feelings of loss in order not to cause their parents any more stress or worry (Mahon and Page, 1995). Second, some siblings develop behavioral problems or withdraw socially as part of their reaction to the loss, and these responses can create other interpersonal problems within their social networks (McCown and Davies, 1995). Third, they may have feelings of guilt, anxiety, and fear in the short term. However, research suggests that, over time, survivors may either socially withdraw from their peers or actually use the loss as a launching pad for their own personal growth (Davies, 1991; Mahon and Page, 1995; Robinson and Mahon, 1997). Fourth, the ways in which parents themselves respond to the loss of a child can have a strong impact on how children experience the death of a brother or sister (Institute of Medicine, 2003).

Worden (1996) outlined thirteen main theoretical differences between losing a parent and losing a sibling, arguing that the distinction between them is important for children's bereavement experiences. However, a more recent study by Worden and his colleagues found no significant empirical differences between parental and sibling loss for children in terms of their total number of problems or the incidence of psychological syndromes, or in the percentage of children defined as "at risk." Instead they did find gender differences in how children responded to the different losses: boys were more traumatized by parental loss and girls were more affected by the loss of a sibling (and by the death of a sister in particular) (Worden et al., 1998).

Children's understanding of death

We have already mentioned that in contemporary society parents often hope to shield children from the realities of death, even in the case of a dying sibling. At the same time, death is a part of our everyday popular culture, and even part of films and cartoons specifically made for children, which can affect how they think about death (Cox et al., 2005). In a world in which children are inundated with fantasies about death but shielded from its realities, how do they themselves think about and understand death? The first attempts to answer this question began in the 1940s and were based on psychoanalytic studies of children in which they were encouraged to talk freely about what they thought about death. The main conclusions of this research were not only that children have a great deal of anxiety and emotion about death, but also that their capacity for really understanding it is limited by their cognitive and emotional immaturity (Slaughter, 2005).

More recently, researchers have focused on children's understanding of three main concepts concerning death: irreversibility, non-functionality, and universality (Ellis and Stump, 2000). Irreversibility is the understanding that, once death takes place, the physical body cannot become alive again. Non-functionality is the understanding that once an organism dies it ceases to function. Universality is the understanding that all living things die (ibid.; Speece and Brent, 1984). The ages at which children develop these various understandings are somewhat debated in the research literature. Studies disagree about how much children between the ages of three and seven understand, although most pediatricians and death researchers agree that children begin to grasp all three concepts by the time they are seven or eight. Various factors can affect children's conceptions of death, including religiosity or religious upbringing, as well as whether or not they have known someone who has died (Ellis and Stump, 2000).

What about children who themselves are dying? How do they think about death and face their own mortality? Practitioners who work with terminally ill children have noted that those suffering from a life-threatening illness appear to have a more mature and advanced understanding of death than other children (Institute of Medicine, 2003; Sourkes, 1995). Perhaps one of the most well-known children in recent history who was faced with a life-threatening illness and whose conception of life and death were beyond that of most adults was Matthew "Mattie" Stepanek. Mattie was born July 17, 1990, with dysautonomic mitochondrial myopathy (DMM), which is a rare form of muscular dystrophy, a hereditary condition that interrupts the functions of the autonomic nervous system.[6] During his lifetime, Mattie had two brothers and a sister who died from DMM, and, at the age of three, he began to write poetry to cope with the death of his older brother. Over the course of his short life, Mattie wrote five books of poetry, many of which dealt with his illness as well as his fears and concerns about death, but also his joy and gratitude about life. The first book of poetry was *Heartstrings*, and all five made the *New York Times* bestseller list; his final book was a collection of correspondence with former President Jimmy Carter. Mattie's consciousness and experience of his disease and the loss of his siblings made him acutely aware of the gift of his life as well as the reality of his and others' mortality. When asked, Do you ever get angry or scared about your disease or dying? He wrote,

> Of course I get angry and scared. I am very human. Some people think I am always brave. I try to be, but I cry like the next person sometimes. I am needle phobic and pain phobic, so that doesn't help. But even if I

get upset, or think, "I can't do this anymore," I get myself together and pray or play or talk with my mom or a close friend, and I get beyond that tough time. I might say, "Why me?" But then I say, "Why not me? Better me than a little baby, or a kid who doesn't have strength or support." I am very blessed to have God and my mom so involved in my life. (Stepanek, 2008)

One could argue that most adults cannot fathom their own mortality the way that Mattie faced his, and certainly most of us do not articulate our feelings about death, dying, and loss the way that he did. Mattie was a poet, a peace activist, and a National Goodwill Ambassador for the Muscular Dystrophy Association. He died June 22, 2004, three weeks before his fourteenth birthday.

Children and mourning

Previously children's experience of grief was ignored, downplayed, or dismissed altogether, but some scholars have recently shed light on this topic (McCarthy, 2007; Morgan, 1990; Thompson, 1997). Thompson argues that this ignorance of children's grief is tied to their ambiguous social status: on the one hand, they are valued and prized yet, other the other hand, they are marginalized and disenfranchised, since they are not given the full rights of citizenship due to adults. This lack of full citizenship translates into a social ambivalence about how children relate to issues of death and dying that is ultimately unhealthy for both them and society (Thompson, 1997).

Researchers have also argued that ignoring children's emotional pain about death is dangerous for their own well-being, since "in reality it is unlikely that any child will grow into his or her own teens without experiencing the pain of loss, the suicide of a friend, or the death of a significant other" (Morgan, 1990: 1, quoted in Thompson, 1997: 61). Although the most frequent loss that young people report is the death of a grandparent or other "second-degree relative" (McCarthy, 2007), about 6 percent of American teenagers aged thirteen to seventeen report having experienced the loss of a parent (Ayers et al., 2003). Furthermore, adolescents are likely to experience the death of a peer (Balk and Corr, 1996; Oltjenbruns, 1996) while a minority experience the death of a sibling (Ringler and Hayden, 2000). How children and adolescents deal with these losses varies according to the type of relationship with as well as the perceived emotional closeness to the deceased (Servaty-Seib and Pistole, 2006).

Not only can children who experience unrecognized or unresolved grief after the death of a loved one or peer become a danger to themselves and others (Morgan, 1990; Lendrum and Syme, 1992), but some scholars argue that excluding them "from issues of death, dying, and bereavement – however well-intentioned – tends to reinforce their non-citizen status and therefore render them vulnerable to a range of problems," many of which can have long-lasting effects on their lives (Thompson, 1997: 62). It is becoming increasingly clear that, although very young children cannot fully understand the concept of death, shielding children from the reality of topics of death and dying, whether in the abstract or in real-world situations, can be detrimental to how they grieve, mourn, and cope emotionally with the eventuality.

Conclusion

In this chapter, we have covered the major topics concerning children and death and dying, ranging from macro-historical social trends in infant and child mortality to the individual coping and bereavement experiences of parents who have lost a child and children's own conceptions of death. At the macro-level, infant and child mortality rates tell us a great deal about the health (and healthcare) of a society and that society's capacity for caring for (and its priorities about) its most vulnerable citizens. It is one thing to talk about children dying in terms of abstract, macro-level trends, but it is quite another to experience the loss of a child in individual terms. Parents who lose a child are susceptible to a range of psychological outcomes as well as substantial changes in their social relationships, and the preponderance of scholarly evidence shows that these kinds of losses are the most emotionally painful and enduring. Losing a sibling is also a traumatic life event, since it can affect the surviving child's identity as well as their relationship with their parents. To this point, enough research has shown that, although very young children may not be able to fully understand what death is, ignoring children's bereavement experiences or assuming that they are immune to the pain of such losses is detrimental not only to individuals but also to the psychological and social health of society overall.

Death and Destruction

CHAPTER
07

Introduction

IN this chapter we examine death by destructive forces that affect numerous lives at once or that take a single life each time. The three main types of event that result in death on a large scale are epidemics, natural disasters, and war. The human toll from each of these catastrophes is immense. Although all of these events produce pain and suffering for individuals, our emphasis here is on the macro-level consequences of large-scale death. Specifically, we focus on the causes and outcomes of these disasters and the ways in which different social groups are more on less vulnerable to catastrophic events and have relatively easier on more difficult times recovering from them. Sociologists will not be surprised to find that the social stratification processes that produce different outcomes in other types of death are also at work in determining which groups are the most susceptible to catastrophic events. In keeping with the focus of this text, our emphasis is on occasions of mass death that have occurred in America, although in the case of epidemics we also discuss some of the historical origins of large-scale diseases that began in Europe and spread to the United States.

Epidemics

Throughout history, epidemics have caused death on a grand scale, and the resulting devastation has changed the future of entire societies and their populations. An epidemic is "a widespread outbreak of an infectious disease where many people are infected at the same time" (DeSalle, 1999: 240), and this is somewhat different from a pandemic, which is "an epidemic that affects multiple geographic areas at the same time" (ibid.: 244). Epidemics usually occur through the dissemination of bacteria and viruses. While medical science has found ways to kill many bacterial infections, scientists are also increasingly concerned about the growth of strains of new bacteria that are resistant to existing drugs and therapies (Levy and Marshal, 2004). Furthermore, researchers have yet to find methods to kill viral infections, rather than merely treating their symptoms. Although vaccines and public health measures have been developed that can either eradicate or hinder the spread of some epidemics, the potential for widespread and devastating mass infections remains – even in advanced societies.

Infectious diseases such as pneumonia, influenza, and tuberculosis were the leading causes of death in the US until the middle of the twentieth century (Wright, 2005). While these afflictions are no longer the main killers of people in the developed world, they remain a cause for concern, particularly since the predominance of rapid, global travel has made the world smaller, more accessible, and therefore subject to an even easier spread of disease. Population growth, as well as technological changes in mass transit and transcontinental travel, facilitate the dissemination of infectious diseases over large areas (and can therefore change an epidemic into a pandemic).

While epidemics may sound like a phenomenon of the past, they still happen today and have profound social and economic effects on individuals, communities, and societies. We now turn to the three main epidemics that have ravaged America at various points in its history, each of which resulted in large-scale deaths: bubonic plague, yellow fever, and influenza.

Bubonic plague: the black death

When most people think about the black death (bubonic plague) they imagine the devastation that ravaged Europe throughout the Middle Ages. Historical evidence shows that the plague was present in China as early as 37 AD, however, as well as throughout India and Asia for hundreds of years. It arrived in Sicily in 1347 and spread throughout Europe over the next three years, beginning a continuous wave of plague epidemics for the next 300 years, until it finally disappeared in 1670 (Scott and Duncan, 2001).

Scholars have produced a large body of historical and epidemiological literature about the human toll caused by the black death over the centuries. The use of the term "black" to describe the disease was meant to describe its dreadfulness (Herlihy, 1997) and also its symptoms, in which the lymph glands (mainly in the groin and the armpits) would fill with pus and eventually turn black (Svendsen, 1997). The infected individual would die within three to seven days. The disease is primarily found in rodents, and it is the fleas that live on these animals that transmit the plague to people. Once individuals are affected they can infect others very quickly simply by coughing, which spreads droplets containing plague bacteria through the air to be inhaled by others (CDC, 2005).

The massive loss of human life in Europe during this age of plagues actually changed the demographic landscape, and in England the population did not replenish itself until 150 years later (Scott and Duncan, 2001). Indeed, in the three years during which the black death ravaged Europe during the mid-fourteenth century it killed an estimated 25 million people, or approximately 30 percent of the population (Kelly, 2005). Although cities eventually recovered from these epidemics, some consequences of the black death were much more profound and long-lasting. In Europe, the plague actually helped improve the socio-economic status of the peasants who survived. Previously the economy was based on cheap labor and the high cost of land. The massive loss of life caused by the plague reduced the size of the available workforce and reversed Europe's economic situation; after the black death, the demand for labor increased wages, and the price of land dropped.

While the bubonic plague ravaged Europe and Asia for centuries, it finally reached America at the end of the nineteenth century. This most recent wave of the disease was called the Third Pandemic (Gregg, 1985). This time, it originated in China, spread to Hong Kong, then to Hawaii, and eventually made its way to San Francisco. In 1894, in Canton, China, an estimated 40,000 people died over a four-month period, and the following year Hong Kong lost about 12,000 people (J. Hays, 1998). Steamships eventually carried the plague to Honolulu in 1899, and it spread to San Francisco that same year.

The trajectory of this epidemic is a fitting example of how changes in technology and travel can help spread disease from one end of the earth to the other. The plague came to San Francisco via rats and their fleas aboard steamships. Before the invention of the steamship, oceanic commerce and travel were limited to sail-powered boats and the journey across the ocean took much longer. Under those conditions, rats and humans who were infected with plague or other disease did not usually survive the trip. In the 1800s steam travel substantially shortened ocean travel times, so that infected fleas, rats, and humans could survive and carry the disease with them. The larger size of steamships also made it possible for larger rat populations to make the journey.

In both Honolulu and San Francisco the disease was confined to Chinatown. In Honolulu, authorities burned down many infected houses in the Chinese areas (J. Hays, 1998). Anti-Chinese sentiments were already causing racial tensions in San Francisco even before the plague arrived. The board of health cordoned off twelve blocks of Chinatown, quarantining the entire area. Later, with the consent of President McKinley, it restricted Asians from traveling on public transportation in the city and also tried to remove the Chinese in Chinatown into detention camps (Marks and Beatty, 1976). Chinese officials in the city sued the federal government and were able to overturn both measures.

The San Francisco epidemic was politically and socially significant particularly because, when plague was initially found in rats in the city, public officials denied that it existed and therefore did not take measures to contain the impending public health problem (Marks and Beatty, 1976). The governor, Henry T. Gage, denied, for both political and economic reasons, that any cases had been reported, and he actually attempted to pass legislation to make it illegal to claim that the plague had stricken the city. This situation lasted until Gage left office in 1903 and his successor fully cooperated with the health board, acknowledged the presence of the plague, and began to assemble forces in order to combat it. When another smaller plague epidemic hit the Mexican district of Los Angeles (killing twenty-eight Mexicans) the denial continued. The local newspapers referred to the outbreak as "malignant pneumonia" (Gregg, 1985).

From a sociological perspective, these epidemics of bubonic plague in the US were noteworthy not only for their virulence but even more so for their social effects. They generated racial unrest as white people felt threatened and, in their respective cases, distrusted both Chinese and Mexicans. The epidemics were also examples of how corrupt politicians denied the existence of any problems, bowing to pressure from powerful business interests, to the citizens' detriment. It is also no accident that those who were most affected by these waves of plague were people of color.

In contemporary America we no longer hear very much about plague. Indeed, most assume that it was a medieval disease that hit Europe and eventually was eradicated. Few Americans realize that it ever made it to this country and actually caused mass death. In reality, however, the plague still exists in many areas across the globe as well as in various rodents and small animals in rural areas of the US. According the Centers for Disease Control (2005) approximately five to fifteen cases of plague are reported in the US each year, most of which are scattered across rural areas and occur during the warmer months of the year. About 14 percent of these cases are fatal, although several modern antibiotics are effective against the disease if it is detected early enough.

Yellow fever

Yellow fever is a highly contagious viral disease that has, at different points in time, ravaged the US as well as Africa and parts of South

America. Both humans and monkeys can catch yellow fever, and it is transmitted primarily through mosquito bites, which explains why subtropical and tropical climates in these parts of the world are particularly vulnerable to waves of the disease (WHO, 2001). Some individuals afflicted with yellow fever experience jaundice,[1] which accounts for the name. The other two primary symptoms include violent fever and black phlegm (produced because the disease attacks the stomach lining) (Powell, 1993). Historians find documents describing epidemics of yellow fever as recently as 400 years ago (ibid.).

In the United States, the first major wave of yellow fever hit the city of Philadelphia in July of 1793. At the time, it was the country's temporary capital and its largest city (Powell, 1993). Between August and October that year over 4,000 people (about one-tenth of the population) died and over 17,000 fled as the disease ravaged the city (Marks and Beatty, 1976; Powell, 1993).

New Orleans is another major US city that has experienced persistent waves of yellow fever outbreaks even more recently than the northern metropolises. In that city, yellow fever was also referred to as Bronze John, Saffron Scourge, and Yellow Jack. The typical season for outbreaks was generally between July and October – the hottest and steamiest months of the year – and as many as a third of the city's population left during that time in order to avoid catching the disease (Powell, 1993). Between 1817 and 1905 more than 41,000 people died of yellow fever in New Orleans (New Orleans Public Library, 2008), where the subtropical climate helped breed the mosquitoes that spread the disease and where close living conditions and poor sanitation systems helped ensure that many people were afflicted. During the 1853 yellow fever epidemic, the local newspaper *The Picayune* provided weekly tallies of the number of dead and the number buried in the above-ground cemeteries (Fenner, 1854).

Physicians were largely unable to do anything to stop the spread of yellow fever or cure those who were afflicted. In his reflections upon the epidemic of 1853 and in making his recommendations for treating the disease one doctor admitted, "in New Orleans may be seen the results of every imaginable course of treatment from *doing nothing at all*, up to the use of *the most potent remedies in heroic doses*; and cases have recovered and died under all" (Fenner, 1854; 57; emphasis in original). Descriptions of the epidemic provide accounts of doctors who stayed with their patients at their own risk, and also acknowledge the apparent connection between the spread of the disease and lack of sanitation in the city.

As yellow fever ravaged New Orleans, officials did their best to keep peace, although some of their tactics for mollifying the scared citizens may seem ridiculous to us now. For example, at one point during the height of the epidemic, the mayor of the city, the council commit-tee, and the board of health began firing a cannon on a nightly basis and burning coal tar as an experiment to purify the air, although citizens began to complain that the cannon fire was detrimental to those who were sick and so the practice was ceased. The last yellow fever epidemic in the US occurred in 1905 in New Orleans. Gradual improvements in city water systems, sewerage, and drainage eventu-ally eliminated a great many of the breeding grounds of mosquitoes in the country.

Across the globe, yellow fever continued to be a threat in develop-ing countries, particularly those in subtropical climates and those with poor living conditions and public health systems. Although it was largely eradicated in the US by this time, a vaccine for yellow fever was developed in the 1930s, and the first large-scale vaccination efforts began in 1934 in what was then called French Africa, south of the Sahara (Vanio and Cutts, 1998). With the widespread use of vaccinations against yellow fever, occurrences of outbreaks seemed largely under control for many years. Nonetheless, the World Health Organization (2001) cautions that the number of epidemics has risen in the past twenty years, and both of the Americas and Africa have large, unvaccinated populations who are susceptible to outbreaks. It suggests that the increase in yellow fever is partly due to changes in the environment as a result of globalization, such as deforestation, that increase interactions between humans and mosquitoes as well as the expansion of worldwide travel.

Influenza

The 1918–19 influenza pandemic was the most devastating pandemic in history, killing between 50 and 100 million people across the globe (Johnson and Mueller, 2002). Although the human loss was massive, the spread of the disease was very quick; most of the deaths occurred in the relatively short period in 1918 between mid-September and mid-December (Barry, 2004). This pandemic of influenza is commonly known as the 'Spanish flu' because it was first reported by Spain, and it received the greatest press attention in that country since Spain was not involved in World War I (which was in its last year when the pan-demic hit) and did not have wartime censorship. It did not originate in Spain, however, but was first reported in Kansas in the US in March 1918 and quickly spread across America (J. Hays, 1998).[2]

Influenza was the first pandemic to begin in America and then spread to Europe and as far as Africa, the East Indies, and Australia. Just like the San Francisco epidemic of plague, this dissemination of flu across countries was largely due to increasing globalization. This time the disease swept across the globe in three waves (Taubenberger and Morens, 2006). America had been involved in World War I since 1917 and had transported thousand of troops to France, where they mingled with European and African troops. Modern transportation then facilitated the rapid spread of the disease to the far reaches of the earth. American troops returning from Europe brought the second wave of the pandemic back home with them.

Influenza is atypical as an epidemic because it spreads extremely quickly, vaccination to protect from it confers very limited immunity, and the virus is unstable, continually presenting itself in different forms (McNeill, 1976). The lifecycle of the influenza virus is short, but the devastation left in its wake was on a grand scale nonetheless. The World Health Organization reports that it is likely to have killed over 40 million people across the world and it was different than other flu pandemics because it killed primarily young people in their twenties (WHO, 2003).

The flu pandemic was influenced by social factors and had a lasting effect on the societies it touched. World War I put a huge amount of stress on both military personnel and civilians and also reduced the quality of life (food, hygiene, shelter) of millions of people, weakening them and making them much more susceptible to infections. In Asia, Africa, and Latin America it was not war but poverty that created substandard living conditions and made people vulnerable to the virus.

HIV/AIDS: a contemporary epidemic

In 1979 doctors noticed a strange and unexpected trend in which a significant number of homosexual men living in Los Angeles and New York began to die in alarming ways. Initially, the deaths were attributed to various causes but the symptoms were remarkably similar: a weakening and eventual collapse of the immune system and the contraction of various types of carcinoma and puzzling infections. At first, scientists named the disease Gay-Related Immune Deficiency (GRID). However, soon they discovered than not only homosexuals but other individuals, including hemophiliacs, intravenous drug users, and Haitians, were afflicted with the same disease (J. Hays, 1998). In 1982, the disease was named acquired immune deficiency syndrome (AIDS) (Grmeck, 1990). As epidemiologists and other scientists accumulated more knowledge about the disease they eventually identified the virus that caused AIDS, the human immunodeficiency virus (HIV). Eventually it was agreed that this virus attacks the immune system and weakens it, causing symptoms that could be taken for influenza. What follows is a latent period of indeterminate length after which the person moves from being considered HIV positive to having AIDS, when the effects of the weakened immune system clearly surface and the patient exhibits other problems, such as carcinoma and various opportunistic infections.

As knowledge about AIDS has progressed over the years, very different public reactions have been encountered, often creating a stigma for those living with the disease. When GRID and then AIDS were first identified and initially associated with homosexual men, panic ensued, and various social groups began to pass moral judgment on homosexuals and others, including intravenous drug users, who were viewed as susceptible to the still mysterious disease. In those early years, various campaigns of misinformation appeared, based on fear, ignorance, and homophobia, that helped to stigmatize people with HIV/AIDS and to blame them for their own misfortunes.

Consider for example, Ryan White (1971-1990), a teenager from Indiana who was a hemophiliac and who contracted HIV and eventually AIDS through a contaminated blood transfusion. In 1984, Ryan was expelled from his school when officials learned that he had acquired AIDS. Since HIV/AIDS was so poorly understood at the time, various members of the community rallied against him out of fear, forcing Ryan and his family to undertake a lengthy court battle in order for him to be allowed to attend his public school. Ryan was one of the pioneers of the HIV/AIDS awareness movement, and his plight galvanized various celebrities to help educate the public about how the disease is transmitted and to stop discrimination against individuals living with it.

By the late 1980s, science and medicine had begun to identify HIV/AIDS in other populations across the globe and to understand that it afflicted heterosexuals as well. Studies of AIDS in other countries helped enlighten the medical community about HIV transmission. Figures from sub-Saharan countries changed the perception of AIDS and showed that it affected heterosexuals and homosexuals, both women and men (J. Hays, 1998). Further, it was becoming increasingly clear that HIV was a sexually transmitted disease and should be defined as such. During this time there was an increasing awareness of the nature of its transmission, the need to protect oneself during sexual encounters, and the necessary imperative of educating the public about practicing "safe sex."

Even with various public health awareness campaigns since the 1980s, HIV/AIDS remains a significant problem in the United States. According to the Centers for Disease Control, in 2005, 37,331 cases of HIV/AIDS in adults, adolescents, and children were diagnosed in the United States (CDC, 2007) and it is estimated that each year approximately 40,000 individuals in this country become infected with the virus (CDC, 1999). Importantly, medical advances since the mid-1990s have improved therapies for people living with HIV/AIDS and have effectively slowed down the progression of infection. As a result, substantial numbers of people are currently living with the virus but have not yet experienced the difficulties of AIDS itself (CDC, 2007).

As with other public health outbreaks, we see significant differences across subpopulations within particular countries. In terms of transmission, in 2005 the group accounting for the largest proportion of reported HIV/AIDS diagnoses was men who contracted the virus through sex with other men, followed by adults and teenagers infected via heterosexual contact. Although women accounted for 26 percent of diagnoses in 2005, men constitute the majority (74 percent). We also see significant differences by ethnoracial category. In 2005, black people accounted for only 13 percent of the US population but comprised 49 percent of the estimated HIV/AIDS diagnoses in that year (CDC, 2007). Indeed, about 70 percent of new cases are among people of color (Office of the Executive Director, 2005).

Since the 1980s, the AIDS pandemic has been escalating at a frightening rate. In 1991 in sub-Saharan Africa the number of reported cases was about 800,000, and in 1992 the same region had 6.5 million people who were living with the disease. In the same region in 2005 there were 25.8 million people with HIV/AIDS, which accounted for 64 percent of the world's cases but only 10 percent of the total world's population. In 2005 in the whole world there were 40.3 million people infected with the virus and in that year 3.1 million people died of AIDS. It is estimated that almost 5 million people are infected every year (UNAIDS, 2005).

As horrible as the figures describing the AIDS pandemic are, the estimates are probably low, since it is likely that many cases are as yet undetected and underreported. For instance, South Africa does not report AIDS among its causes of death, but a sharp increase in the nation's death rates and the stated causes of death strongly suggest that AIDS was to blame for many. In some groups the death rate is extremely high, for instance among men aged forty to forty-four it is up to 28 deaths per 1,000 people (Wines, 2006). On a positive note, the Bill and Melinda Gates Foundation is spending hundreds of millions of dollars in fighting against AIDS in Africa. New effective antiretroviral drugs are being used for HIV treatment today. Yet, the experts argue that, unless we find a way of quickly delivering these new (and expensive) drugs to those in need in developing countries, we will have failed in our humanity (Gates Foundation, 2006).

Natural disasters

History is filled with dramatic and tragic examples of natural disasters and catastrophes that have resulted in massive losses of life. In this section, we focus on one of the most recent catastrophic events to affect America: Hurricane Katrina. In keeping with the overall themes of this book, it is important that we underscore the social nature of natural disasters and their aftermaths. As the historian Ted Steinberg argues, although the tendency is to explain natural disasters simply as random acts of God or some higher power, this view obfuscates the ways in which government and business leaders have a hand in determining who are best able to protect themselves from catastrophes and who fare the worst under these circumstances: almost always the poor, the elderly, and ethnoracial minorities (Steinberg, 2006).

The worst natural disasters in American history have tended to be tornadoes, earthquakes, hurricanes, and fires. Out of the various types of natural disaster that have occurred, hurricanes have caused the greatest number of casualties in the US. Of the ten deadliest natural disasters in American history, six were hurricanes (Gibson, 2006).

Hurricane Katrina

The most infamous and deadly hurricane in recent history was Hurricane Katrina. It began as a category 5 hurricane, made landfall near New Orleans, Louisiana, on August 29, 2005, and was responsible for 2,057 deaths (Gibson, 2006). In addition to the staggering loss of life, there was extensive damage to the city's residential and non-residential property, estimated to cost about 21 billion dollars, with another 6.7 billion dollars in damage to public infrastructure (ASCE, 2007). The local economy was devastated as more than 400,000 people fled the area, many of whom have yet to return.

The force of the hurricane itself weakened when it hit land (it was downgraded to a category 3 storm). However, the massive storm surge that followed caused the most damage, stretching from Louisiana along the entire Mississippi Gulf coast and into Alabama. In Louisiana, the federal flood protection system of levees, designed and maintained by the Army Corps of Engineers, failed in more than fifty locations (ASCE, 2007), allowing water to flood into New Orleans, which sits below sea level.

Conspicuously, while some parts of the city were spared from the rising water, the poorest areas – primarily in African-American neighborhoods – suffered the worst devastation and loss of life. New Orleans has had explicit patterns of racial segregation since it was founded. Land value has always been strongly associated with elevation, and African Americans have always been relegated to the lowest-lying areas that are the most vulnerable to flooding. Although the number of deaths from Katrina was striking, even more traumatic was the fact that, in contrast to other devastating natural disasters that have occurred over the past century, this event was both predictable and televised (Brinkley, 2006). In keeping with Steinberg's argument about the unnatural nature of natural disasters, even the American Society of Civil Engineers acknowledges that "the levees and floodwalls breached because of a combination of unfortunate choices and decisions, made over many years, at almost all levels of responsibility" (ASCE, 2007: v).

As they watched the images of hurricane victims on television, it was immediately apparent and shocking to most Americans and people across the globe that it was poor black people who were most affected by the floods. Image after image showed African Americans standing on their roofs, waving to helicopters, pleading for help. Other images showed over 20,000 people existing in squalor for six days in the New Orleans Superdome and in the Convention Center. The local and federal responses to the disaster were painfully slow in arriving, and criticisms were launched at the mayor of New Orleans, Ray Nagin, the governor of Louisiana, Kathleen Blanco, and particularly at George W. Bush and his administration, which was heavily censured for its delayed and inadequate response to the disaster. In particular, the White House was harshly criticized for having appointed Michael Brown as the director of the Federal Emergency Management Agency, even though he had no experience in emergency management or preparedness (Brinkley, 2006). The images of suffering, devastation, and abandonment in Louisiana and Mississippi highlighted the racial and economic inequality that existed before Katrina's landfall and how those inequalities exacerbated the atrocities that occurred in the wake of storm.

Census figures from 2004 estimate the pre-Katrina population of the New Orleans area to be about 1 million people, comprised of about 67 percent African American, 28 percent whites, and very small percentages of Hispanics and Asians. Post-Katrina reports are that about 580,000 people lived in the city in 2006, which is a drop of about 44 percent (ASCE, 2007: 9).

Many of the deaths that occurred during Katrina and in the weeks following were due to the direct effects of the storm. Many people drowned as the floodwaters rose. Some fled up to the attics of their homes as the water climbed, only to find themselves breaking through their roofs in order to reach a dry place to stand and await rescue. Others fled their homes altogether and died in other locations awaiting food, medical care, or water. The elderly were among the hardest hit: across all races, people over the age of seventy accounted for 60 percent of those who died (ASCE, 2007: 35).

From a sociological perspective the traumatic events surrounding Hurricane Katrina perfectly illustrate how structured inequalities that exist pre-disaster can be exacerbated during and after a disaster. Others have noted these trends as well, and have pointed out that "farthest from the reach of telegraph, phone, or radio, the poor have also had the flimsiest housing and most limited access to transportation. So with no warning of impending doom and no way to escape, indigents have often been trapped in shacks that offered little protection" (Gibson, 2006: 26). This was certainly the case in New Orleans when Katrina struck. The citizens who had access to transportation or who could afford to leave the city did so and weathered the storm and its aftermath in areas that were not severely hit. But for those who did not have access to a vehicle, the only option provided was to seek shelter at the Superdome. Because in New Orleans economic means are highly correlated with race, America was confronted with the stark image of thousands of black refugees trapped in the flooded city.

Other scholars stress the relationship between economic disadvantage and how people fare in the face of natural disasters. In the case of Katrina, poor people, who were also more likely to be African American, were disproportionately affected by the devastation in terms of their economic standing as well as their health (Walker and Warren, 2007).

War

A huge literature exists about the history, nature, causes, and consequences of war. For our purposes in learning about death and dying we will focus on the large-scale casualties of wars as well as the effects of war on survivors.

During the twentieth century, an estimated 216 million people died in wars or military conflicts across the globe (Leitenberg, 2005). Some scholars have envisioned that the twenty-first century will be just as rife with armed conflict and no less brutal than the last (Hirst, 2002; Lindsey, 2007). America has not been involved in every violent conflict in the world, but we certainly have been pivotal players in many of them. In keeping with our theme of social stratification, some authors have argued that the future of conflicts across the globe hinges on how the most powerful and rich countries choose to wield their military might and have wondered about the consequences for the less affluent countries (Lindsey, 2007).

Scholars and historians often make the distinction between *limited* war and *total* war. Limited wars are conflicts in which the daily lives of citizens are not involved even though their armed forces are. These types of war are more common than total wars (Clausewitz 2005). Indeed, many are unaware that, at virtually every time in its history, the US has been engaged in some sort of armed conflict (clandestine or overt) in some part of the world or another, and most citizens' lives are unaffected (at least on the surface) (Chomsky, 2003). Most of these conflicts would be considered limited wars. In limited wars, a central idea is that the fighting should occur between military forces and that civilians are not legitimate targets.

In contrast, total war is one in which nations mobilize all of their available resources and no one is excluded from the fighting; that is, everyone becomes part of the war effort, either as a soldier or as part of the extensive support system necessary to bolster the war itself. Although definitions of what constitutes a total war vary, most historians agree that both World War I and World War II were total wars (and many argue that the American Civil War also meets the criteria), particularly because not only did the fighting involve several countries but also because there was significant mobilization on the home front in terms of economic production, rationing, and exten- sive propaganda encouraging all civilians to support and participate in the war efforts. In these wars, civilians are asked and encouraged to support their troops not only symbolically, but by making changes in their own lives and sacrificing for their country. Thus, according to this definition, civilians are just as essential to the war effort (and just as legitimate as targets) as the soldiers themselves (Chickering, 1999).

American wars and military casualties

The American Civil War (1861–5) between the Union North and the Confederate South, is usually depicted as the most brutal, violent, and deadly conflict in our history. An estimated 620,000 soldiers lost their lives, which if an equivalent proportion of today's population were killed would equal about 6 million (Faust, 2008). There has been a debate among some historians as to whether killing on a such a massive scale was actually provoked by the war or whether a predisposition toward brutality already existed in the country (see, for example, Neely 2007, Schantz, 2008).

The US Department of Veterans Affairs provides statistics on the numbers of service members mobilized and killed in this country's various official wars throughout its history. The first World War (American involvement 1917–18) engaged almost 5 million people, and by the end of the war 116,516 of them had died either in battle or in other service (US Department of Veterans Affairs, 2007). World War II (American involvement 1941–5) engaged 16 million people worldwide and lost 405,399 in fighting and other service. The Korean War (1950–3) engaged almost 6 million soldiers and service people and 54,246 were lost. The Vietnam War (1964–75) had almost 9 million people in service across the globe (3.4 million who were deployed to Southeast Asia), and American casualties in battle and other deaths amounted to 90,209.

In the early 1990s, the US began Operation Desert Shield, which was eventually named Desert Storm (1990–1). That conflict engaged 2.3 million service members worldwide, with almost 700,000 deployed to the Gulf region; 1,972 of those died in the conflict.

The "Global War on Terror" (GWOT) is currently underway and began in October 2001 in response to the terrorist attacks on September 11 in New York, Pennsylvania, and Washington, DC. The GWOT is actually being fought on several military fronts and includes Operation Enduring Freedom (against the Taliban in Afghanistan) and Operation Iraqi Freedom (against the late former dictator Saddam Hussein in Iraq), which are ongoing conflicts and have been highly politicized and controversial (particularly in the international arena) since they began. Current data from the US Department of Defense spanning the period from October 7, 2001, to January 17, 2009, reports that across all branches of the US military 636 service members have lost their lives in Afghanistan, while 2,664 others have been wounded; 4,218 service members have been killed in Iraq,[3] with 30,984 wounded in action (US Department of Defense, 2009).

One way of thinking about death in the context of war emphasizes the loss of soldiers' lives, which certainly gives an indication of the extent of violence and the sacrifices made for the country. Another aspect of death and war to consider is the loss of civilian lives during wartime, which adds to the overall picture of how war devastates not only those who carry it out but also those who are innocent bystanders. As we have noted above, the government keeps track of military casualties. However, in the current wars in which we are engaged, they do not keep track of civilian casualties and do not offer any official estimates. Thus, in order to assess the loss of life among Afghanis and Iraqis, for example, we must rely on journalistic reports and estimates based on newspaper accounts, which are likely undercounts.

To date there are wide discrepancies in estimates of the number of civilian casualties in the Iraq war. Despite the range of numbers it is clear that the number of Iraqi dead is much higher than the number of US and coalition military forces who have died thus far. The British-based nongovernmental organization (NGO) Iraq Body Count reckons that 82,000 Iraqis have been killed, although they admit that it is likely an underestimate since they base their numbers on available public sources of data, meaning that they are capturing only the number of reported Iraqi deaths in published news sources. Another NGO, the British-based Opinion Research Business, conducted face-to-face interviews with 2,400 Iraqi adults around the country and estimates that the number of civilian casualties in the conflict is upwards of 1 million (Opinion Research Business, 2008).

Some analysts argue that wars are increasingly causing more rather than fewer civilian deaths. Marc Galasco, a military analyst for the NGO Human Rights Watch, argues that in World War I civilians accounted for approximately 10 percent of the total death toll, in World War II they comprised about half of all deaths (including those prisoners who died in the death camps), but in the current conflict in Iraq may account for approximately 90 percent of the total (cited in Clark, 2008). Given these trends in civilian casualties compared with military deaths, politicians and the military are increasingly interested in how media coverage of civilian deaths influences public opinion about wars (Larson and Savych, 2006).

War death also has broad implications for survivors on a social scale. Monuments are traditionally erected to commemorate the deceased. Washington, DC, the center of American government and politics, is also the center for commemoration of the nation's fallen. We have the Lincoln Memorial, the Washington monument, Arlington cemetery, the Vietnam Wall and the newer monument to women fallen in Vietnam. The most impressive of them all is the "Wall," a long, sinuous, black granite wall that is powerfully evocative:

> Approaching the long, black wall . . . we are overwhelmed by strong feelings of sorrow, nostalgia and frustration, as our throats become parched and our eyes moist. We slowly and silently walk along it, passing men in uniform and whole families, flower-bearing teary-eyed survivors, touching those stark names on the wall flanked by the final and irrevocable dates of their sudden demise. (Fontana and Collins, 1995: 197-8)

The very presence of the wall ensures that society will never forget what happened and never fully heal.

Fallen soldiers and their survivors

The soldiers who lose their lives may be "casualties of war," but we should also include their friends, family, and other survivors in the list of casualties. The death of a soldier has significance for the country and his comrades, as well as for his immediate family and friends. Unlike other routine deaths that occur in society, such as traffic accidents or those due to illness, military deaths are practically the only kind of death that we routinely feel "should" have meaning. Furthermore, although the military as an organization is associated with violence and death, and it has institutionalized expectations and practices for anticipating and dealing with soldiers' deaths, from the viewpoint of family and friends the suddenness of a soldier's death can often intensify feelings of anger and even manifest as protest (Ben-Ari, 2005). Much of how survivors experience, interpret, and find meaning in the death of a fallen soldier hinges upon their feelings about the war itself. In this context, family and friends who lose a loved one during wartime may experience "complicated grief" (Beder, 2003).

Very little of the research on bereavement and grief has addressed how people cope with the death of a soldier to whom they were related. Of the studies that do address bereavement and war death, the majority focus on parents and their adjustment after the loss of a child.[4] However, it is also clear that war death has implications for spouses and partners, children, friends, and also other soldiers.

Parents of fallen soldiers – As we discussed in chapter 6, age is also a significant factor in how people interpret the loss of a soldier. Since most military personnel who die in combat are young, and may even be at the height of their physical power, survivors, particularly parents, often interpret the death as "unnatural" or against the natural order of things (Ben-Ari, 2005). Some research suggests that the parents' age matters for how they respond to such a death. Those who are younger and who may still be able to have another child have lower levels of grief than those who have aged out of their reproductive years (Rubin, 1990). Other research has found evidence that parents' grief over the loss of an adult-child soldier does not necessarily fade away over time (Florian, 1990; Rubin, 1992), which is consistent with other research findings regarding parental bereavement.

Surviving spouses and the death gratuity – We address how spousal loss affects widows and widowers in chapter 9. Specifically in the case of war, the difficulty for those at home may begin with being aware that the spouse is deployed in a dangerous area but not knowing how or where they are. The constant uncertainty about the safety of a partner can be unnerving, challenging, and even traumatic. In this tension-filled context, then, the death of a spouse may be even more difficult to handle than, for example, an unexpected death in non-wartime circumstances. Conversely, the strong military culture and community may provide a group of people who have also experienced such a loss, which survivors may find comforting.

While some widows and widowers in civilian life may collect life insurance or survivor's benefits from Social Security after the death of a spouse, military spouses who lose their partner in active duty are entitled to what is commonly known as a "death gratuity," in addition to other types of financial support. The death gratuity is a one-time, non-taxable payment of cash assistance of up to $500,000 that is made available in the period directly after a service member's death (Burelli and Cornwell, 2005). It is designed to kick in before any other sources of income from the military become available, and practically all designated survivors of military personnel receive this benefit.

For some, this financial infusion is welcome, while, for others, it may feel like the government is putting a dollar amount on their lost loved one's life and fuel their feelings of resentment. It may also add to the surreal experience of losing a partner and make the grieving process more complicated. For example,

> for the family of Corporal Ryan, 25, who was killed in Ramadi on Nov. 15, the gratuity became an emotional hurdle, "We were very shaken up about depositing this check," Lauren Ryan said. She remembers driving to the bank with her mother. She remembers the everyday nature of the transaction; the teller did not even look up. And she remembers the anxiety about spending the money. (Barron, 2005).

For some of those left behind, the sudden influx of cash is dis-combobulating as they try to cope with their loss and grieve their deceased spouse while at the same time handling their finances and learning what to do with the sudden windfall of money (Foderaro, 2008). The money comes with no strings attached – "for many families, the check is something of a mystery: modest but meaningful, and coming without any real guidance on what it is meant to represent or how it is customarily spent" (Barron, 2005). In the face of bereavement and financial inexperience, some widows have even spent their entire $500,000 within the first year and have had to ask the military for a loan (Foderaro, 2008).

Some people describe how, with the arrival of $500,000, long-lost family and friends emerge asking for money and handouts, which makes their spouse's loss even more painful. Another difficulty with the death gratuity is that the service member must designate who the beneficiary is, and although it may be their spouse it might also be their parents. There have been cases in which surviving spouses with children have expected the payment from the government but the money was left to their parents. As a result, the surviving spouse and the deceased soldier's parents may fight over the money, causing long-term rifts within the family. The ensuing conflicts can be heartbreaking and traumatic – particularly in the context of bereavement. In order to address this problem, in 2005, the military began notifying spouses when an active service member designated someone other than them as the beneficiary (Foderaro, 2008).

In addition to the death gratuity, surviving spouses (and family members) may receive a lump sum payment from the service members' Group Life Insurance. Other economic support may also be available from the Veteran's Administration Dependency and Indemnity Compensation and the Survivor Benefit Plan, both of which are intended to provide monthly income over the long term (Burelli and Cornwell, 2005).

Homicide, suicide, and accidents

Death rates

Data reported by the National Center for Health Statistics (NCHS) provides information that describes the health of the population, including birth rates, death rates, and morbidity rates. For our purposes we are concerned with death rates, which are calculated as a ratio of the number of deaths to the number of people in a population (that is, the number of deaths in a year divided by the number of residents in that population), expressed as the number of deaths per 100,000. In the following sections we provide some macro-level snapshots of the death rates by different causes for the US population and some subpopulations.

Homicide

The death rate from murder for the entire population declined throughout the 1990s, from 9.4 to 5.9 in 2000. It had increased by 2001 to 7.1, but decreased again to 5.9 in 2004 (NCHS, 2007: table 45). While these macro-trends tell us something about the level of murders in the US for the overall population, they mask differences in rates among different groups. For example, among young African-American men (aged fifteen to twenty-four) the homicide rate decreased dramatically over the 1990s, during which time it ranged from as high as 157.5 to as low as 84.7 (note that these figures are dramatically higher than those for the general US population). Since 2000, the rate among this group of young men has remained relatively stable (from 83 to 85), and in 2004 was 77.6 (ibid.). For young black men in the US, homicide continues to be the leading cause of death.

Suicide

The rate of deaths by suicide in the United States has hovered between 10 and 12 since the mid-1980s (NCHS, 2007: table 46). Psychologists have long noted gender differences in both suicide attempts and successful suicides. Men are much more likely to die from suicide than are women (the rate is 18 for men compared with 4.5 for women).

In addition we see how suicide rates differ between men and women and among men and women by their age groups. Young men (aged fifteen to nineteen) are significantly more likely to kill themselves than are young women, in part because boys are more likely to use a firearm (NCHS, 2007: tables 46 and 62). Among men, the overall rate of death from suicide tends to increase with age, and those who are eighty-five or older have the highest rates (45). In contrast, among women the rate tends to be highest at midlife, during the ages thirty-five to fifty-four (ibid.: table 46). To complicate this picture even more, we find race differences, such that the suicide rate for white men of all ages is 19.6, compared with that for African-American men of 9.6 and that for Hispanic and Latino men of 9.8. Among women we find similar race-based patterns of suicide (ibid.).

One the most powerful examples of mass suicide comes from Jonestown, where an estimated 900 Americans died by drinking a very American drink, Kool-Aid, laced with cyanide. The dead were members of the West Coast-based People's Temple, a cult that had prospered under the leadership of Indiana-born Reverend Jim Jones, aged forty-seven. Disenchanted with the American way of life, its members moved away from the chaos of the US and built its Shangri-La in a remote corner of the jungle in Guyana, creating the hamlet of Jonestown. When a California congressman, Leo Ryan (fifty-three), along with a number of the cultists' parents, flew to Jonestown to investigate rumors that some of the members were being coerced to remain there, things began to unravel. One of Jones's followers attacked Ryan with a knife and was barely subdued. Fearing the worst, Ryan and his party left for the airstrip. It was then that the folly began. Reverend Jones went berserk when he learned that fourteen of his followers (totalling 1,200) had decided to leave with Ryan, and issued the death order. Many of the cultists followed the instructions to commit suicide by drinking the lethal punch. Children were killed first, then adults took the devilish cocktail and wandered off to die. Others, apparently reluctant to follow their example, were seemingly forced at gunpoint by Jones's gunmen to drink the poison. Jones himself was found dead from a pistol-shot, the victim of apparent suicide. The colony became a multicolored carpet of bodies as the haven of happiness turned into an arena of death.

Deaths from accidents and injuries: cars, guns, and work

In the period from 1950 to 1990, the overall death rate from motor vehicle-related injuries ranged from between 18 and 27, but in the early 1990s it began a downward trend. Throughout that decade, the death rate from car accidents declined, from 18.5 to 15.4 in 2000, and remained at 15.4 in 2004 (NCHS, 2007: table 44). We do find some significant age differences in the incidence of deaths, such that younger people (aged fifteen to twenty-four) and older people (seventy-five years or more) have higher rates than those in other age groups (ibid.).

The US has such high gun ownership rates that it is not surprising that a significant number of deaths occur from firearms. From the 1970s to the late 1990s, the death rate from firearm-related injuries hovered between 12 and 15, though from 1997 to 2004 it declined, from 11.8 to 10.0 (NCHS, 2007: table 47). While these trends are heartening, we must also note that men are much more likely to die from gun-related injuries than women, and that this is consistent across all ethnoracial groups.

It may surprise some people to find out how many work-related deaths there are in the US, as we may consider occupational and industrial hazards to be a thing of the past. In 2005, 5,734 people died as a result of occupational injuries, and they were much more likely to be men than women. In 2005, 5,328 men died at work or through injuries incurred on the job compared with 406 women. This puts the death rates at 6.9 for men and 0.6 for women (NCHS, 2007: table 49). In addition to gender differences we see variation among workers in terms of age, race, and industry. Older workers had higher occupational death rates than younger ones (highest among those sixty-five or older), Hispanic or Latino workers have slightly higher rates than those of other ethnoracial groups, and workers in agriculture, forestry, fishing, and hunting, mining, transportation, warehousing, and construction have higher rates of occupational deaths than those in all other industries (ibid.).

Conclusion

In this chapter we have discussed various types of death by destruction in the US that affect large groups of people or individual lives and we began by examining three of the main causes of large-scale death: epidemics, natural disasters, and war. Although our focus has been on events that happen within the United States, we should also note that other countries face many of these challenges as well. Epidemics continue to affect the stability and health of less-developed nations across the globe. While the US faces its own ongoing health and healthcare problems, the forces of globalization ensure that Americans' health and well-being will continue to be linked to economic development and public health in other parts of the world.

Hurricane Katrina devastated New Orleans and the Gulf region, killing many people in the process and shining a spotlight on existing economic, racial, and social inequality in the United States. Although scholars and engineers had been aware for years of the vulnerability of the citizens (and particularly of the poor black residents), political and economic interests helped ensure that, once a natural disaster on the scale of Katrina hit the region, the death and destruction would be unequally distributed through the population. This outcome of this "natural" disaster was not natural and inevitable, but predictable and socially constructed. Other regions across the globe routinely face these kinds of threat, and the most underprivileged members of those societies also face the most extensive losses, deaths, and damages.

Even a cursory glance at American history demonstrates that war, violence, and death have been ongoing themes since before our nation's founding. Many American lives have been lost in battle, yet the thanatological literature does not often address the specific experiences of death during wartime. Some studies do attempt to provide guidance to healthcare providers and social workers who deal with the families of fallen soldiers, although this specialized area remains largely underdeveloped in the American context.

Next, we examined death by homicide, suicide, and various types of accident. Death by murder as been declining in the US but it still remains high; there are important racial differences in the rate of homicides. The rate of suicides is also very variable, depending on the sex, age, and race of the individuals. Examining deaths by accidents, we found marked aged differences in those caused by automobiles. Deaths by firearms are declining, but remain high and are primarily a male phenomenon. A surprisingly high number of deaths occur at work, showing once more that social class affects our life chances.

PART IV

COPING WITH DEATH

CHAPTER 08

Giving Bad News

Doctor: Your mother's condition is deteriorating, and we don't expect her to do too well.

Family member: Thank you, doctor, we know you are doing your best.

Doctor: Well, so far we've been able to keep her blood pressure up with pressors.

Family member: That's good isn't it? At least the blood pressure isn't a problem.

(Physician leaves)

Family members to each other: Thank goodness he didn't say she is dying.

(Campbell, 1994: 1052)

Introduction

Giving bad news to patients and family members is the most difficult aspect of the physician's role (Coulehan and Block 1997; Nguyen and Weinreb, 2002). In the above quote, it is clear that the doctor is evading the complete truth about the patient's situation. Indeed, he attempts to "soften the blow" by trying to give family members moderately good news about the patient's blood pressure without clearly stating that she will die anyway. Until about thirty years ago doctors would not readily tell patients they had a terminal illness, particularly cancer (Smith, 1998; Thomasma, 2003). Today they give the bad news more readily, but we are not sure how good, sensitive, and clear their explanations may be (Groopman 2002; Smith, 1998; Thompson, 2000; Zuger, 2006). Currently, few doctors receive training in how to talk about death and dying with patients or how to provide patients and loved ones with a terminal diagnosis (Groopman, 2002).

Times have changed. The context in which death takes place has altered dramatically over time and so have the ways in which we inform dying people and their loved ones about their impending death. From the Middle Ages to the nineteenth century death was considered an unavoidable natural event that came to us calmly in our bedchambers, where we waited for it among friends and relatives, who provided us with support in the waning moments of life (Ariès, 1974). Today we tend to die in aseptic hospital rooms, among hired strangers for whom we are "just another patient." And yet, we need these strangers to give us more than medical and technical aid. We need them to extend a helping hand, to share a kind word, to "soften the blow" of our demise. To be left without any form of support as we face death may be too hard to bear for many of us.

In this chapter we examine the techniques used by occupational groups whose job it is to manage and disseminate bad news about disease and death. In their roles as professionals, doctors, nurses, lay counselors, ministers, and coroners' assistants must attempt to reconcile dying people with their impending fate, as well as to assuage the fears of spouses, relatives, and friends. Most of these individuals are totally sincere in their efforts to help. The larger question is whether they have any training in delivering this kind of bad news and what kinds of decisions they make about how and how much information to provide (Groopman, 2002). Indeed, some physicians and counselors may act in a calculated and deliberate manner, albeit with good intentions, as they try to find a reasonable way to impart bad news without actually being forthright with a diagnosis. The way professionals interact with families and friends is just as important as how they relate to the patients themselves. For example, doctors may attempt to minimize the pain associated with the dying process in their explanations, such as telling a new, distraught widow, "Your husband died peacefully, without any suffering," knowing full well that the patient suffered to the very end (Sudnow, 1967).

Techniques of giving bad news

Before examining techniques of how professionals give patients bad news, let us briefly examine some attitudes and values toward death, which are paramount in deciding what techniques to use. For instance, a priest can tell a religious person that her death will place her in a better situation as she will soon be with God; however, the same consolation would not work with an agnostic or an atheist patient. Charmaz, in her classic study of coroners' deputies (1975), found that their beliefs and values toward death shaped the ways in which they divulged bad news to the relatives of the deceased. For instance, in order to insulate themselves from the harshness of having continually to announce that someone has died, the deputies come to believe that death is incidental, rather than central to their work. As a deputy stated, "That's not a body lying there. *It's an investigation*. You have to look at it as an investigation, not a person lying there" (Charmaz, 1980:184).

Jacques Choron presented three different types of fear of death: what happens after death, fear of dying, and fear of ceasing to be (Choron, 1974). Then he addressed some of the ways in which individuals attempt to alleviate the fear of death for the dying. He proposed a number of alternatives, the primary ones being: (1) individuals *minimize life* by considering it only a brief temporary period, juxtaposed with the eternity of being in heaven; (2) individuals *minimize* death in order to soften human fear – for example, by equating it with eternal sleep or by using euphemisms such as eternal slumber, passing on, or resting with angels rather than the dreaded word – death; (3) individuals *ignore death*, engaging instead in positive thoughts and emotions, such as spending time with your grandchildren, taking the last trip to visit a desired site, or even helping other dying persons who are less positive about it (Feifel, 1977); (4) individuals *familiarize* themselves with death and its markers in order to overcome the fear of it – for example, they might do so by taking a class in death and dying.

Erving Goffman (1952) suggested some techniques of "softening the blow" following bad news, which he refers to as "cooling out the mark," the situation in which a "cooler" has to reconcile a "mark" with a negative situation without becoming too upset. In the following quote, notice how the coroner's deputy announcing a death over the phone uses a progressive strategy and actually lets the relative be the first to use the word "dead":

> I tell them that he collapsed today while at work. They asked if he is all right now. I say slowly, "Well, no, but they took him to the hospital." They ask if he is there now. I say, "They did all they could do – the doctors tried very hard." They say, "He is dead at the hospital?" Then I tell them he's at the coroner's office. (Charmaz, 1980: 186–7)

Goffman's primary focus is on individuals' adaptation to loss in many areas of life, from a swindle, to the loss of a job, to rejecting a potential lover. In his view, some people in these situations have the role of the cooler and have the duty to give the bad news to others. He examines how coolers sugar-coat bad news and the different techniques they use in different situations to keep the recipients calm. For instance, the job of employees in "complaint departments" is to settle buyers who have purchased a defective product or have had something go wrong in their transactions with the store. Goffman addresses the role of the cooler as it relates to the process of dying:

in some cases, as in those pertaining to death, the role of cooler is given to doctors and priests. Doctors must frequently help a family, and the member who is leaving it to manage the leave-taking with tact and a minimal of emotional fuss. A priest must not so much save a soul as create one that is consistent with what is about to become of it. (1952: 457)

Some of Goffman's more general categories can be applied to the study of the dying and the bereaved: (1) the telling of bad news is given to the *highest-ranking* person available, to provide a sobering effect in a potentially volatile situation. For instance, in the movie *Saving Private Ryan*, a mother who just had three sons die while fighting in Europe during World War II, is told the sad news by a three-star general (one of the highest rankings in the US military); (2) a change in the *status* of the dying is invoked – such as transforming into an immortal soul; and (3) dying or grieving individuals are allowed to *blow their top*, venting volatile emotions, which has a cathartic effect and helps them to deal with their anger and sorrow.

Besides those suggested by Goffman, there are other devices used in giving bad news. These may be nonverbal, such as the serious expression on the face of the person doing the telling, or prefacing their words with an apology, "I'm sorry but . . ." Conversational analysts have studied the importance of turn taking in conversations that address bad news (Maynard 2003) and have found that the manner in which it is told has a profound effect on how the information is taken. Just imagine receiving bad news in the following way:

It was awful. We'd gone to see her, my daughters and me and the wife had first gone along the corridor to go to the toilet . . . and a nurse came out of the office and just said "You know your wife is dying, don't you, and the doctor wants to see you tomorrow" and she went off. We were completely shattered. We had to hide in the corridor as my wife came back and went into her ward. We couldn't let her see us. We were in tears. Then I went to see the doctor the next morning and told him what the nurse had told us. (Maynard, 2003: 50)

Reconciling individuals to bad news goes beyond caring for an individual or a family. Since about 80 percent of all Americans die in an institution (NCHS, 2002), attempts to tone down public expressions of anger or grief are also meant to avoid disrupting the smooth organizational flow of hospitals, because such outbursts upset both other patients and the staff. Individuals who refuse to remain calm upon receiving bad news may find themselves heavily sedated, moved to a private room, or simply avoided by staff members (Sudnow, 1967). Relatives who are being told something distressing are often moved to a "disclosure space" (Glaser and Strauss, 1965: 153) such as a private office or the hospital chapel (Clark and LaBeff, 1982). Thus, professionals giving bad news accomplish two tasks: they help the dying individual or the grieving family cope with the situation but also allow the work flow in the organization to continue with minimal disruption. Although the business of death is simply part of the regular business of healthcare organizations, it is nonetheless surprising to find how little training healthcare professionals have in how to talk with patients and family members about end-of-life issues, and also how much variation exists in how the information actually gets disclosed. We now turn to a discussion of how the various occupational groups whose job it is to tell people about their impending death, or otherwise provide bad news, and to manage the consequences actually impart the facts to patients and their relatives.

The physician

As we noted in the chapter tracing the historical circumstances of death, doctors have only relatively recently become the buffer that modern Americans place between themselves and death. As we showed earlier, this has not always been so. For many centuries the white-clad figure of the physician did not inspire much confidence in patients (Magner, 2005). For a long time healing the sick was the enterprise and vocation of a wide range of individuals: self-appointed healers, barber-surgeons, herbalists, charlatans, and the few university-trained doctors to be found. The favorite cure consisted of bloodletting and the use of drugs to bring about purging, sweating, and vomiting. It was believed that all diseases were produced by the accumulation in the body of putrid material that caused constriction of the blood vessels. This method of curing goes as far back as the days of the Roman Empire and lasted well into the nineteenth century both in Europe and America. The autopsy of a French soldier who died of yellow fever in the late 1800s revealed the following:

> On the first day the patient was given a large dose of castor oil, an enema, and several doses of calomel, while leeches were applied to his temples. On the second day, in addition to a large dose of calomel, the patient was bled by leeches and lancet. On the third day, the patient was given several enemas . . . before he died. (Magner, 2005: 309)

The fact that a great many patients died did not aid much in bolstering patients' confidence in their physicians. It took major changes in the American medical system for doctors to acquire the prestige, tools, and training necessary to beat out the competition of these various other healthcare providers and consultants and take their place at the top of the list (Starr, 1982).

It was not until the scientific boom of the nineteenth and twentieth centuries that doctors became successful in forestalling and redefining death. Over time, the image of death was transformed from the grim reaper, who inexorably mowed everyone in its path, into various other images, all bearing such medical names and features as carcinoma, myocardial infarction, cardiac arrest, fulminating necrotic hepatitis, and perforated peritonitis (Illich, 1976). Doctors successfully reduced the instances of death from these types of illness, thus leading patients to believe (or hope) that eventually physicians would eliminate death itself. The more success physicians had, the more their social status and power increased (Starr, 1982).

The advance and success of medicine led to the medicalization of life, as more and more aspects came under the aegis of physicians. Phobias, excessive drinking, obesity, and many other behaviors came to be redefined as medical ailments, to be controlled by doctors (Davis, 1972). Also, physicians were the only ones who could translate the complex jargon and the intricate knowledge of medicine into everyday language. Thus, the public relied increasingly on the physician as a knight in a white coat to protect them from illness and keep death at bay (Illich, 1976). Doctors found themselves in a delicate situation; being in a position of great authority, they faced onerous responsibilities. They were faced with the task of announcing vital information about the medical condition of their patients, and, at times, that included giving bad news. Indeed, one study estimates that "over the course of a career an oncologist [a doctor who specializes in cancer] will break bad news to patients about 20,000 times, from the first shocking facts of the diagnosis to the news that death is near" (Zuger, 2006).

Even though imparting bad news to patients is an integral part of their work, by and large doctors are trained and held accountable only for their technical skills; they have no substantial grounding to fall back on when dealing with the announcement of death (Fallowfield, 1993; Groopman, 2002). In fact, as Dr Anthony Back, an oncologist, has recently put it, "the general feeling is that these are not teachable skills – that you either have it or you don't" (Zuger, 2006: 1). This attitude is probably not much consolation to patients and family members. While one may argue that the doctors' primary job is to administer to the sick and use their skills to prevent or delay death, most of us would likely also prefer that they have some positive communication skills that allow them to talk about illness, death, and dying in a human way. This is particularly the case when it is ourselves or our loved ones who are afflicted. But giving bad news tends to be an uncomfortable aspect of the physicians' job. They tend to view death as the enemy, which they fight against by engaging in life-saving procedures and "heroic measures." Therefore, saving a patient tends to be seen as a victory while a patient's death is perceived as a loss, not only for the patient but for the doctor as well. Given this scenario, doctors often endure a great deal of stress as they try to save their patients. Losing a patient tends to be an emotionally disturbing event, not only on a human level but on a professional level as well. The doctor loses on two counts: a human life and a battle with death (Coombs and Powers, 1977).

It is ironic, in a way, that at this moment of personal turmoil the doctor is called upon to be calm and give bad news to their patient and to family members. Doctors are expected to be unemotional, and the social norms surrounding interactions between them and their patients prohibit them from crying or showing their own intense feelings. Their role demands scientific detachment, composed demeanor, and a calm front (Buckman, 1992).

Doctors generally face two very different situations: telling the patient that their illness is terminal and telling the relatives that the patient has died. The former entails announcing a change of the patient's status from "acutely ill" to "terminally ill." Part of the physicians' job requires that they should spare patients from suffering whenever possible, including when faced with terminal cases (Nguyen and Weinreb, 2002). To ease the stress of the situation, doctors employ a number of strategies in announcing death. They may make the pronouncement in a written form by placing the patient's name on the hospital's critical list; couch the telling in obscure medical jargon, leaving the patient puzzled and confused (Gillotti and Applegate, 2000); let the patient do the announcing, as the following quote exemplifies:

> "What is it? Tell me."
> "I don't know."
> "You ought to."
> "But I don't."
> "What should I . . .?"
> "It needs to come out."
> "No!"
> "Be sensible. It may be . . ."
> "Cancer."
>
> She had said it first. All along it had been a game, not unlike choosing sides by gripping a baseball bat to see who wins first choice. He [the doctor] had won; she had said it first. (Selzer, 1974: 22)

Doctors can be vague, withholding such details as the time of death or the specific consequences of the illness, or they can be brutally frank and blurt out the news, often leaving the patient stunned: "The doctor started speaking without preface or explanation, 'Mr. DeBaggio you have Alzheimer's,' he said with the bluntness of a hammer. He offered no details of the tests or of their results. I gasped, as much at his hurried diagnosis, as at the death sentence his words implied" (DeBaggio, 2000, quoted in Maynard, 2003: 50). Finally, doctors can engage in a situation of "mutual pretense" by stalling, whereby patients learn slowly about their condition without being directly told. They sense that they are dying, but do not really want to know, and learn about their impending death by cues and clues given by the doctor. For instance, being moved to a bed right next to the nursing station is a sign of needing continuous monitoring.

In a groundbreaking study, a team of researchers funded by the Robert Wood Johnson Foundation conducted a large, multi-year clinical study of dying in America. The goal was to "improve end-of-life decision making and reduce the frequency of a mechanically supported, painful, and prolonged process of dying" (SUPPORT, 1995: 1591). One of the most comprehensive and innovative studies of death and dying in hospitals, its findings revealed how, despite attempts to increase the communication about patients' end-of-life preferences to doctors, these efforts had little to no impact on the terminal care provided (Oddi and Cassidy 1998). In the initial phase of the study, researchers documented problems in communication between doctors and patients and found that doctors frequently used aggressive treatments, and that

> only 47% of physicians knew when their patients preferred to avoid CPR; 46% of do-not-resuscitate (DNR) orders were written within 2 days of death; 38% of patients who died spent at least 10 days in an intensive care unit (ICU); and for 50% of conscious patients who died in the hospital, family members reported moderate to severe pain at least half the time. (Ibid.)

Phase II of the study found that, after implementing efforts to improve communication between doctors and patients, patients experienced no improvements in communication or any other outcomes. The results of the SUPPORT study were very discouraging to the medical community and helped spur on a patients' rights movement in the US.

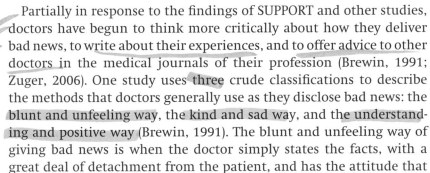

Partially in response to the findings of SUPPORT and other studies, doctors have begun to think more critically about how they deliver bad news, to write about their experiences, and to offer advice to other doctors in the medical journals of their profession (Brewin, 1991; Zuger, 2006). One study uses three crude classifications to describe the methods that doctors generally use as they disclose bad news: the blunt and unfeeling way, the kind and sad way, and the understanding and positive way (Brewin, 1991). The blunt and unfeeling way of giving bad news is when the doctor simply states the facts, with a great deal of detachment from the patient, and has the attitude that nothing can be done to soften the truth since the patient will be upset at the news no matter what. The kind and sad way is "to be private, concerned, and unhurried, but to regard the matter as just a painful duty. The bad news is given gravely and solemnly, with little positive support or encouragement" (ibid.: 1207). Finally, the understanding and positive way is grounded on several characteristics and communication skills, including "flexibility, based on [the patient's] feedback, while giving the bad news; and positive thinking, reassurance, and planning for the immediate future, all blended with the bad news, not just saved for later" (ibid.). Clearly, this third way is the ideal scenario for both the doctor and the patient. Its strength is that it hinges on the idea of a real and genuine conversation between the two parties about the end of life and the patient's preferences about their care.

Some physicians have realized that practice and tuition may indeed be helpful in giving bad news. Dr Back and his colleagues recognized the need for improvement, fully aware that only 5 percent of all oncologists had had any communication training (Zuger, 2006). With a grant from the National Cancer Institute they began coaching physicians willing to learn the art of communicating bad news. The trainers use actors to portray the role of dying patients. Students and doctors learn valuable things, such as:

> never to give bad news while standing up, never to do it in a public corridor, always to have a box of Kleenex at hand. They learn not to try to cheer up patients who have every right to be grief-stricken. They learn to address the question behind the question, "How long do I have?" rather than just reciting numbers that are invariably inaccurate. (Zuger, 2006: 2)

Telling relatives that the patient has died is the other task that awaits doctors, though they may use the prerogative of their rank and have someone else relay the news: "Disclosing to a family is not simply beneath the doctor's dignity, it is simply a difficult task that his superior status may allow him to delegate to nurses" (Glaser and Strauss, 1965: 148). At times, doctors may assign the unpleasant task to a nurse with such paternalistic comments as "you're a woman, you're more sensitive with people." When the doctor makes the announcement to family members, she or he usually uses the same general methods that are used in talking with a patient about their terminal illness. The concerns are different, however, since, with the patient no longer alive, it is likely that there are details to be taken care of, such as autopsy permits to be completed as quickly as possible, thereby closing the case. A relationship exists, however, between giving bad news to patients and to family members. While doctors may give more information to a patient than a family member (or vice versa), how they handle the situation with the patient is likely to impact how the family takes it as well. For example, if the patient died from a terminal illness rather than an abrupt accident, and the doctor and patient were able to engage in a constructive and supportive conversation about end-of-life care and subsequent plans, the discussion with the family and the details to be arranged may be much easier. Doctors may be inadvertently role-biased and look for a male family member, who may, for example, turn out to be a distant cousin, even if the woman standing right there is the new widow.

David Sudnow (1967), in his classic study of dying, observed that a language game takes place between the doctor and the relatives when death is announced. After the bad news has been given and the relatives have recovered from the initial shock, a series of questions pertaining to cause, pain, and preventability ensues. The same questions are always asked and the same answers always given: "he died peacefully with no pain," and "we did all we could," are stock answers, regardless of their veracity, which are intended to allow the family to feel better while also removing any doubt of incompetence regarding the doctor. According to Sudnow, the subject matter of the conversation is unimportant; what is important is that it is a staged ritual, aimed at letting the relatives recover following the initial shock.

Giving bad news can be impromptu but can also be a carefully orchestrated event, preparing the relatives as to the inevitability of death, attempting to have them accept the situation as calmly as possible, and with the additional intent of reducing their suffering, minimizing the doctor's liability, and allowing the flow of work to continue uninterrupted.

Doctors have the main role in giving bad news, since they control the definition of patients and the flow of work, yet there are other groups involved in the process, and it is to them that we now turn.

The nurse

Nurses, like doctors, are trained to place a high priority on curing illness and preserving life (Whaley, 2000). Nurses' training with dying patients focuses on medical procedures. Yet, while the doctor makes brief sporadic appearances, nurses are constantly present, adding considerable burden to their situation. A number of features affect a nurse's relation with a dying patient, some of them of institutional in nature, outside of the nurse's control (Sudnow, 1967). Some wards, such as the intensive care unit (ICU), are geared to cope with emergencies, providing highly technical care at a very fast pace. In these settings, patients tend to be unconscious or semi-conscious, they are hooked up to a number of monitoring and life-support machines and tubes, and they are usually heavily sedated. These conditions can make the nurse–patient contact rather brief, leading to little personal interaction and an aura of technical depersonalization.

On other wards where patients are chronic or terminal, the pace is much slower and allows for longer periods of interaction (Sudnow, 1967). The nurses in these longer-term settings are placed in the position of establishing familiarity and ties with the patient who is dying. In this context, the patient is not a faceless, unconscious stranger but acquires a face and a personal history. Nurses are expected to follow the guidelines of their training and maintain a professional distance from the patients, as well as remaining continually calm and controlled (Bugen, 1979). At the same time, nurses can play an intermediate role between the doctor and the patient, offering optimistic and hopeful support and leaving the bad news to the doctors. The following are typical answers that nurses give to patients who are asking about their condition: "'You're doing so well now. You don't have to feel this way', 'You don't really mean that . . . You're not going to die. Oh, you're going to live to be a hundred', 'Let's think of something more cheerful. You shouldn't say things like that; there are better things to talk about' " (Bugen, 1979: 83).

A potential problem in the relationship between a nurse and a dying patient hinges on the fact that part of the nurse's work is very intimate and requires them to provide physical care such as bathing, feeding, and grooming (doctors do not generally engage in this kind of hands-on caregiving). This level of intimacy may make such tasks even more emotionally draining for the nurse. At the same time, from a more meso-level perspective, the logistical and organizational aspects of the job, specifically those pertaining to staffing issues, may further complicate the nurse–patient relationship. Some nurses, when faced with overwhelming tasks on account of chronic understaffing, may find it necessary to routinize how they handle and care for their patients in a matter-of-fact way. In these situations, they may have to cut back on the time and energy they spend with a dying patient, particularly if they perceive that the patient will die shortly (Strauss and Glaser, 1970b).

Recent studies have found that staff shortages and lack of supervision in nursing homes are related to lower quality in end-of-life care and that sometimes residents have not received basic care such as bathing, repositioning, and oral hygiene (Kayser-Jones et al., 2003). In response to increasing concerns about the availability of nurses to care for dying patients, particularly those in ICUs, as well as their ability to provide adequate end-of-life care, some practitioners have begun to call for nursing practice that includes a model of terminal care that emphasizes both cure and comfort and a decision-making process that is shared between patient, doctor, and nurse (Miller et al., 2001).

Nurses' contact with dying patients may be further reduced as death approaches, in order to avoid having directly to face questions that they may not feel up to answering, creating a "mutual pretense" situation. In order to avoid direct disclosures and upsetting the patient, the nurse, along with the doctor, may "snow" (heavily sedate) the patient so as not have him or her upset others in the ward by volatile emotional behavior. The sedated patient will not be troublesome but will remain, instead, in a semi-conscious state of stupor. For some, this may take on a drug-induced sense of merriment: "Later in the afternoon I was talking to another nurse who said that Mrs. Abel is now euphoric, that it must be due to the amount of morphine she is getting . . . It was then too, that she was put on Ritalin, which is sort of a mood elevator" (Strauss and Glaser, 1970a: 41). The patient may be jolted out of the "mutual pretense" situation that the doctor and the nurse have orchestrated by another patient, as illustrated by Solzhenitsyn's classic novel *Cancer Ward*, when a new patient on the oncology ward, Pavel Nicolayevich, states quietly, in reply to another patient's inquiry, "I have cancer of nothing. I have no cancer whatsoever," to which the other patient loudly replies, for all to hear, "Stupid fool! If it's not cancer, what the hell d'you think they put you in here for?" (1968: 9). Coyle and Sculco (2003) suggest that the "mutual pretense" between doctors and nurses and patients does not necessarily have to be a negative type of interaction.

The nurse may decide to drop her professional mask and extend herself to the patient, well beyond her professional obligations: "Then the night nurse said that she realized what was happening so she took Mrs. Abel in her arms and let her cry . . . It was the crying of real despair" (Strauss and Glaser, 1970a: 118); she could just sit and patiently listen to the patient reminiscing; she may well provide a continuity of interaction for the patient, acting as a mediator between the latter's medical world and their personal world; finally, she could continue to provide meticulous physical care for the patient, in an effort to bring a glimmer of a positive hope to a self who has already been dimmed in so many ways (Nguyen and Ash, 2002). By continuing to treat the patient on a physical and a social level as a living person, the nurse minimizes the change in status from living to dying.

Counselors and ministers

Doctors and nurses are trained to cope primarily with the physical demise of their patients. Ministers and lay counselors are the people who attempt to provide the dying and the bereaved with psychosocial and spiritual care. Clergy, social workers, and counselors are an integral part of an end-of-life care team as they assist patients with their psychological, logistical, and social needs and also relieve doctors and nurses of the full responsibility of helping patients and family members deal with bad news.

A number of hospitals have hired chaplains as members of the staff; this provides added comfort to both the dying patients and their families. While various studies have documented that death, dying, and terminal illnesses often invoke a spiritual component in patients and family members, little research has specifically examined the extent to which patients' spiritual needs are met. One recent study showed that only about 20 percent of hospitalized patients are visited by chaplains (Flannelly et al., 2005). Chaplains can also function within this context to help smooth out possible emotionally charged scenes and uncooperative behavior on the part of patients or family members. Furthermore, the chaplain frees some of the more valuable (as viewed by the hospital administrators) time of physicians. For example, a minister in a hospital in a large Western city told one of the authors that it is typical for doctors who are on their way to announce a terminal diagnosis to a patient to take him along with them for support. According to one informant, the doctor typically stands close to the door, utters the diagnosis in medical jargon, introduces the chaplain as one who will answer further questions, and leaves the room.

While some hospitals have a paid chaplain on staff, others rely on both lay and religious volunteers for counseling services for patients and family members. A few private groups were organized to provide trained "death companions," individuals who keep the dying company for a few hours a day. One such group was Threshold, formed in Los Angeles in the mid-1970s by Robert Kavenaugh, a former Catholic priest and licensed psychologist, to "help ease lonely, dying clients out of the world" (*Time*, 1975). Threshold companions would sit, for a fee, with dying patients in hospitals and chronic care facilities. However, since medical insurance companies do not reimburse for "grief care," many of these groups were doomed to fail, since very often dying patients do not have the extra financial resources to pay for a "companion."

Groups such as Shanti (from the Hindu word for peace through understanding) provide a more successful and less costly alternative. Operating out of San Francisco for over thirty years, Shanti has a volunteer telephone service to help various groups of terminally ill or grieving individuals (*Time*, 1975). However, its focus in principally on breast cancer and HIV/AIDS (www.shanti.org).

Lay groups are rare, thus the brunt of looking after those who are dying and the grieving falls upon religious ministers, whose task may be fraught with problems. Unless they are employed by the hospital, ministers have no access to the patients' medical records and are often uninformed about their exact medical condition. Also, they have only a vague notion of how much the patients themselves know about their terminal status. Thus, they must go through some deductive reasoning and guesswork in order to assess the situation. For instance, one of the ministers interviewed by Juanita Wood reported:

 I went in and she greeted me and I sat and she looked like she was thinking very profoundly – a bit pained in her expression – and I said to her, "Barbara, you look as if you are thinking very deeply and feeling very deeply right now." And she said, "About what I have to face." And then so it could be open to be dealt with explicitly, I said, "And what's that?" And she said, "My dying." And that opened it up to talk about her feelings. (1976: 139)

 Ministers are also confronted with the problem of time. The dying patient many feel that they have all the time in the world, while in fact they have a demanding work schedule to be followed. Thus, they must counsel the patient in the little time that they have while giving the impression that time is not important (Wood, 1976).

Both lay and religious groups minister to the dying in similar ways. They both employ the popular method of client-centered therapy, listening to the patients and providing empathy and support while remaining non-judgmental. Having an attentive listener allows the patients to relive their past, vent their emotions, and ultimately share their angst with someone else who seems to care for them.

Counseling and the stage theory of dying

Counselors and ministers tend to rely on their personal skills to help the dying; as one minister put it: "moving beyond professionalism to the point of caring is the key" (Gibbs, 1976: 173). However, both groups require that members receive training in psychosocial counseling before ministering to dying people. One of the most accomplished and famous scholars on death and dying, Elisabeth Kübler-Ross, a neo-Freudian psychiatrist, had extensive experience working with dying people and developed a model of the process of death that has become an important part of counselors' formalized psychosocial training.

Having conducted interviews with 200 dying patients, Kübler-Ross introduced the notion of "stages" of dying in her seminal book *On Death and Dying* (1969), which was well received both in academia and by the public at large. According to Kübler-Ross, although patients retain their individuality in the face of death, the process of dying tends to follow a similar pattern for most people. She identified five psychological stages: (1) people experience denial and isolation and

5 stages of grief

assert that "this can't be happening to me"; (2) they feel angry and ask, "Why me?"; (3) they move into a period in which they wish to bargain for a cure or more time. At this point they would like to make a deal and promise that, "I'll be good if only . . ."; (4) they experience depression and a powerful sense of loss; and (5) leading up to the death they move into a period of acceptance in which they resign themselves to their fate and no longer attempt to deny or change it. While this stage theory might sound like a universal progression through which every dying person moves, the process is not necessarily linear. Kübler-Ross acknowledged that her model of the stages of death is not set in stone. Individuals may experience some or all of these stages, the time that any one person spends in a particular stage varies greatly, and people may not move through them in the particular order that she outlined.

Whether or not Kübler-Ross intended to create a rigidly structured model (Moller, 1996), many counselors and ministers saw it as a way to structure their own understanding, since relying on the stages greatly reduced the ambiguity of the process of death. The orderly progression offered by the model provides the counselor or minister with a guide within which most of the patient's behavior can be interpreted and controlled. Many professionals turned to the stages as a way to think about death and dying, and some devised similar models for other situations; for instance, Kavenaugh (1972) proposed seven stages of grief for survivors. Indeed, Kübler-Ross's model has become an important part of the way in which counselors and people attending to the dying think about death, though some scholars argue that it has had a limiting effect on counselors' abilities to think creatively about death and individuals' variation in the process of dying. Indeed, one writer argued that, "her five-stage theory has become established and institutionalized as the unopposed American credo of human dying" (Moller, 1996: 47).

What about the patients? Although counselors may have been trained in the stage theory of dying, the model is so widely known in American culture that patients themselves are likely have some familiarity with it. They too are apt to place some order in their confused minds, restructuring their emotions and behaving according to the "script," the stages furnished by the counselor or minister. Or they may experience increased confusion and anxiety if they suspect they "ought to" be in a given stage, for example anger, when in fact all they feel is depression. Some patients may reject this definition of dying by stages and continue to freely vent their emotions, regardless of any theoretically imposed sequential expectations for their behavior. However, such venting of emotions may be a cry in the wilderness, since the counselor or the minister may be interpreting and filtering information from the patient in terms of the expected stages, either not seeing or dismissing information that contradicts his or her expectations (Moller, 1996).

Kübler-Ross's main contribution to the field was to sensitize people working with the dying to the fact that the feelings of the terminally ill must be viewed carefully, as they are likely to be very different than those of others; additionally, and perhaps most importantly, she made it possible for Americans to actually talk about the feelings of dying people. But many others pushed her work too far, were too eager to formalize dying. America has a tendency to quantify all information (Cicourel, 1964). Since everything and everyone is given a value and attributed a number, why not have people die in a proper and orderly manner?

Coroners' assistants

Coroners' assistants (also called deputies) have perhaps the hardest task in giving bad news. Coroners' assistants are part of a large bureaucratic organization that attempts to manage the volatile and disruptive situation of an unexpected death. The roles of those involved are clearly spelled out. In fact, in many counties police officers are not allowed to impart bad news (perhaps because of their lack of training on the matter), thus, even if they are the first to contact the family, they will not divulge information but stall until the arrival of the coroner's assistant. The latter's tasks are: (1) finding the right person to whom the disclosure of bad news must be made; (2) attempt to minimize and control emotional outbursts; (3) ensure that funeral arrangements are made; (4) leave the grieving person with someone to ensure their safety.

Imagine, for example, this scenario: when the assistant rings a door bell to tell a young woman with a toddler in her arms that her 28-year-old husband has died in a car accident near the Golden Gate bridge, that young woman has no expectations that she is about to receive this news. The assistant cannot use euphemisms or other methods to "soften the blow," but must make sure the woman understands what has happened, so is completely blunt and uses the word "death." Assistants, when faced with a potentially highly volatile case, may call on a neighbor to be present (before or after the announcement is made) to help console the relative.

Coroners' assistants use a different tactic depending on their views of humanity; some believe that individuals need to be helped through this difficult situation, while others are convinced that people are more rational and accepting than is generally believed (Charmaz, 1975). They gauge their tactics depending on the situation and the person who is about to receive the news; it also depends on whether the announcement is being made in person or by phone. The first task at hand is to make sure the individual approached is the right one; then it is the assistant's role to convince them of his or her credentials. Although it is not always the case, the assistant usually will be abrupt, in an attempt to convince the person that his or her loved one is dead. A progressive strategy may be used, disclosing a bit of information at a time (ibid.). When the information is imparted in person, serious facial expressions give a strong clue of what's coming. If it is given on the phone, opening sentences such as, "I have some very bad news to give you" alert the listener to the nature of the call.

Military notifications

It is interesting that large organizations adopt similar tactics. For instance, the Israel Defense Forces (IDF) handle giving the news of a soldier's death in a similar manner to the US coroner's offices. They make use exclusively of officers in the reserve to "knock on the door" of families, thus removing such possible recriminations as "why is he alive and my son is dead?" The "announcers of casualties" (Vinitzky-Seroussi and Ben-Ari, 2000: 392), as they are called, use all possible subterfuges to ensure they have contacted the appropriate party, then help prepare the funeral and the burial in a military cemetery, and assist the grieving family. The military has come a long way from World War II days, when both British and American armies announced bad news through a letter written by a high-ranking officer (Kennet, 1987) (the Israeli army followed the same procedure).

In the United States army, notification is handled by the Casualty and Memorial Affairs Operations Center. Next of kin are informed by an officer, a warrant officer, or a senior noncommissioned officer in dress uniform (CNO), under the supervision of the casualty area command (CAC). The CNO is instructed to deliver the news as soon as possible, to be natural, not to hurry, not to keep looking at his or her notes, and not to interject personal opinions. The CAC also assigns to the next of kin (and also to the parents if the deceased was married) a casualty assistant officer to help them handle all the necessary arrangements. The United States armed forces, and especially the army, have recently come under criticism for providing little training to personnel handling the notification and assistances processes. A small number of notifications have gone badly and have recently received publicity in the press. For instance, some families were not told their loved one had been killed by 'friendly fire' when this was the case or through some oversight were not assigned a casualty assistant

(Alvarez, 2006). These mistakes have prompted the army to intensify its training of CNOs and provide increased support to families, beginning in January 2006.

The recipients of bad news

We have looked at the individuals whose profession involves them in being the bearers of bad news. What about the other side, the recipients of bad news? After all, the bearer's task is fleeting; he or she may be uncomfortable, even sad, for a while, but once the message is delivered, the messenger can abandon that role, or at least see it ending. The recipient is left with the burden of what was said – "your cancer has spread to the liver," "your husband has died in a car crash on the turnpike" – and that moment of telling may remain indelibly etched in their memory for life. "Baby boomers," for instance, will never forget where they were when they heard the news that president John F. Kennedy had been assassinated (1963). Similarly, younger individuals remember where they were and what they were doing when the World Trade Center collapsed on September 11, 2001. Older people used to remember Pearl Harbor (1941) in the same way and younger ones remember the moment when the shuttle Challenger blew up (1986). Other examples are the death of stars, such as Elvis Presley (1977) or John Lennon (1980). In the popular television show *Six Feet Under*, Claire has a flashback of her brother Nate crying and listening to CDs, grieving the death of the rock star Kurt Cobain in the 1990s.

There is a whole literature on "bad news," mostly found in organizational psychological studies (Kanter, 1977; Lewis, 1987). Reviewing it is outside our present scope, yet the most important point that emerges from these studies is that giving bad news depends strongly on *power* and *distance* (Lee, 1993). The literature speaks of *power* between the bearer and the recipient of bad news, in our case, for example, the power differential between a high-ranking doctor and a patient or a military officer and a young widow. *Distance* refers to how close or how far apart the bearer and the recipient are, such as your pastor and yourself or a masked resident in ICU and a dying patient.

We would like to add another dimension of power, that of the telling in itself. The bearer decides how, when, and where to divulge the information while the recipient is totally at the bearer's mercy. In this unbalanced situation what may work well for the organization may not fit so well for the individual recipient. Again, in our case, the common practice of having the highest-ranking doctor or military officer impart the news usually works well organizationally, as it is likely that the recipient will accept it calmly, striving to control herself or himself, intimidated by the interaction with the important person. Yet, the *distance* between the two is so great that there is no sharing of the "pain" (Lee, 1993) of the telling, meaning that the bad news is relevant only to the receiver while the bearer has no invest-ment in it.

A recent study (Lautzenheiser, 2007) found that female coroners' assistants are advantaged over their male counterparts in giving bad news to female recipients, since they can reach out and hug the desolate women, thus sharing, if fleetingly and briefly, the pain of the information. *Gender*

We can only hope that the bearer of the bad news will be competent if not compassionate. Otherwise, the interaction will become a worse nightmare for the recipient, as in the following case:

> After Neil Santorello heard the news that his son, a tank commander, had been killed in Iraq, from the officer in his living room, he walked out his front door and removed the American flag from its pole. Then, in tears, he tore down the yellow ribbons from his trees.
>
> Rather than see it as the act of a man unmoored by the death of his 24-year-old son, the officer, an Army major, confronted Mr. Santorello, saying, "Don't be disrespectful," Mr. Santorello recalled. Then, the officer,whose job is to inform families of their loss, quickly disap-peared without offering any comfort. (Alvarez, 2006: 1)

The bearer of the news needs to step out of his or her official role, to take an existential stance, and temporarily to look at the world through the eyes of the recipient. Very often the recipient of such an announcement feels that the world is falling around him or her and desperately needs the bearer to extend a helping hand – not just to say "He died," but to also to add, "I'm sorry."

Conclusion

This chapter has analyzed the various ways that people give bad news and the main occupational groups that have to impart it to dying patients or the relatives of recently deceased individuals. It began by looking at general techniques employed in the telling, in the effort to "soften the blow" of the disclosure. The chapter then examined the roles of physicians, nurses, ministers, lay counselors, and the influ-ence of Elisabeth Kübler-Ross's work on the process of addressing dying patients. We further examined how coroners' assistants and the military notify families of casualties. The emphasis is on the ways these groups accomplish their tasks in an effort to buffer the terrible news they have to give and simultaneously to care for both the dying and the bereaved.

While the majority of this chapter has emphasized the micro-level experience of telling and learning about the news of death, we also discussed various ways in which these processes have been institutionalized at the macro- and meso- (organizational) levels. Doctors' lack of training concerning death, dying, and counseling is indicative of larger institutionalized aspects of the medical profession. Indeed, while there are many sensitive, sympathetic, and even loving doctors who care deeply for their patients, the lack of coaching in how to counsel patients concerning death is part of the wider culture of Western medicine. In this context, with such a lack of cultural and educational supports, doctors are left to find their own ways of discussing death and dying with their patients, which, of course, creates wide variations in their methods and their effectiveness.

Similarly, our discussion of the impact of Kübler-Ross's stage theory of death and dying shows how the model has been institutionalized and used at the macro-level, so that it dominates much of counselors' training and our common understanding about the "correct" way to die. These macro-level trends in society and in the helping and healing professions have micro-level implications for how individuals experience their own process of death and the quality of the participation of the people around them.

The Grieving Process

Introduction

IN many ways one could argue that death is as much about the living as it is about the dead. Although everyone ultimately has to die alone, the death of an individual impacts others' lives as well, and those who are left behind are the ones who have to deal with the loss. The dead person's work is done, but the living are left to cope and find ways to continue with their lives.

Bereavement can change with the social importance of the deceased, for example a president or a pope, or with a large number of people dying at the same time, such as in an earthquake. Grief varies tremendously based on the culture of those involved, and in many cultures there are different grieving social expectations for men and for women. Similarly, individuals and societies express their mourning in a great variety of ways, at times unfortunately viewing women as possessions of the deceased to be treated as objects. This chapter examines different forms of bereavement, grief, and mourning, with an emphasis on the Western and American expressions.

Bereavement, grief, and mourning

First, we need to clarify the differences between bereavement, grief, and mourning. In our popular culture people tend to use these three terms interchangeably; however, those of us who study death recognize that they are distinct experiences. Understanding what they mean will help us gain a better understanding of what happens when a death takes place. In a nutshell, bereavement is the state of having lost someone through death, grief is the mental state of distress or suffering as a result of the death, and mourning is individuals' social display of their response to the death of a loved one.

Bereavement

Bereavement takes place as the result of losing a loved one through death and is not limited to specific relationships or deaths within family; often the death of a close friend results in a shocking and saddening loss. On occasion, entire communities or even nations enter a state of bereavement due to war, terrorism, natural disasters, or epidemics.

The social world cannot exist without daily interactions between various individuals. Through these interactions we both receive and provide a wide variety of needs: emotional, economic, protective, nurturing, and more. Life course theorists emphasize how these social relationships link people's lives together so intricately that a disruption or alteration in one individual's life produces ripples of change that affect many others (Elder, 1994). Bereavement is a clear example of how lives are linked. When bereavement occurs, some individuals change their social status; for instance, a wife becomes a widow, a daughter or son becomes an orphan. In a famous example, when the American President John. F. Kennedy was assassinated in 1963, his wife Jacqueline became a widow, while vice-president Lyndon B. Johnson immediately became president. The English language does not always provide a label for people affected by bereavement, especially for those experiencing grief for a loss in a non-socially recognized relationship, such as the loss of a gay partner. Even for socially acknowledged losses there is at times paucity of words: "There is no term to describe a parent who has lost a child – there are no words adequate for that pain" (Sebba, 2004: 4).

Marital partnerships are intimate, social, and economic in nature, and the loss of a spouse can precipitate the loss of many parts of one's life: "the loss of a husband, for instance, may or may not mean the loss of a sexual partner, companion, accountant, gardener, baby-minder, audience, bed-warmer, and so on" (Parkes, 2001: 8). At times the death may severely affect the financial standing of the survivor, when the 'bread-winner' was the deceased individual. Bereavement may also bring about other changes in others' social relationships and social status. For example, a widow may find that her position in her social group has changed with the death of her spouse, as people may feel embarrassed and uneasy around her, proffering awkward gestures of sympathy and vague offers of help (Doka, 1989). Although she and others may hope that their relationships continue unchanged after the death of her spouse, the nature of her social life may be altered. The widow may find herself cut off and isolated from her group of friends and social relations.

Grief *internal*

Grief is the typical response to bereavement for most people after the loss of a loved one. Grief is defined as the mental state of extreme distress or suffering, especially following the death of an important and meaningful person to the individual. It affects the survivor on both physiological and psychological levels. The emotional impact of grief may include a sense of numbness, sorrow, despair, guilt, disbelief, and shock. Among physical symptoms can be tiredness, backaches, and fatigue. While most people experience some or all of these emotional or physical signs of grief, under some circumstances the passing of a loved one may actually trigger a sense of relief (Keene and Prokos, 2008) or indifference.

As with other emotional experiences, grief occurs within a particular cultural milieu that colors and even dictates how we as individuals experience different life events. In modern-day America the grieving process is anchored in a rationalistic, scientific, and medical ethos that has helped create and perpetuate a specific medical model – that is, a proscription for the right and wrong ways to grieve and the notion that when individuals do not grieve "correctly" there is something wrong with them that must be fixed. While this is the prevailing conception in our culture, there is also an increasing realization that grief can manifest itself in a variety of different manners in different cultures and times. The many various ethnic and racial groups in America tend to express these feelings in different ways. Also, there are different expectations of grief from men and women, with women expected to freely vent their emotions while the men attempt to remain stoic. In the second half of this chapter we return to the concept of grief and examine the various ways in which doctors and clinicians have studied it and have formulated definitions of the right and wrong ways in which to grieve.

Mourning *external*

Grief and mourning are so very closely intertwined that at times it is hard to separate them. After all, we learn how people feel inside (grief) by their outward expressions of it (mourning). Thus, it is really difficult to provide specific examples of grief, since the moment it is expressed it becomes mourning.

Mourning is the period following the death in which survivors socially communicate the impact of their loss. Just as with bereavement and grief, different cultures have their own rituals and expectations regarding how to reflect sorrow appropriately when

lamenting the death of loved ones. Consider this example among the
Warramunga aborigine tribe of Australia:

> A piercing cry suddenly came over the camp: a man was dying there.
> At once the whole company commenced to run as fast as they could,
> while most of them began to howl . . . Some of the women, who had
> come from every direction, were lying prostrate on the body, while
> others were standing or kneeling around, digging the sharp end of a
> yamstick into the crown of their heads, from which the blood streamed
> down their faces, while all the time they kept a loud, continuous wail.
> (Durkheim, 1965: 435–6)

The ways in which individuals mourn their dead is thus a mirror
of the values of the society in which they live. Some prominent signs
of mourning are wearing black clothes or black armbands and flying
flags at half-mast. The ancient Romans hired professional mimes that
would wear wax masks duplicating the features of the deceased in
order properly to eulogize him or her at the funeral. They also hired
women, who, for a fee, would "wail" in order to provide the proper
amount of public display of grief (Friedlander, 1913).

We see the difference in the role of women in mourning in these
early cultures; women caused themselves more bodily harm than the
males among the aborigines and were expected to be the ones expressing deep emotions (if for a fee) among the Romans.

As exemplified above, self-inflicted injuries were not uncommon.
Hair, considered by some to be the symbol of growth and life, has
historically played an important part in mourning. People who
commonly did not cut their hair or shave their heads did so as a
sign of mourning. So common were these practices among the
ancient Israelites that the religion forbade them: "ye shall not cut
yourselves, nor make any baldness between your eyes for the dead"
(Deuteronomy 14: 1–2). At other times, the Israelites were encouraged by their sacred book, the Talmud, not to cut their hair until
the first thirty days of mourning were passed (a period called the
sheloshim) (Tigay, 2007).

Cultural arguments about the acceptability and appropriateness
of public versus private displays of mourning may also be political
in nature. For example, in 2004, rather than publicly mourning its
fallen soldiers, George W. Bush's administration placed restrictions of
the viewing of flag-draped coffins of the military personnel who were
being brought back from the war in Iraq to avoid further criticism of
the military effort in the Middle East. In particular, the administration did not want photographs of the coffins displayed in the press,
since such powerful images would emphasize the wartime loss of life
in the mind of the public. Nonetheless, the restrictions did not stop
families and comrades from publicly mourning the fallen ones. What

follows is the description of the memorial service at Camp Pendleton (San Diego) of the 100 Marines from the 5th Regimental Combat Team who died in Iraq in 2006:

> A Marine called out each name in a somber voice, followed each time by the single chime of a giant bell . . . As is Marine tradition during such services, each service member's dog tag hung from the pistol grip of a ceremonial rifle . . . The service concluded with another tradition: a three-volley rifle salute and the playing of taps. (Roth, 2007: 1–2)

Colors and mourning – As we mentioned above, the color black is an important cultural sign of mourning, and it seems to be the predominant color associated with it in many societies across the world. It was first introduced by the Catholic Church in the sixth century. For Christians, black symbolized the "spiritual darkness of the soul . . . first used by St. Benedict . . . his Benedictine monks became known as the 'black monks' because of their black habits" (Taylor, 1983: 251–2). Women in small villages in Sicily and other rural areas of Italy wear a black dress as a sign of mourning for the loss of any relatives and, given the extended structure of the family in such villages, some dress in black forever. The men, however, do not engage in such extreme displays but simply wear a black armband or a black lapel button, or even black shirt buttons. Historically, blackening the face or parts of the body is a common mourning practice among some groups. For instance, in the American Chippewa tribes, "a man in deep mourning painted his entire face black; in less extreme mourning he painted a black circle covering each eye" (Densmore, 1929). White is also associated with mourning, symbolizing purity and innocence. White garments were used in ceremonies in ancient Rome, China, and Japan (Puckle, 1926) and are still worn today in China, India, and Japan (Taylor, 1983). In Borneo, white was associated with the color of bone and thus is tied to mourning customs. In the second century, Christians wore white at funerals as a symbol of resurrection (Huntington and Metcalf, 1979). In China, where white has been worn at funerals for thousands of years, black is making an inroad, as funerals now see mourners wearing a mixture of white and black (Taylor, 1983). In the US, while customs have become more lax about what color to wear, black remains the dominant color at funerals.

Gender and mourning – As with most aspects of our popular culture, individuals and society have different expectations for how women and men mourn. In most cultures men are expected to be rational and unemotional, while women are supposed to be irrational and emotional. These stereotypes also apply to the ways in which women and men are expected to mourn, which may be considered to be displays of extreme hyper-masculinity and hyper-femininity: real men don't cry and real women cry a lot. The masculine ethos of American society labels crying as unmanly, and therefore men rarely cry publicly after the loss of a loved one, internalizing their grief, although they may feel totally devastated (Doka and Martin, 2001; Parkes, 2006). Furthermore, the expectations surrounding men and mourning are so strong that men may even resist private displays of emotion as part of their grieving process. In contrast, women are encouraged to externalize their grief and are expected to cry and mourn openly. Our culture's expectations about the appropriate ways for women and men to act are very strong, and, when men do cry or women do not show "enough" emotion over the loss of a loved one, others may censure them.

In keeping with women's subordinate status in most cultures, mourning rituals often invoke women's suffering and require that they make personal sacrifices to show their debt and loss after the death of their husband or child. For example, in the traditional culture of the Warramunga of Australia, women were expected to be silent for at least twelve months and use only sign language during mourning. Durkheim reported a case in which a woman had not spoken for forty-four years after the death of her husband (Durkheim, 1965: 437).

Women's traditional roles as caregivers and homemakers also color their relationship to the dead and the ways in which they are expected to mourn. Women have traditionally been expected to not only to attend to the sick and dying but also to prepare the body after death. In one example among the Australian aborigines it was the elder sister of a woman who had lost her child who buried the corpse (Meggitt, 1965). Also, among the Murua in Australia, women were the ones who buried the dead (Bendann, 1930). Even today women are expected to do the "dirty work" after a death:

> When I returned from the hospital after she'd died from the stroke, she'd been incontinent all over the floor. No one had touched it. I suppose it was too awful for father, who had found her. I'd always dealt with the grot [mess]. The mess was stinking. Two days it had been left. I cleared it up, then I found all the vomit on the sheets. I changed them in case my brother wanted to sleep in her room. He didn't, so that night I slept in her bed (Marge, daughter, fifty-seven). (Cline, 1996: 98)

In keeping with stereotypes about women's emotional ties to others and their selflessness as caregivers, during mourning women are not only expected to cry and be emotional, they are also expected to be composed and rational caregivers to the dead and to the survivors around them.

Another powerful example of the conflicting roles facing women in mourning comes from American women's diaries during the great continental migration between 1840 and 1870 (Schlissel, 1982). The trip west was perilous, and births and deaths were daily events. Women's duties as caregivers to the sick and the dying made them acutely aware of the dangers of disease and accidents and the overall loss of human life. As Schlissel notes: "whereas men recorded the death in aggregate numbers, the women knew death as personal catastrophe and noted the particulars of each grave site, whether it was newly dug or old, whether of a young person or an adult, whether it had been disturbed by wolves or by Indians" (1982: 15). The diaries from this time recount again and again the incidence of births and deaths. Losing a child while en route was an overwhelmingly common experience, and women wrote about having to bury a child at the side of the trail: "within the space of three days, Mrs. Henderson saw one child buried and another born. There was no time to mourn and no time to grieve; the journey was relentless" (ibid.: 51). In this rugged and treacherous atmosphere, stopping to give the dead a proper burial put the rest of the group in danger, which added stress made the trip all the more difficult.

Historically, women have often been treated as objects and used as props in order to display appropriate signs of mourning. After a king died in the Congo, twelve young women were buried alive with him. Similarly, in Mexico, when a king died a number of women were buried with him to "amuse him" (Puckle, 1926: 55–6). Finally, there is the infamous practice of "sati," or "widow burning," in India, in which the favored wife of a deceased man would be burned on the husband's funeral pyre. Traditionally women were expected actually to throw themselves, out of devotion and obligation, on the funeral pyre. Although the British rulers in India banned the practice in 1829, it occasionally occurs in modern days. The following event took place in the northern Indian village of Deorala in 1987:

> A pretty, young bride of eight months, Roop Kanwar, gained universal fame September 4th . . . She became a sati – burning herself to death on her husband's funeral pyre. The reaction in India was an unresolved mixture of shock, admiration, outrage, reverence, and embarrassment over the young's girl action. (*Hinduism Today*, 2007: 1)

As a reaction to Kanwar's suicide, in 1987 the Indian government passed an anti-sati law, which treats the woman as an offender who is attempting suicide and prescribes a fine and/or imprisonment for up to one year (igovernment, 2007). Efforts to amend the law to treat women as victims have thus far failed. This state of affairs demonstrates the persistence of gender inequality. The prescribed mourning rituals for Indian women have changed from their being required to sacrifice their own lives as a display of subordination to their husband to being treated as criminals for adhering to traditional sati practices.

Thus far we have discussed the three main processes that survivors go through after the loss of a loved one, and it is clear that bereavement, grief, and mourning vary across cultures, gender, and history. It is also important to note that, even within a particular culture, not everyone grieves the same way. We now turn to a discussion of the various types of grief that scholars have identified and social science theories about the process of grieving.

Types of grief

Studies of bereavement and grief as well as clinical research have attempted to identify different types of grief and to define what was considered psychologically healthy as opposed to unhealthy. Social norms and social roles are two sociological concepts that are centrally relevant to this discussion.

Norms, roles, and grief

Sociologists often study social norms. Norms are shared expectations and rules about what is acceptable and socially desirable. Talcott Parsons was one of the first sociologists to provide an explicit example of behavior that deviates from the norm. In his description of "the sick role," Parsons argued that the norm is for people to be healthy and able to take care of themselves (Parsons, 1951). When people are sick they deviate from the norm and adopt the role of an unhealthy person, which brings with it an entirely different set of acceptable and normal behaviors. However, sickness is an undesirable behavior, and therefore people are expected to move into and out of the sick role very quickly – prolonging the sick role is unacceptable. Parsons proceeded to outline steps through which a patient must go to conquer the illness and return to being healthy. This medicalized view of normalcy and the notion that a person progresses through steps (or stages) in order to get well is applicable to views about how people process their grief during bereavement (we return to this idea later in the chapter).

Normal versus pathological grief

The prevalence of the medical model of grief in America has led experts to define some types of grief as pathological, meaning unhealthy or as a disease. It is important to note the relevance of the social context in which grief is defined as normal or abnormal. In the US, the high social status of the medical establishment means that doctors and medical practitioners are viewed as the most qualified to evaluate normal versus abnormal behaviors. Some scholars have pointed out, however, that these evaluations are made within particular social, cultural, economic, and organizational contexts: "for organizational reasons of supply and demand of services, clinical lore needs to differentiate abnormal from normal grief . . . clinical lore draws on both clinical practice, research and popular cultural ideas of abnormality to create its own . . . notions of what is normal and what abnormal" (Walter, 1999: 165).

Definitions of pathological grief vary considerably, since there is no clear-cut definition of what constitutes normal grief. For instance, grief can be defined as pathological if it is too intense or lasts too long, but it could also be considered pathological if it is not intense enough or does not last long enough (Middleton et al., 1993). To help clarify this issue, one prominent bereavement scholar, Margaret Stroebe (2001), proposed that normal grief is culturally specific and that the grief process can be considered normal if it takes the typical trajectory and duration of a particular culture.

Definitions of grief have evolved over the past century. It was Freud ([1919] 1959) who first made the distinction between grief (normal) and melancholia (pathological). Later on, Lindemann (1944) distinguished between normal and morbid forms of grief, defining normal rather narrowly. Parkes (1965) outlined various types of pathological grief: (1) *chronic grief*, when years after the death the survivor is still very preoccupied and/or severely distressed with memories of the deceased; (2) *inhibited grief*, when the person avoids confronting the loss as a way to distance themselves from the pain and the usual markers of grief are largely absent; and (3) *delayed grief*, when the survivor first goes through a period of numbness in which they do not express their anguish until later. More recently, Parkes (2001) further refined these categories of pathological grief by adding other qualities, such as anxiety, panic attacks, and self-blame. Grief is only one of many psychological states that people experience after a loss, and it co-exists with syndromes such as depression, anxiety, and post-traumatic stress, making it hard to gauge the true state of the individual.

Probably the most famous type of pathological grief is now known as post-traumatic stress disorder (PTSD). PTSD is a collection of symptoms that individuals experience usually in response to a traumatic event. Its diagnosis has evolved over time, and at various historical points its symptoms have been called "railroad spine syndrome," "shell-shock syndrome," and various types of "war neuroses" (Lamprecht and Sack,

2002). Regarding the relationship between PTSD and the trauma of losing a loved one, Middleton and colleagues (1993) argue that the circumstances of the death are important for how people grieve. Indeed, if the death is unexpected or results from violence, such as a disaster, homicide, or suicide, people are more likely to experience PTSD during the grief process than if the death took place over a long time period and was expected.

In light of the contextual nature of definitions of normal and pathological grief, scholars have proposed alternative terms for describing these states, including complicated grief, which occurs when the bereaved person does not recover from their loss and make progress in life (Stroebe, 2001), or traumatic grief, which occurs in response to sudden or unexpected losses (Range, 2002).

Disenfranchised grief

Although individual people experience pressure to conform to societal norms, norms themselves also exist as part of our larger, macro-level social structure. Thus, the structure of society also impacts the ways in which people grieve and what is considered to be acceptable, healthy grief. Sociologists have long struggled to explain this tension between an individual's free will and their relationship to the larger social structure. Durkheim emphasized, perhaps too much (cf. Pine, 1989), the weight of society on the mourning person:

> Mourning is not a natural movement of private feelings wounded by a cruel loss; it is a duty imposed by the group. One weeps, not simply because he is sad, but because he is forced to weep. It is a ritual attitude which he is forced to adopt out of respect for custom, but which is, in a large measure, independent of his affective state. (Durkheim, 1965: 443)

The concept of disenfranchised grief recognizes that societies have sets of "grieving rules," which are norms that attempt to specify who, when, where, how, how long, and for whom people should grieve (Doka, 1989: 4). In our social context, we as individuals also make value judgments about the relative importance of different losses and the appropriate form and duration of grief that people should experience. Indeed, the higher the status of the deceased, the more acceptable it is for prolonged and emotional displays of grieving to be enacted. Losses that are considered legitimate by society, such as the loss of a spouse, afford those left behind more institutionalized channels of mourning (such as viewing the body, the funeral, and receiving greater social support).

These value judgments also mean that some losses are not valued as much as others and that society judges some people's behaviors more negatively than others, depending on the nature of their losses. Thus, not all losses automatically merit rights or privileges for grieving behavior. When society does not consider a loss to warrant the expression of grief these occasions are referred to as disenfranchised grief. Formally, disenfranchised grief is defined as "grief that persons experience when they incur a loss that is not or cannot be openly acknowledged, publicly mourned, or socially supported" (Doka 1989: 4).

Society generally does not recognize or validate grieving when a person is not related to the deceased, such as a lover, a friend, a co-worker, a neighbor, an ex-spouse or partner, a homosexual partner, a complete stranger, or even a pet. We also have socially sanctioned age limits for displays of grief such that we often do not validate such emotion among young children or the very old. Additionally, the very private nature of the loss of a fetus through miscarriage and the social stigma that is associated with abortion often mean that women and families who experience these events have to endure them privately and alone, without socially recognized avenues to express their grief.

Disenfranchised grievers are not allowed to "work through" their feelings and receive support in their sorrow, thus being thrust deeper into despair. These people are denied support because their claims to grief are not seen as legitimate for the reasons mentioned above. An ironic twist is that the grievers, often themselves influenced by societal values, may suppress any kind of public demonstrations because they feel ashamed that their deceased loved one was gay, or an extramarital lover, or a dog. As Kauffman puts it, "in self-disenfranchised grief one is disenfranchised by one's own shame" (1989: 26).

Lack of grief

In some cases, individuals who experience losing someone close fail to demonstrate grief, and just as society judges overt displays as more or less appropriate, a lack of grief can also be problematic. Consider the following case:

> In Arizona, John Henry Knapp was convicted of the murder of his two young daughters, who died in a fire that destroyed their one-bedroom trailer. The principal evidence offered against Knapp was that immediately after the fire, he was outwardly calm and talkative and showed no overt display of distress. He was ultimately sentenced to death and remained in prison for 13 years. At that point, new evidence emerged about the origin of the fire that exonerated Knapp, and he was released. (Wortman and Silver, 2001: 405)

In some instances people may not show symptoms of grief because they have already begun the grieving process and experienced anticipatory grief. Anticipatory grief happens when someone begins to grieve for the loss of a loved one before that person actually dies (Beder, 2002). Many scholars believe that anticipatory grief does not entirely remove grief after death (see, for instance, Fulton and Fulton, 1971), but, by allowing for preparation and reducing most of the shock, its intensity is lessened. The survivor may be emotionally spent after helping the dying person through a long declining illness, or the amount of time this has taken may have helped the process of gradually detaching him- or herself from the sufferer. Pine (1989) observes that, while anticipatory grief serves a positive function, it rests on a delicate balance; if it is "too successful too soon," it may disconnect the living from the dying too early and isolate the dying person as a result. Not all scholars agree on the benefits of anticipatory grieving. For example, Fulton (2003) finds little evidence to support the theory that it diminishes stress.

It is also possible that survivors feel a sense of relief at the passing of a loved one, which is an emotional reaction that conflicts with our typical expectations about responses to death and dying. Still, in some situations we can understand how a person may feel relieved by a death. The cessation of prolonged illness, where the dying person has been in pain or suffering, as well as of an intensive caregiving situation, may actually be welcomed (Keene and Prokos, 2008). This may be the case, for example, with caregivers of Alzheimer's disease patients who have spent years witnessing the slow deterioration of their loved one to the point that he or she no longer recognizes them.

As we have established, grieving takes many forms and is dependent upon the situation and the circumstances of the loss. Nonetheless, psychiatrists, psychologists, and counselors who try to guide people through the grief process have identified various patterns and have theorized about the utility of grieving in different ways. We now move on to discuss these specific theories.

Theories of grief and bereavement

Having seen the complexities of grief and the widely different responses to bereavement, it is clear that attempting to explain and predict how people will react to bereavement is a difficult and problematic task. Nonetheless, we will briefly survey some of the major theoretical explanations. Stroebe and Schut (2001a) review the current theories on grief. Just as Freud speculated that grieving individuals need to do "grief work" to return to a "normal" life, the authors believe that how people cope with grief will have consequences for their health status. Thus they focus on the adaptive strategies people employ that are aimed at offsetting the negative consequences of grief. In their review, they identified three main categories of theories: stress and trauma theories; general theories of grief; and models of coping specific to bereavement.

Stress and trauma theories

Stress and trauma theories of grief are general in nature and focus on a broad spectrum of events that cause both emotions, for example war, accidents, and bereavement. In looking at bereavement and the stress it causes, these theories examine the ways that people cope. For instance, the cognitive stress theory (Stroebe and Schut, 2001a) considers bereavement as the stressor, and the people can address the emotional problems caused by grief either by confronting them (feeling guilt at how they, on occasion, treated the deceased) or by avoiding them (such as refraining from crying); they can also turn their attention to practical problems deriving from the loss (such as earning money to overcome financial losses as a result of the death). Trauma theories address people's reaction to stressful events, including post-traumatic stress disorder. In reviewing the work of Janoff-Bulman and Berg (1998), Stroebe and Schut state that "The fundamental assumptions people hold about themselves, the world, and the relation between these two, which normally go unquestioned and unchallenged, are shattered by traumatic events such as the death of a loved one" (2001a: 383). Coping, according to Janoff-Bulman and Berg (1998), would involve reassessing one's beliefs in themselves and the world and challenging the negativity surrounding the death by finding new life meanings.

Grief theories

Grief work – In contemporary society, grief is viewed as something that survivors need to "work through." It is no longer acceptable to continue the grieving process for an extended length of time. Rather, in our culture we now consider prolonged grieving to be dysfunctional, since it disrupts people's lives and causes psychological and physiological distress (to themselves and those around them). Now we tend to expect people to move on with their lives, develop new bonds (Parkes, 2001), and reinvent their identity as they progress (Lopata, 1979). When they appear to languish too long in the grieving process we tend to look for medical and psychological strategies for helping them to move on. An entire industry of counseling and psychological professionals has emerged in the US (Groopman, 2004). In this context, we use medical imagery and terminology to describe individuals who fail to work through their grief in a timely fashion, and their condition is described in terms of syndromes, suggesting disease.

Theories of grief mark the beginning by social scientists to attempt to explain this phenomenon. In his early work on grief, mourning, and depression, Freud recognized four elements of normal grieving: "profoundly painful dejection, loss of capacity to adopt new love objects, inhibition of activity or turning away from activity not connected with thoughts of the loved person, and loss of interest in the outside world" (Middleton et al., 1993: 45). Freud argued that the only way for patients to improve their condition was literally to work through the grief in order to overcome it. In his view, this had to be done through hard work, leading to the acceptance of the irremediable loss of the loved one (Freud, [1919] 1959).

Building on Freud's work, the psychiatrist Eric Lindemann coined the term "grief work" to describe the process of dealing with one's emotions after a loss (Lindemann, 1944). During World War II, Lindemann studied 101 people who had survived the fire at the famous Coconut Grove nightclub in Boston. Through his observations he determined that grieving was a normal psychological state and suggested that patients who suffered from prolonged or acute grief should seek therapy in order to return to normalcy. According to his theory, failure to face and resolve one's feelings will result in pathological grief. Lindemann built on Freud's notion that people needed to work through grief and, in his own clinical work with patients, found support for the idea that clinicians could help with this (Parkes, 2002).

Stage theories of grief

In the 1960s and 1970s, Elisabeth Kübler-Ross pioneered the notion that terminally ill patients progress through various "stages of dying" that lead them finally to accept their own impending death (see chapter 8). Bowlby and Parkes (1970) applied this idea to the notion of working through grief in stages. They identified four distinct phases: numbness, yearning and searching, disorganization and despair, and reorganization.

Despite the popularity of stage theories, grief (like death) may not be so easy to categorize, and people in mourning often do not progress through the stages of grief in a linear fashion. Grief waxes and wanes over time and in response to different dates, events, and memories. For example, various markers can trigger memories of the deceased – a picture, a song, a movie, an anniversary, a birthday – as can various objects, such as the deceased's favorite chair or car. Memories can stimulate positive feelings, reminding people to cherish that special moment or object, or alternatively may elicit a new wave of sorrow, causing some to steer clear of anything that might have this effect (Parkes, 2001).

Task and growth models

Worden (1991, 2002) considered that the stage theories require an ordered sequence from the first to the last stage, which may be taken too literally and be too constraining. Mourners, he felt, engage in a number of tasks in no given order and often revisit one or another. This approach breaks away from the previous linear models and the notion that, once a mourner goes through a stage, he or she doesn't look back – that stage is done. Worden's model is much more fluid, and also drastically changes the common belief in grief theories that we need to move away for good from the deceased or our mourning will be considered pathological. His last task is "to relocate the dead person within one's life and find ways to memorialize the person" (1991: 15). Thus he considers an emotional tie between the bereaved and the deceased to be normal.

Other researchers, beginning in the 1980s, followed a path similar to Worden (for a review of the various models, see Rothaupt and Becker, 2007) and challenged the traditional concepts of mourning. They accepted a bond in the relationship between the bereaved and the deceased rather than seeking closure. Bereaved individuals will follow a unique path of mourning that involves their personal relation with the deceased and even with objects that belonged to the deceased. Even a lack of a display of emotions by the bereaved now becomes acceptable (Stroebe and Stroebe, 1991).

Growth models go beyond the task models by taking an existential approach to mourning (Davies, 2004), that is, by stressing the unique meaning that the bereaved individuals make of their mourning and by allowing even more fluidity, moving away altogether from linear and rigid models. Rothaupt and Becker (2007: 10) summarize these models thus: "This new orientation allows ongoing relationships and emotional connections with the bereaved, supporting ongoing rituals, marking of special occasions, and recognizing the uniqueness in individuals' experiences of grief and mourning."

Bereavement theories

Dual-process model – One of the most popular bereavement-specific theories is Stroebe and Schut's dual-process model. This theory focuses on two broad types of stressor (those elements that cause distress): loss-orientation, in which the bereaved person concentrates on some aspects of the loss itself, and restoration-orientation, in which their attention turns to the tasks of restoration. If the person engages in avoidance behavior, ignoring one of the stressors, successful recovery will not be possible. An example would be keeping very busy at work so not to have to think about the loss (the stressor). In the dual-process model, in order to make a successful recovery, the grieving individual must oscillate between the two stressors, attending to personal emotions and feelings but also reconstructing their daily life (Stroebe and Schut, 2001b).

Stroebe and Schut (2001b) also explain how women and men experience grief differently according to their model. Men tend to follow restorative coping mechanisms as they focus on "getting things done" and take on new roles and relationships. Women, in contrast, usually fix on the emotional loss and the events and feelings surrounding it. In order to grieve, then, women are inclined to concentrate on positively reinterpreting past events and the emotional aspects of their loss. Men place more emphasis on restoration-oriented stressors, which involve getting things done, such taking on new roles and making new relationships. Women focus more on loss-oriented stressors that underline emotional events surrounding the loss and feelings, such as positive reinterpretation of past events. Despite its value, this theory of grief closely follows American stereotyped conceptions of role differentials between men and women.

The processes of bereavement, grief, and mourning do not merely involve the internal resolution of pain and emotion. For example, the loss of a spouse also requires adjustment to the new social role of widow or widower, to which we turn next.

Widowhood

The death of a spouse is arguably one of the most stressful life situations that people endure. For many of us, thinking about losing our life partners is one of the most painful experiences to ponder. Recall our discussion on life expectancy from chapter 2 that showed that, on average, women outlive men. Since women have longer life expectancies than men, it follows that the majority of research about spousal loss and bereavement focuses on women's experiences (Lopata, 1986), although some studies do examine widowers' lives after the death of their spouse (Bennett, 2005).

It is well established that widowhood is an event that has negative effects on psychological outcomes (Miech and Shanahan, 2000). Losing a spouse has been linked to a temporary increase in depression (Umberson et al., 1992). However, the death of a spouse does not mean that survivors are depressed for the rest of their lives; research has shown that bereavement and adaptation to widowhood is a process like other types of grief (Bodnar and Kiecolt-Glaser, 1994; Carr and Utz, 2002; Kramer and Lambert, 1999). Although the surviving partner's mental well-being generally declines during the first year after the loss, by the second year of widowhood their mental health generally recovers (Mendes de Leon et al., 1994; Umberson et al., 1992). As time passes the negative effects on their well-being tend to decline (Lee et al., 2001; Mendes de Leon et al., 1994; Stroebe and Stroebe, 1993). Overall, research has found little or no long-term effects (Harlow et al., 1991).

Studies of how individuals adapt to widowhood examine various aspects of adjustment, including bereavement, loneliness, depression, grief, anxiety, stress, self-esteem levels, and coping. While widowhood is commonly associated with depression (Carr and Utz, 2002), some of the critical factors that can affect this are an individual's level of social support, their physical health, their financial situation, their gender, whether the death of the spouse was sudden or anticipated, and the quality of the marital relationship (Bennett, 1997; Carr and Utz, 2002; Field and Sundin, 2001; Levesque et al., 1995; Zisook and Shuchter, 1991). We turn to a brief discussion of each of these factors now.

From a sociological perspective, it is important to consider the physical and material conditions of survivors' lives and how those factors may impact their experience of widowhood. First, it should not be surprising to find that better physical health predicts better psychological adjustment in widowhood (Ozawa et al., 1984). Second, the deceased spouse's health before death may also be important. The kind and duration of their illness explains some variation in survivors' psychological adjustment (Carr et al., 2000; Keene and Prokos, 2008; Norris and Murrell, 1987). One study of widows found evidence that those whose spouses were ill before death were able to engage in anticipatory grieving and begin to adjust to the notion that their spouse would die. This helped reduce the effect of widowhood itself on depression for as long as three years after the death (Carnelley et al., 1999). Related to the dying person's health is the issue of whether or not their partner acted as caregiver. Some research has shown that the length of such caregiving before death (Keene and Prokos, 2008) and the specific characteristics of the situation (Prokos and Keene, 2005) have an impact on survivors' depression over time.

As most sociologists would guess, higher income may help protect against depression among widows (Arens, 1982; Carr et al., 2000). For many women, marriage provides a financial safety net that may be lost with the passing of their husband. Also, the cost of healthcare, medical bills, and funeral expenses may exacerbate widows' financial problems. Indeed, one study found that financial strain lead to higher grief, depression, and anxiety (Utz, 2002). Financial insecurity or health problems may also force widows and widowers to move in with relatives or into institutional settings, both of which can be disruptive to their lifestyles and can cause personal and familial stress.

We also know that men and women differ in their adjustment to losing their spouse: men yearn for deceased spouses if their wives died after a prolonged illness, whereas wives yearn more if their spouse died suddenly (Carr and Utz, 2002). The perceived quality of their marriage affects how both men and women grieve. Happier marriages lead to more grief, whereas troubled marriages are associated with lower levels (Carr et al., 2000). We might even suggest that, although even among unhappy marriages the death of a spouse can be painful, it could also bring about a sense of relief for the survivor.

Patterns of mourning have changed over time. While there were once strict rules for how women should behave (including the colors they wore – or the lack thereof, and the duration of the mourning process), as values become more fragmented Americans find less guidance of this kind. Women are no longer required to wear black garments or arm bands, and people frequently remarry after the loss of a spouse, although men are even more likely to remarry.

Conclusion

Death is as much about the living as it is the dead. For those of us who are left to go on after the passing of a loved one, the journey through bereavement, mourning, and grief can be difficult. We also know that the immediate emotional and physical symptoms of grief tend to lessen over time and that it is possible to continue with life after a loss. As they say, time is a great healer. Social scientists have identified various pathways that people take through the bereavement process. While there is some controversy about what constitutes "normal" grief, and grieving is different for different people, researchers have also shown that some experiences are more typical than others. For some people counseling and therapy is a useful and necessary part of the grieving process, while others move through bereavement on their own.

We have seen that men and women are expected to behave differently in the face of loss, often perpetuating stereotypes of women as the "weaker" sex. Women also were, and still are, expected to carry out the "hard" work that arises with death situations, both as caregivers of the dying and in caring for the body. In some cultures women were considered merely as possessions of the deceased and treated as expendable. Men and women also experience widowhood in dissimilar ways, given their different societal expectations and resources.

CHAPTER 10

Life after Death

J UAN Ponce de Léon, the first Spanish explorer to set foot in Florida, wandered for years in the New World searching for the fabled fountain of youth, which was rumored to be in the island of Bimini off the coast of Florida. Allegedly, those who drank the water from the fountain would remain young forever. What the conquistador found, instead, was death from the arrows of hostile American natives (Segerberg, 1974).

Oscar Wilde's (1974) Dorian Gray, a handsome young man, asked the devil that his beauty should not be spoiled, and so his portrait began to age instead of the man himself. Gray lived a life of pleasures and cruelty, and with each vile deed he committed the painting grew older and more ugly. Eventually he realized that he was in an unwitting pact with evil forces and turned to a pious life, but he could not change the situation. Finally, desperate, he lunged at the painting and began to slice it with a knife. A servant heard horrible screams and rushed into the room, only to find the painting intact but portraying a handsome young man again; in the corner an old, withered man was dead with a knife through his heart.

These are but two famous examples of the human quest for immortality, which has taken many forms and has suffered many setbacks, both in fictional accounts and in real life. But the search goes on undaunted. In this chapter we examine the question of life beyond death. The sociological queries raised by the quest for immortality concern notions of how realities are constructed, how they are legitimated, and how they affect the self. We examine some of the accounts put forth by various disciplines to illustrate how people structure their systems of belief and thus their everyday lives and their thoughts, fears, and beliefs about life after death. Experiencing and interpreting everyday reality depends to a great extent upon the assumptions about the world that one considers legitimate (Schutz, 1971). For example, people who believed the earth was flat lived in a reality shaped by the conviction that the terrestrial orb was shaped like a pancake, and therefore acted as if they lived on a flat planet.

If an individual, group, or society legitimizes a cluster of ideas that present a particular view of the world, that view will become reality for those who accept its legitimacy (Weber, 1974). Likewise, if a system of beliefs encompassing the existence of immortality becomes legitimate for a particular group, that group will share social values and actions based on that belief. In other words, people who believe in immortality are socially immortal, for their lives are acted out as if they lead to a future without death.

The ways leading to the legitimization of immortality are varied. They range from attempts to validate the supernatural scientifically to religious, dogmatic faith in an afterlife. This chapter examines some of the attempts to transcend our finitude: "A finite universe is unimaginable, inconceivable. An infinite universe is unimaginable, inconceivable. Doubtless the universe is neither finite nor infinite, since the finite and the infinite are only man's way of thinking about it" (Ionesco, 1968: 25).

The ancient beliefs

The Greeks

Almost all societies have some form of belief in immortality. The first evidence of this in the Western world was found in ancient Greece. The Greek word *psyche* translates into English as "I," "self," or "soul," embodying in itself a complex gamut of meanings. The ancient Greeks worshiped their dead with offerings of food and drinks, by placing weapons and other ornamental objects in graves, and, at times, by sacrificing slaves to dead heroes (Moore, 1963).

Homer's epic works the *Iliad* and the *Odyssey* provide us with some evidence of the Greek concept of the afterlife. People's deaths were lamented and respected, but little remained of the pleasures of life. Odysseus visited Hades, (the land of the dead) during his peregrinations and reported the existence of a bleak world where the souls of the dead wandered. There seemed to be no reward or punishment in Hades, but instead an overwhelming dullness. The greatest of ancient warriors, Achilles, now dead and wandering through Hades, tells the visiting Odysseus: "Rather would I live on ground as the hireling of another, with a landless man who had no great livelihood, than bear sway among all of the dead that be departed" (Homer, 1965: 176).

The spirits of the dead in ancient Greece were depicted as incorporeal shadows that maintained their former human semblance

(Odysseus recognized Achilles and many others). Greeks did not view transcendence into an afterlife as a positive event. The emphasis was rather toward life on earth with a glorification of living. Even inscriptions and scenes found on sepulchers describe terrestrial events rather than projections of an afterlife. Important statesmen and warriors were awarded much more elaborate burials, often with weapons and other earthly valuables being placed alongside the dead body (Moore, 1963).

The Egyptians

Other ancient civilizations also believed in the immortality of the self. The Egyptians provide an interesting example. They did not distinguish very clearly between the natural and the supernatural, and seemed to vacillate between a real belief in an afterlife and a mythical concept of the beyond and the gods. Egyptians believed that each person has a double within themselves, the *ka*, a human-like figure with the head of a bird. The *ka* left the mortal body at death.

Different types of embalming were practiced, depending on the social class of the deceased (Hardt, 1979) – the higher their social status, the more elaborate and expensive the embalming. This procedure allowed the body to withstand decomposition and gave the soul time to reach the gods in the world of the afterlife. The voyage of the soul was aided by burying, alongside the body, food, drinks, and the worldly riches of the departed. Gold was especially helpful; it was considered the metal of the gods since it captured the golden radiance of the sun god. The supreme rulers of Egypt (the pharaohs) were completely encased in gold after their death to help their journey to the great beyond. Archeologists found the young pharaoh Tut-Ank-Amen sheathed in gold when they unearthed his tomb. The Egyptians also left *The Egyptian Book of the Dead* in the tombs of important people; the book describes the voyage of the soul to the world beyond.

The mythical belief in immortality, among ancient Egyptians, was rooted in the story of Osiris, the ruler of Egypt and the lord of creation (Budge, 1961). Osiris was murdered by his enemy, Seth, and his body was dismembered. From the torn limbs rose Osiris' son Horus, the god of the sun, who defeated Seth in battle, and night gave way to the day.

The mystery created by the strange mixture of natural with supernatural in ancient Egypt has continued in popular folklore to modern times (Fodor, 1964). Allegedly, many of the individuals who desecrated the burial places of the pharaohs, whether thieves or archeologists, were struck by the "Egyptian curse" and died under strange circumstances. The latest episode occurred when archeologists discovered Tut-Ank-Amen in 1922. As the party entered the pyramid, a hawk, the symbol of the gods, hovered above. This was taken as an omen of doom for the discoverers, who, allegedly, were later struck by severe misfortunes.

Religious beliefs

There are numerous religions that portray their own particular view of the afterlife. They all rely on dogma rather than empirical elements, and they all share a conception of a world beyond earthly life. Because this is a topic unto itself we examine only four major religions: Judaism/Christianity, Buddhism, Islam, and Hinduism. They encompass a large portion of the earth's population, and therefore they shape the lives (and the dying) of millions of people. Judaism and Christianity combined comprise over 2.2 billion believers, Islam has 1.3 billion adherents, Buddhism has 376 million, and Hinduism has 900 million (Adherents, 2005).

Judeo-Christian afterlife

Judeo-Christian theology provides two different views of immortality. The Jews envisioned a golden era of a kingdom of God on earth, but, when time passed and this promised kingdom failed to materialize, hope shifted to waiting for a spiritual kingdom either on earth or in heaven.

In the Old Testament there was little to rejoice about death. The first humans, Adam and Eve, had a choice in the Garden of Eden. But, rather than seeking the fruit from the tree of life that would have given them immortality, they sought the fruit from the tree of knowledge, thus condemning themselves and the human race to mortality. Having been doomed to a finite life, they could not find salvation in an afterlife, since the choice made in Eden was irreversible (Choron, 1964). The afterlife was not that important in the Old Testament; when mentioned, it was a place neither of reward nor of punishment for terrestrial deeds. Instead, the spirits of the dead wandered aimlessly, just as Achilles and the other Homeric shadows did in Hades. The Old Testament presented comfort in the face of death not so much through hope of salvation as through absolute faith in God.

The New Testament introduced the possibility of the resurrection of the body. Jesus himself spoke of the kingdom of God on earth and its continuation in heaven, but had little to say about the relationship between body and soul. This relationship was clarified in Christ's resurrection from the dead, which provided the Christian cornerstone for the belief that resurrection was in both body and spirit. Contrary to the Greek and Egyptian religious systems, which favored the wealthy and the famous, Christianity favors the poor and the down-trodden, promising a them a glorious life beyond. Christians do not place expensive earthly goods alongside the deceased; the emphasis is more one of "you cannot take it with you."

It was Jesus' disciple Paul who elaborated on the notion of body and soul. It should not be ignored that Paul had been a Pharisee before his conversion, and Pharisees had strong beliefs in the resurrection of the dead. Paul envisioned human beings who had received the spirit of God as possessing both body and soul. For Paul, though, the body was not a mere vessel carrying the soul. He considered the two inextricably bound together and that a resurrected body that was incorruptible and heavenly would rise along with the soul after final judgment. Faith in the resurrection of Jesus was all the proof that was needed to support Paul's argument (Moore, 1963).

In summation, for some Christian denominations (but not all), the self undergoes three stages: (a) a mortal body and soul during life; (b) after death but before judgment day the self is an incorporeal shadow; and (c) after judgment day the soul is reunited with a new, immortal body.

Buddhism

Buddhism originated in India from the teachings of Gautama Buddha. The belief in Buddhism spread widely in the East and to some extent in the West, taking a variety of forms. Buddha in Sanskrit means "fully enlightened," and there is no single god-like Buddha that is compa-rable to the Christian deity. Instead, there are numerous Buddhas, who periodically abandon the state of nirvana where they are fully enlightened, and house their consciousness in a body to spread their teachings concerning the meaning of life. All individuals, according to Buddhist teachings, possess an essential element that does not die with the body, but changes form from time to time, like an eternally reborn butterfly shedding its cocoon:

> There is not *one* person, indeed, not *one* living being, that has *not* returned from death. In fact, we all have died many deaths, before we came into this incarnation. And what we call birth is merely the reverse side of death, like one of the two sides of a coin, or like a door which we call "entrance" from outside and exit from inside a room. (Govinda, 1960: liii)

To ensure that humans do not forget their continuous journey through life, many are made to remember glimpses of their previous lives. These glimpses fade away, forgotten, in the minds of adults, but are often lucidly clear in children.

One of the Buddhas is the Dalai Lama, the exiled spiritual leader of Tibet, a land remotely placed among the highest and most inaccessible Himalayan mountains. Tibetan notions of immortality are to be found in *The Tibetan Book of the Dead* (Bardo Thödol). This book is a guide for the dead; there are three stages from birth to death and three from death to birth (Govinda, 1960).

Buddhism is wrongly stereotyped as a world-denying religion. Yet, poverty is a negative element in Buddhism. Poverty causes *dukkha* (suffering/unhappiness), and the goal of Buddhism is to end unhappiness. To be poor makes it difficult to follow the Buddhist spiritual quest, for the poor are unhappy. Wealth is also a negative element, since it is often abused, and again stands in the way of a spiritual quest. The right Buddhist path is to accept one's condition and remain detached from worldly preoccupations (Payutto, 1994).

Islam

People of Muslim faith comprise a great variety of national, ethnic, tribal, and other communities. Islam is the name of the religion found in the Holy Koran, preached by the prophet Muhammad. It is monotheistic, centered on the god Allah. Like Christians, Muslims believe that the quality of life of earth will determine one's fate in the afterlife and that body and soul will be reunited after the final judgment day.

There are, however, differences between these two. There is a Muslim concept of the life of the grave, where the dead person is visited by two angels who decide whether the deceased will go to heaven or hell (Gilanshah, 1993). Thereafter, the dead person remains unconscious until the day of final judgment (Smith and Haddad, 2002). Martyrs for Islam go directly to heaven. The faith of women is more problematic: "Reflecting a misogyny that became more intense in the later eras of Middle Eastern Islamic history, the collected sayings of the prophet commonly hold that most women, lacking reason and self-restraint, will end up in hell" (Lapidus, 1996: 153).

Muslims believe that death is another test of their faith, and that it is not the end of life but leads to life beyond and to Allah. The spirits of the dead can communicate with the living by apparitions or in dreams. The Koran describes the wonderments of heaven but not the tribulations of hell. It is believed that in the end the great Allah will forgive even the most heinous sinners.

Islam encourages its followers to gain property and income as long as they use it without arrogance and pride. It does not place a great value on poverty but it recognizes it as a social evil. Every Muslim is asked to pay a tax, *zakat*, which is distributed among the poor and the needy in order to alleviate poverty (Güner, 2005)

Hinduism

The third largest religion on earth, Hinduism, is difficult to categorize. There is widespread belief that Hindus worship many deities
(polytheism), though others view Hinduism as monotheistic, since
there is only one supreme god, Brahman. Still others view the three
aspects of the supreme god as a triad, three gods, with Brahman as the
creator of all things, Vishnu as the preserver of creation, and Shiva as
the destroyer (Rinehart, 2004). Basically, Hindus have a supreme god
and many other deities who are forms or manifestations of Brahman.
Additionally, villages have their local goddess who oversees fertility
and disease (hence life and death).

An important component of Hinduism is the caste system; although
it was outlawed in 1949 it maintains considerable influence in India.
Each follower belongs to one of four social castes (called *varna*). The
system is rigid and there is hardly any intermingling within members
of different castes, thus regulating strictly all walks of life. A fifth
group is "the untouchables," who are relegated to the lowest jobs and
are shunned by all others. Today the law prohibits discrimination
based on caste, yet the system remains a powerful force, often control-
ling marriage, occupation, and many other aspects of life.

While Judeo-Christians have a linear concept of life and afterlife,
in which an individual moves forward from one to the next, Hindus
believe in a cyclical concept of time and in reincarnation; humans
shed body after body until their immortal soul finishes its cycle
and comes into the presence of God. Everything one does affects a
person not only in the present life but also in all other lives. *Karma*,
our destiny, based on cause and effect, affects all our actions and
determines our fortunes, and if we will be reborn in a better situation. There are many different heavens and hells, but heinous sinners
remain in hell only until they are purified, rather than forever, as in
Christianity (Rinehart, 2004).

Scientific "immortality"

The awareness of mortality permeates the life of humans (Brown,
1959; Heidegger, 1962). This self-reflexivity is a blessing in that it
allows human beings to transcend their biological self, but it can also
be a curse, since humans know they are doomed to die. As we have
seen, religious beliefs create realities based on a transcendental self
and a life beyond. Another powerful belief that shaped people's sense
of reality in the late twentieth century and into the present day in
America is science. Many Americans believe that science, if employed

judiciously, can do great things, even greatly prolonging life and possibly, if not likely, help us reach immortality. However, there is a difference between the immortality of religion and that of science. The difference is time. There is urgency in the quest of scientific followers, since the "immortality" that science will bring them is not in a future afterlife but in this one. The key to the mystery of death must be unlocked now or it will be too late for the current generation. As Alan Harrington (1969) put it, "We have circled the moon, harnessed nuclear energy, artificially reproduced DNA, and now have the biochemical means to control birth; why should death itself, the Last Enemy, be considered sacred and beyond conquest?"

Fictional accounts

We mentioned Dorian Gray, the handsome young man who made a pact with the devil to remain young. Eventually he rebelled against the sybaritic life he was leading and died as a shrivelled old man. Another classic quest for immortality is the Jewish legend of the Golem. While there are many versions of the legend, a common one tells us that, in the sixteenth century, the Rabbi Löw made a man with clay and gave him the breath of life. However, the Golem ran amok and had to be destroyed. Mary Shelley ([1818] 1983) presented a more recent version of the Golem in her popular story *Frankenstein*. The pathetic figures of the Golem and Frankenstein present a clear message to humanity: humans should not tamper with life itself lest they unleash the fury of forces beyond their control.

The message conveyed by Aldous Huxley ([1932] 1989) in *Brave New World* was less melodramatic, but far more chilling. In his novel, Huxley portrays genetically pre-programmed children whose parents are not humans but chemical solutions. While mass production of children in laboratory bottles may be a nightmarish vision, scientists have made great progress toward unlocking the genetic secrets of life.

Scientific experiments

A nineteenth-century French scientist, Charles-Edouard Brown-Séquard, attempted to create an artificial elixir that would give him immortality. Troubled by his aging and diminishing physical prowess, Brown-Séquard conducted a number of experiments with endocrine glands. The aging physiologist, in his seventies, repeatedly injected himself with extracts from the minced testicles of sheep, dogs, and guinea pigs, diluted with water, as a result of which he claimed to be greatly rejuvenated. The year was 1889; he died five years later at the age of seventy-seven. Brown-Séquard's claims gained some temporary public notoriety, but his scientific credibility was marred by his obsession with what other scientists derisively called "the Brown-Séquard elixir" (Comfort, 1964). Two other scientists felt that the previous experiment had failed for the lack of human testes; however, failing to be able to recruit donors, they used any animal available, from billy goats to chimpanzees, with no lasting success (Segerberg, 1974).

More recently, some have put forward a collagen theory of aging. Collagen is the substance present in connective tissues in much of our bodies; it loses elasticity with time, causing a deterioration of the organs it connects, allegedly resulting in aging. Others claim that aging is related to the immune reaction of our body's cells. Still others point to mutations in the genetic material (DNA) of our bodies as the key. A few believe that the pituitary gland may control the process.

There is even less agreement on the methods used to retard or arrest aging. Some place their faith in pharmaceutical products, while others swear by vitamins. In Romania, Dr Ana Aslan has used Novocain injections to try to restore youth, while in Switzerland Dr Paul Niehans has used the cells of extracts from unborn lambs (Segerberg, 1974).

Science has made giant strides at the other end of the spectrum – the creation of life. In 1961, an Italian scientist, Daniele Petrucci, successfully fertilized twenty human eggs outside the womb. Seventeen years later, on July 24, 1978, the world's first test-tube baby, Louise Brown, was born, in the town of Oldham, England. Patrick Steptoe, a doctor, and Robert Edwards, a physiologist, are the two scientists behind the Brown case. They perfected a procedure called embryo transfer, which calls for the fertilization of an egg outside the body. The egg is removed from the ovaries and fertilized "in vitro" with sperm; the fertilized egg is then implanted in the womb to complete the process of pregnancy.

The newest procedure is the asexual reproduction from a single parent – "cloning." It is based on the fact that practically every cell in the human body possesses the information necessary to create a complete human being, thus re-creating a replica of an animal or person from a single cell, called a clone. American ethical concerns have kept cloning at bay but other nations are moving forward, large animals, such as a sheep (named Dolly) and dogs, have been successfully cloned. Some groups have overtly claimed to be close to having the technology for cloning human beings. While some of these efforts are blown out of proportion and are at times sensationalist, cloning may be one of the possible scientific avenues toward some form of immortality.

In America the benefits of science vis-à-vis retarding death, or at least temporarily restoring the looks of youth, today take place within the context of a consumeristic society, as we have seen through this book. Scientific development is expensive, and scientific, especially medical, procedures and products that can forestall or hide the aging process are heavily marketed and costly. "Miracle" drugs that allegedly can remove the effects of old age form a thriving industry, and surgery, from liposuction to face lifts, is very popular, despite its high cost.

Extrasensory experiences

The immortal self sought by science is a tangible, empirical entity. The problem of credibility arises when we turn to incorporeal forms of life or extrasensory perceptions. There have been a variety of beliefs in these: apparitions, hallucinations, ghosts, near-death experiences and out of body experiences. Some individuals claiming these experiences reject scientific affirmations altogether; others seek scientific legitimacy, which is problematic since apparitions cannot be weighed, measured, or classified. Ultimately, extrasensory experiences are subjective experiences which do not meet scientific rigor. They are seen by many as eccentric and their claims are often viewed as outlandish.

Ghosts, apparitions and hallucinations

Some beliefs in the spirit world, such as in apparitions, hallucinations, and ghosts, have been part of popular folklore for a long time. Ghosts have been traditionally portrayed as incorporeal forms that wander restlessly, waiting for their time to move on to the afterworld. The writings of William Shakespeare, for instance, are replete with ghosts. In *Hamlet*, the young prince of Denmark faces the ghost of his father, who says:

> I am thy father's spirit,
> Doomed for a certain term to walk the night,
> And for the day confined to fast in fires,
> Till the foul crimes done in my days of nature
> Are burnt and purged away. (Act I, scene v)

In *The Tempest*, Prospero consorts with spirits, and in *Macbeth*, the ghost of Banquo torments his murderer, Macbeth. The accounts of ghosts and haunted mansions are far too numerous to examine.

Ghosts belong to the realm of fantasy, yet some scientists have attempted to interpret extrasensory phenomena such as hallucinations and apparitions through physiological explanations. Studies have shown that individuals in a state of sensory deprivation experience sensations that transcend the physical realm, such as body distortion, floating on air, or looking down at one's body from some-where above it (Moss, 1974). Similar experiences have been shown to happen under the influence of hallucinogenic drugs. These are called autoscopic hallucinations and are also linked with pathological disor-ders, such as alcoholism, cerebral lesions, brain tumors, and mental illness (Zamboni et al., 2005).

Near-death experiences

Near-death experiences (NDEs) refer to those events reported by people who have been pronounced clinically dead from a variety of causes – cardiac arrest, electrocution, coma, near drowning, and more (van Lommel et al., 2001). Similar experiences may be the result of psycho-logical factors, such as depression, or a combination of physiological and psychological factors. They do not seem to vary across cultures, nor do they differ in respect to demographic factors such as age, sex, and race (Ring, 1980). While out of body experiences (OBEs) occur only occasionally in NDEs, the two terms are often used interchangeably. In a study published in *The Lancet*, Dr van Lommel and some colleagues studied 344 patients who were resuscitated from cardiac arrest in ten Dutch hospitals. The research team found that 18 percent (sixty-two) of the patients reported NDE. The eight most reported elements by the patients were: (1) positive emotions (56 percent); (2) awareness of being dead (50 percent); (3) meeting a dead person (32 percent); (4) moving through a tunnel (31 percent); (5) seeing a celestial landscape (29 percent); (6) OBE (24 percent); (7) seeing a light (23 percent); and (8) seeing colors (23 percent) (van Lommel et al., 2001: 2041).

Many personal accounts present NDE as wonderfully enriching: "I floated or walked down the tunnel, moved into another tunnel – it wasn't very long – and I stood there and saw a huge mass of colour . . . It could have been a garden, it could have just been colour, but it was beautiful, one of the most wonderful things I've ever seen" (BBC News, 2001: 2). Not everyone finds that NDEs are a wonderfully enriching. Blackmore (2004) found that a significant minority of people reported that they are very unpleasant, even horrifying.

Parapsychological out of body experiences

OBEs, while not as common as NDEs, are more interesting from a tran-scendental point of view. An OBE allegedly consists of transference from a physical body either to an incorporeal one (Mishlove, 1975) or to a consciousness outside the body. The belief in the duality of the self and that the incorporeal part can leave the physical part and travel outside of it has been shared by many cultures:

> The Greeks called it the eidolon, the Tibetans the radiant body, the
> Egyptians the ka, the Germans the doppelganger, the Norwegians
> the verdoger, the occultists the astral or etheric body, Inyushin the
> energy body. Descriptions of this subtle body, whatever it is called, are
> remarkably similar. (Moss, 1974: 281)

Regardless of name, this self seems to possess some core features: it is
invisible, it weighs little or nothing, it is capable of floating in air, and
it can travel, at times covering great distances.

In the mid-twentieth century Jarl Fahler attempted to prove OBEs
by the use of hypnosis (1958). In ten years of experiments he achieved
some measure of success with a single subject, Mrs S. The woman was
hypnotized and her sense of pain was transferred to a water glass.
When Fahler jabbed Mrs S's arm with a needle she did not react in
any way, but when the needle was inserted in the glass of water the
subject reacted by jerking, even when the experimenter moved the
glass to another room.

A parapsychologist at the university of California at Davis, Dr
Charles Tart (1968), engaged in multiple experiments to prove the
existence of OBEs. In one of them, a woman was closed in a room with
a number of electrodes attached to her head to preclude any undetected movements on her part. A five-digit number was placed on a
high shelf, out of sight from the subject. Tart expected the subject to
leave her body and travel near the ceiling and read the number. After
several nights in which nothing unusual occurred, the subject finally
told Tart the exact numbers.

The two individuals who have popularized OBEs are Raymond
Moody and Elisabeth Kübler-Ross, both physicians. Moody (1975) presented a number of accounts of individuals, from all walks of life, who
were clinically dead or close to dying and allegedly underwent OBE,
and who provided remarkably similar accounts of the experience. The
OBE seems to begin with a feeling of quiet and peace that takes over
from pain sensations. At this time the subject experiences noises or
sounds, often pleasant. Then the subject travels through a void or dark
tunnel after leaving his or her body behind. The subject no longer has
any physical sensations and hovers high above while looking down at
his or her body. The experience reaches its high point as the subject
sees a bright light (body of light, God, angel, being of light). Eventually
the subject is returned to his or her body, often unwillingly.

Kübler-Ross also discussed OBEs and provided many accounts from
her patients, very similar to Moody's descriptions. She herself claimed
to have enjoyed an OBE:

> By about five-thirty I was in my room, about to sleep . . . I stayed on the
> bed and in about two minutes – I really have no time concept – I was out
> of my body and I was gone. I had an incredible experience, as if there

were a lot of beings who took all the tired parts out of me and replaced them with new parts . . . an hour and a half later I woke up and felt as if I were twenty years old – no tiredness, no fatigue . . . Later I . . . read the books about out-of-body and learned that one part of you can separate from the body. That was my first experience. (Kübler-Ross, 1978: 145)

Scientists have been very skeptical of these OBE accounts. Fahler was dismissed for using a single subject. Tart was strongly doubted, although the statistical probability that the subject could actually guess the identical number was 1 in 100,000; many felt the subject could have seen the number though a reflection on a clock or that she had used telepathy, since Tart had set the numbers himself. Moody's remarks were based on the accounts of his patients rather than scientific data. Kübler-Ross became embroiled in a scandal involving sexual allegations toward a preacher who practiced on her 40-acre California retreat, and the adverse publicity resulted in widespread skepticism toward her OBE claims.

Some scientists believe that the "bright light" described in OBE experiences could be related to a variety of factors: anoxia (oxygen deprivation) has been shown to produce bright light in a number of subjects. Others believe it possible that the body's endorphins (painkillers) may affect the optic nerve and create the effect (Koerner, 2002). Mainstream America remains very cynical about OBE accounts and tends to relegate them to the world of fiction. In the US, individuals claiming to have extrasensory perceptions or to have had extraordinary experiences are often seen as charlatans, attempting to swindle a gullible public by reading their future or some other scam. There is also a great cultural difference among groups. The majority of people have been socialized in a scientific reality and the monopoly of Western medicine, that is, if you're sick you go to a physician. Other groups may believe that their illness is the cause of supernatural powers, such as an evil spell cast upon them, and may seek help from a *curandero* rather than a physician (Payer, 1996).

The philosophical explanation

Our concern is with life after death, and thus we focus on a few important philosophers who uphold the duality of the self and acknowledge an afterlife. The forefather of this group of philosophers who maintain the dualism of mind and body is Plato (1969, 1973). He was partial to the powers of reason and considered the mind (or soul) as the essential element of the self. The body, for Plato, was a mere receptacle with a number of limitations, to which individuals must adapt for the period of their terrestrial stay.

René Descartes' work can be considered one of the clearest examples of a dualistic philosophy of the self. His famous statement "cogito, ergo sum" (I think, therefore I am) established, for him, that thought was the essence of human beings. Descartes (1958) considered the body as an element of the material world while the soul (or mind) belonged to a separate world, that of thought. Being aware of the relationship between soul and body, he attempted to explain how these two elements, which are in separate worlds, could influence each other. He "solved" his dilemma by locating the incorporeal soul in the pineal gland of the human brain. The soul, for Descartes, departed its material locus upon the death of the body. But departed for where? Many dualistic philosophers said little about the afterlife.

The problem of immortality and the nature of the afterworld also beset Immanuel Kant (1949, 1956). He felt that human beings create an "objective" reality by attributing meaning to things through their experiences. Thus, things become what we make of them and our world is a world of experiences. Kant thought that there must be a consciousness in human beings that is separate from the realm of experiences, since it is consciousness that organizes the world of experiences in a meaningful way. Kant called this consciousness a "transcendental unit of apperception," in other words, an incorporeal self.

Insofar as immortality is concerned, Kant said that human beings cannot know the future. We can only believe in immortality, or "future life," as he called it, as a moral imperative rather than as a logical proof. In a Western concept strikingly similar to the Eastern quest for nirvana, Kant stated that human beings strive in a moral search for perfection. But perfection may be only achieved, according to Kant, if we are allowed to strive toward perfection forever, without interruptions; therefore if we are to achieve perfection we need to be immortal.

Ludwig Wittgenstein (1958) provides a different perspective on immortality. Wittgenstein's inquiry addressed ordinary-language philosophy and his philosophical concern was with the use of words in everyday language. For Wittgenstein, to understand a word means to understand how that word is used in language, but that this understanding tells us nothing about the object it describes. Thus, people will raise exclamation to "God" when they are in trouble, providing us with an understanding of when and how the word "God" is used in everyday language, but that tells us nothing about the abstract notion of "God." Similarly, when we speak of death:

> To understand what death is we should look and see how and in what context death language is used. Its meaning will only be its use. To know what death is is to know how to speak the language. The meaning of death can only fly out of its use as the soul flies out of the body. That is, it doesn't. Only the arrogants have souls. (Shibles, 1974: 79)

In ordinary-language philosophy, to speak of death and immortality is merely to understand how the words are used in language. But we cannot know the meaning of the notions described by these words since they are non-experienceable. To be awed by immortality or fearful of death is nonsense, since we are speaking about metaphors and their use in language, not the experiencing of death or immortality. We can only experience living. Even when we say we are dying we are really addressing a state of living in which severe deterioration is occurring (Wittgenstein, 1958).

Ernest Becker, in his Pulitzer prize-winning book *The Denial of Death* (1973), articulates the existential view toward death. For Becker, who synthesizes the thoughts of a great many important existential thinkers, humans are terrorized by the thought of death.[1] William James felt the same way and addressed the fact that humans are reflexively aware that they shall die and that this knowledge spoils the beauty of life for them. José Ortega y Gasset elaborated further by pointing out that this knowledge of our mortality throws humans into a state of uncertainty, of chaos. To escape this state we become social and fill our lives with social goals, in the hope of alleviating the terrible knowledge of our mortality. "Social reality" takes over for humans, and we use it and its goals as a shield to hide the horrible truth, that all is for naught, since we shall die.

Constructionist sociologists[2] follow Ortega y Gasset's path. Peter Berger notes that the knowledge of human mortality throws into doubt every belief about society, for its existence is based on the fragility of the human condition: "Death radically challenges *all* socially objectivated definitions of reality – of the world, of others, and of the self. Death radically puts in question the taken-for-granted, 'business as usual' attitude in which one exists in everyday life" (1969: 43). For Berger, humans find themselves having to legitimate life in the face of death and turn to religion.

The human paradox, that we are mortal but can transcend mortality with our cultural achievements, has been discussed by many other existentialists. Søren Kierkegaard saw the ambiguity of being partly an animal and partly an angel as the cause of terrible *dread* in life. Martin Heidegger referred to the ambiguity of both being-in-the world and being-of-the world (*Dasein*) and Maurice Merleau-Ponty (1962) saw humans as irremediably embedded in their bodies (*être-au-monde*).

Immortality and the self

Macro-beliefs in immortality affect societies at large. For example, the recent increase in suicide bombers across the globe comes from the belief that that kind of death is martyrdom and will lead to rewards in the afterlife (Atran, 2006). Yet, on a micro-level, individual lives are also greatly affected by whether one believes or not in immortality; a Buddhist's belief in reincarnation will allow him or her to tolerate setbacks in this life, confident that they will improve in the next life; a firm believer in the progress of science will believe that it is just a matter of time before we unravel the mystery of eternal life and conquer death; a devout Christian will endure adversities such as poverty in this life, steady in the belief of a future glorious life in Heaven. The following quote comes from a hospice patient, whose strong religious beliefs allow him to retain a positive attitude in the face of nearing death:

> And if it wasn't for God, I would be lying in bed all day long, but he is the one that boosted me to get around ... it is just wonderful to talk to him. Cause you feel good. It is amazing how your body, how my body perks up ... I feel like when I am in the bed and I pray in the bed, you know that he is right on the corner of it sitting there. (Nakashima and Canda, 2005: 115–16)

We have seen that, from ancient civilizations to the present, the debate on immortality and the self has taken many forms. In a nutshell, beliefs vary from drastically negative ones to faithfully positive ones. At one end are the beliefs espoused by Sigmund Freud, who saw the child going through various stages until he undergoes the "castration complex" and accepts subjugation to his elders. He then takes refuge in the "lie" of social reality, devoting his life to social endeavors that are but screens intended to allow the child, and later the adult, to forget that he shall die (Freud, in Becker, 1973). At the opposite end we find complete individual faith in immortality, as exemplified by the following quotes: "Only a person who has never seriously thought about death does not believe in immortality" (Tolstoy, in Cote, 2000: 16); or "The human soul cannot be destroyed when the body is. What will remain is eternal" (Spinoza, ibid.: 14).

We rely on people's beliefs since there is no actual eyewitness data of life beyond – unless one accepts out-of-body-experiences. Consider the following account of a woman who had heart failure and was pronounced clinically dead:

> All of a sudden I was just somewhere else. There was a gold-looking light, everywhere ... there was music. And I seemed to be in a countryside with streams, grass and trees, mountains ... There was a sense of perfect peace and contentment; love. It was like I was part of it. That experience could have lasted the whole night or just a second ... I don't know. (Moody, 1977: 16)

The woman came back among the living and told her story about the great beyond.

Language and culture at times provide support for the notion of immortality of the self – *psyche*, the Greek word for self embodies in its meaning both body and soul. Trilling (1972) noticed that the French developed the word *je* (I) at about the same time, the early Renaissance, that the Venetian artisans produced mirrors for the population at large, suggesting the importance of reflexivity in viewing the totality of the self and of looking inward to search for the "true" self. It was also during the Renaissance that painters seeking their "soul" began to paint innumerable self-portraits, led by Rembrandt, who left over ninety portraits of himself.

The lack of personal accounts of life beyond is compensated by the fictional media, which produced and still produces an immense amount of books and movies about various aspects of what individuals do after death. A quick reference on the internet yielded eleven pages of movies about various forms of immortality, from the fountain of youth (*Death Becomes Her*), to artificial life (*Bram Stoker's Dracula*), to parapsychology (*The Mummy Returns*), to life across centuries (*Highlander*), and we can add more of our own, such as belief in angels (*Michael*), reincarnation (*What Dreams May Come*), and of course the astronomically successful *The Lord of the Rings* series, with its belief in various forms of mythical life.

A sizable number of individuals also believe that we can communicate with the dead, from holding séances in order to summon the spirits of the deceased to actual appearances of people from the great beyond. A recent study (Britt, 2008) found that, in a survey of 3,000 people, a whopping 58 percent believed in the supernatural, including ghosts. Americans actually celebrate (and so do many other cultures) a day to the spirits of the dead, although probably many of them are not aware of this fact. Halloween, on October 31, is a tradition which stems from the English Hallows Eve, when, fearing that the spirits of their ancestors would come back and haunt them, people disguised themselves in costumes and masks so that they would not be recognized.

In conclusion, a belief in a life beyond death can be a great equalizer, overcoming[3] the handicaps that life has placed in one's way – poverty, discrimination, oppression, hunger, and more. When Fontana (1977) studied the poor elderly living in SROs (single room only) he was surprised to find that a number of them not only endured poverty and failing health but actually looked forward to being with the Lord. One of them, Nora Simpson (not her real name), was paralyzed and her husband took care of her. The husband died twenty years before Fontana interviewed Mrs Simpson, who was eighty-one years of age, ill, frail, and living in abysmal conditions. He had been self-employed and did not contribute to Social Security or Medicare, so his widow was left alone with no help. She learned to walk again (if haltingly): "That's what the Lord did with my body. I learned to walk. Just like a baby learns to walk" (Fontana, 1977: 136). She looked forward to living in the next world: "I look forward to the coming of the Lord . . . we don't worry about death because we're ready to meet the Lord . . . it's so wonderful to be ready to meet the Lord" (ibid.: 137).

Conclusion

We have seen that humans have attempted to solve the dilemma of life beyond death in many different ways. People attempt to legitimize immortality by relying on ancient tradition, on religious belief, on scientific assertions, on psychic belief, and on philosophical analysis. We have but scratched the surface of the multitude of beliefs in immortality. What emerges is that we do not all live in the same reality; some of us live peacefully, awaiting a wiser self or eternal bliss, while others live frantically, attempting to win the race with time and decay; still others live in denial, unwilling to confront the possibility of human finitude.

There is no single way to answer the question of immortality. It has been reported that Thomas Edison invented a machine to contact the dead: "The apparatus depicted consisted of an aluminum trumpet, and an aerial, a microphone, and a chemical electrolyte to generate an electric current for amplifying the supposed etheric waves from the spirit world" (Ebon, 1969: 128). If the machine had worked, many of our queries about life after life might have been answered. But the machine did not work, and we have no answers.

We do know that death may be an abstract and irrational concept in linguistic terms. Yet, everyday people construct their realities, not only their verbal realities but their entire life worlds, upon abstract concepts such as death, finitude, and immortality. Thus, even if these words are empirically nonsensical, they are a powerful nonsense around which most of us structure our lives.

Even when dealing with beliefs in a life beyond, social class and wealth are of great importance. The ancient Greeks and Egyptians paid homage and lavished expenses on the wealthy and powerful upon their death. Religious beliefs also addressed the notion of wealth and poverty, albeit in different ways, from the elevation of the poor in Christianity to the strong remnants of a rigid caste system in Hinduism in India.

Finally, science, especially through medicine, markets youth, or at least its semblance, at a very high price.

Conclusion

IN our journey through this monograph we have seen death and people's relation to it changing continually through history, through social changes, and through natural calamities. The rich and powerful have always had special treatment, even in the face of death, from the ruler of Egypt, the pharaoh, to the president of the US, such as John F. Kennedy, to the head of the Catholic Church, such as Pope John Paul II. The poor, on the other hand, were disposed of in common graves or died shriveled on the slab of a dingy hospital room (see George Orwell's description in chapter 4).

We have followed death and dying through two lenses, a macro one, through which we saw the multitudes swept away by hurricanes or decimated by the plague, and a micro one, which brought death close up, as a child died in the home or an old woman stopped breathing in a nursing home. Let us, in concluding, continue this pattern and briefly discuss modern-day trends of death in the US. We examine three individual deaths in today's world.

Death in America today

Senator John Edwards recently pointed out (in Sack, 2008) that there are two Americas, in relation to both wealth and health, and that the two are growing further apart. This book has shown that Mr Edwards is absolutely right about wealth and health, and that the same pattern pertains to dying. Rich and poor Americans live and die in different ways and the healthcare they receive is vastly different. In the consumeristic ethos of the US we no longer "provide" healthcare but "market" it; in the American dream it is distasteful to speak of death, so now "death" workers (especially in hospices) refer to themselves as "end-of-life" specialists (Henig, 2005).

We are two Americas. In the wealthy America the newest buzzword in healthcare is *boutique* (or concierge) medicine. Patients pre-pay a retainer fee, ranging from $1,500 to $10,000 per year. In return they get same-day doctor's appointments, 24-hour telephone access to their doctor, and, in more expensive plans, home visits by the doctor and home delivery of medicines (Zuger, 2005). Life can often be prolonged for as long as the patient can continue to pay for medical attention (Anspach, 1993).

In 2005 in the other America, almost 19,000 patients died due a virulent, drug-resistant bacterium that spread out of control in hospitals and nursing homes, largely unnoticed by the media (Sack, 2007). In this other America poor people live on average 4.5 fewer years than the affluent ones, since they are less likely to have health insurance, to eat healthy food, and to live in a safe neighborhood, and are more likely to smoke (Pear, 2008).

The healthcare industry is growing at extremely high rates in the US, while the death industry remains fairly constant. Yet, with the aging of the baby boomers, those 78 million Americans born between 1946 and 1965 who comprise almost 30 percent of the population (Ein, 2004), business in death-related services is expected to flourish. Funeral businesses have traditionally been small and family-owned, but are now being taken over by large corporations, thus gaining more professional management. There is a strong trend in pre-planning arrangements, as more people buy in advance a "package," inclusive of funeral service, memorial, and plot. Cremation is on the increase, and members of the Cremation Association of North America are expected to corner 20 percent of the burial market by 2010 (Hyperstrategy, 2007).

The business of dying will become more customized, as the baby boomers are likely to insist on a range of individual choices, such a choosing their music, writing in advance their eulogies, publishing memorials on the web, customizing their funeral on line with Mywonderfullife.com in Minneapolis or Yourdeathwish.com in London, and even arranging for grief therapy (Ein, 2004). Again, there will be class differences; the poor and indigent are buried by the state in plain boxes in unmarked graves for less than a $1,000, while an average funeral costs between $2,000 and $8,000 and there can be an additional cost between $500 and $20,000 for memorials, such as headstones (Hyperstrategy, 2007).

The many choices available to customers today – interment or cremation, type of casket or urn, classical or pop music, temporary or permanent memorials, and much more – have taken away some of the control over death from the funeral business and returned it to individuals. As we have seen, the choices tend to be consumeristic, but some of them are also ecologically friendly. Green burials are becoming trendier, as more people do not wish to be buried along with a hunk of metal (the casket), filled with chemicals (embalming) and surrounded by half a ton of concrete (the vault) (Dicum, 2006).

Death itself seems to be trendier. The HBO series *Six Feet Under* (2001–5), about a California family that ran their funeral business from their home, was a tremendous success. The German show Body Worlds, the traveling exhibition that displays plastinized human corpses preserved and displayed in various ways to showcase muscles, organs, etc., has attracted an audience of over 20 million people across the globe in a decade (Barboza, 2006) and has been copied by a similar show in Las Vegas that uses Chinese corpses. The 2002 novel *The Lovely Bones*, by Alice Sebold, has as its narrator a dead girl and was on the *New York Times* bestseller list for over a year. Mitch Albom's *Tuesday with Morrie* (1997), detailing the author's weekly visits to his dying sociology professor, has sold millions of copies.

Some cemeteries are attracting increased revenues by presenting themselves as necropolises that cater to tourists in various ways. An interesting case is the town of Colma, south of San Francisco, which went into the business of memorial parks when San Francisco passed ordinances removing all cemeteries from the city limits. Colma occupies only 2.2 square miles, 73.5 percent of which is zoned for cemeteries. The town has 1,500 residents, but there are another 1.5 million people buried there (Pogash, 2006). The cemetery chapels do a brisk wedding business, as do flower growers and monument makers. Another case is Laurel Hill cemetery in Philadephia. According to its executive director, "We're rebranding ourselves as a heritage tourism destination" (Brown, 2007: 2). It recently held a nine-course meal re-creating the last supper on the *Titanic*, followed by a tour of the mausoleum, an event which was sold out. Other available tours are "Dead White Republicans" and "Birding among the Buried," for birdwatchers. Both Colma and Laurel Hill are diversifying services since they have almost no more room to expand in the traditional sense. In Colma an acre of undeveloped land goes for over 2 million dollars (Pogash, 2006), while at Laurel Hill's 78 acres only a minuscule 1 percent is still available for new burials.

But death in America is not all a business venture. We can wrap it in glittery props and sing away, but ultimately it is the end of our mortal life. In concluding, let us see some of the ways in which individuals die in today's world.

How individuals die today

The following are just some of the stories that might reveal something about the many directions in which society is moving with regard to death and dying. We have no answer to definitively explain or clearly predict the future. In closing this book we would like to quote from Dr James Hallenbeck, a palliative care expert: "Studying death is somewhat like studying a black hole. You can study around it, but with death, like with black holes, there's something intrinsic in the very process that defies our ability to analyze it" (Henig, 2005: 8). But we *can* show what happens. Dan Berry followed a dead man's journey after Hurricane Katrina (Berry, 2006). American military personnel wear a "dog tag" around their neck, a metal necklace with their ID number, so when they die their bodies can be identified – civilians do not. When havoc struck in Louisiana, well over a thousand bodies went unidentified, scattered on the streets or floating in the muddy waters, largely disfigured by the heat and the water. Forensic experts meandered confusedly through this macabre scene in search for clues to the lost identities of all these bodies. Here is the one Berry followed:

> The dead man, a black man, had been sprawled like carrion on dry Union Street, just outside a parking garage, for several hot-crazed days after the late August hurricane. The only dignities granted him were a blue tarp across the face and orange traffic cones near the head, placed by a state trooper to keep the milling soldiers and reporters and law enforcement officials from driving over him like a speed bump. (Berry, 2006: 2)

Berry follows the trek of the dead black man, interweaving his story with that of the larger one, filled with bureaucratic foul-ups and a general governmental inability to solve the problems caused by the hurricane. Finally the dead man comes to rest in a warehouse, along with another eighty-five corpses: "In one of the silvery-caskets, lies a man who was effectively washed clean of his name and role in life. About all that is known about him is that he was found on Union Street in New Orleans, facing up" (ibid.: 6). The man on Union Street died alone and unidentified.

The next case described is very different, as the girl in the story is killed by someone from her own family. The events took place outside the US, in Syria, but its message is universal; the story is an extreme case of the sexism that pervades, to different degrees, many of parts of our planet. Zahara, a sixteen-year-old wife, was asleep on the floor of her apartment, after her husband left for work. When her older brother Fayyez managed to enter in the apartment, this is what followed,

> He raised the dagger and stabbed her five times in the head and back: brutal, tearing thrusts that shattered the base of her skull and nearly severed her spinal column. Leaving the door open, Fayyez walked downstairs and out to the local police station. There, he reportedly

turned himself in, telling the officers on duty that he had killed his
sister in order to remove the dishonor she had brought on the family
by losing her virginity out of wedlock nearly ten months earlier.
(Zoepf, 2007: 1)

Zahara's dishonorable act was simply that she had been abducted
and raped when she was fifteen. In Syria, "honor killing," the killing
a female relative who has committed an "immoral act," is not pros-
ecuted. Zahara's death would have been of little consequence, but
both her husband and her father refused to accept the situation,
sought recourse in the courts, and made the matter public. Thus the
case became very popular and a rallying case for women advocates in
Syria. Fayyez was arrested and his future is unclear. "Honor killings"
are under scrutiny in Syria (and neighboring Jordan) but, until the
powers that be make a decision, it is estimated that across the world
about 5,000 young women are killed every year for such "crimes" and
the killers go largely unpunished (Zoepf, 2007).

Not all deaths in today's society are horrific. The following story
has a powerful message, that, as the US grows older as a nation, on
account of increased longevity and the large number of baby boomers,
more Americans will have disabilities, and intolerance to them is not
the answer.

In June of 2008 Harriet McBryde Johnson died of a congenital
neuromuscular disease that ravaged her muscles, nerves, and limbs
(Rosen, 2008). She had been a social activist all her life. She was very
open, perhaps too much so for some people, about her disability and
disabilities in general. She knew people were uncomfortable looking
at her gnarled body, but she was a firm believer that a disability does
not preclude a meaningful life. She was active in a number of disability rights movements. She spoke against Jerry Lewis's famous and
successful telethon approach to individuals with disabilities, such
as calling them "cripples." She was also outspoken against efforts to
terminate Terry Schiavo's life. Her beliefs in the sanctity of life often
placed her alongside conservative and evangelicals in the public
arena, but she was a liberal and an atheist, and her words could not
be dismissed as bigoted. She felt strongly that it is wrong for society to
condemn parents who choose not to terminate a pregnancy that may
result in a child with disabilities. Rosen (ibid.) poignantly captures
Johnson's message: "As our scientific powers to eliminate disability
grow, our acceptance of disability wanes."

Johnson's life and her death are examples of an indomitable spirit
fighting for recognition to be seen as a person; Zahara's death exposes
the injustice and evil of discrimination; and the death of the man in
Union Square portrays the squalor of dying alone and unrecognized
on a public street. They all exemplify the interrelation between life

and death; the way we live, our cultural beliefs, our poverty or wealth, and many other social factors impinge upon our death. In a way death is a mirror of our life.

When we turn to the US we see that Americans are both strongly individualistic in their beliefs and strongly oriented to consumerism. They are surrounded by consumer choices in their daily life and they are increasingly treating the final farewell as a statement of individuality within their culture. In the face of death Americans respond as they know best – by invoking their uniqueness in prepared eulogies, idiosyncratic music choices, and themed funerals revolving around their favorite hobby, such as football or hunting (Bates, 2007). They also continue the behavior that defined their lives; they spend to the very last. If you can't take it with you, you can show those remaining behind that you had it in the first place. For what other reason would the singer Tina Turner have buried her dog at Pet's Rest Cemetery, wrapped in a posh fur coat (Pogash, 2006)?

Notes

Chapter 1   An American View of Death

1 We discuss the implications of healthcare inequality for death and dying in more depth in chapter 2, and indeed it is a recurring theme throughout the text.

Chapter 3   Where Dying Takes Place

1 The Adelson Hospice, which is directly adjacent to the University of Nevada, Las Vegas (the campus of the authors of this book), is a large square building with living quarters for guests and patients in the four corners. These are connected by corridors that flank the open middle of the building, which originally was a large aviary filled with doves, whose cooing provided a soothing sound and created a gentle ambiance.
2 Medicare is the federally funded national health insurance system for people over the age of sixty-five.

Chapter 4   Dying

1 We further discuss Hurricane Katrina, the death and destruction that it caused, and how it is linked to larger patterns of social inequality in chapter 7.
2 Nevada has a Nevada Living Will Lock Box, whereby the state government keeps a list of residents with a living will, which can be accessed online by hospitals or medical personnel.

Chapter 5   Funeral Practices

1 Most of the information on cremation is gleaned from Prothero (2001).
2 Ariès (1974: 17) points to the bishop of Amiens who died in 540 AD as the first recorded example of a person to be buried within a church.
3 The tomb of Julius II was never placed in St Peter's Basilica in the Vatican. It can be found instead in the church of St Peter in Chains, near the Coliseum.
4 In this section we rely primarily on Jackson and Vergara (1989).

Chapter 6   Children and Death

1 Although it is beyond the scope of our discussion here, we must also emphasize that changes in the conception and experience of childhood are intricately linked to changes in cultural conceptions of motherhood and definitions of what it means to be a "good mother" (S. Hays, 1998; Wyness, 2006), as well as the

rise and dominance of capitalism as a social system and the concurrent separation of work and family spheres (Ferree, 1990; Lasch, 1995).

2 Not to mention the differences between pregnancy, labor, and birth for free
(white) women compared with the experiences of enslaved women, who
endured horrible living conditions, hard physical labor (even up to the moment
of giving birth), and the reality of having their babies and children taken from
them and sold elsewhere. The differences are immeasurable.

3 We discuss at length the typical characteristics of bereavement in chapter 9 on
the grieving process.

4 Perinatal death (defined as death that occurs between five months before and
up to one month after birth) due to miscarriage or termination as a result
of fetal abnormality is a unique type of traumatic loss that comes without
warning. It is different than other types of losses on account of the fact that
often there is no visible child for parents to mourn or any shared memories
with the child (Keefe-Cooperman, 2005). However, as with other types of child
deaths the effects of such a loss for parents are long-lasting, and the significance of the loss is often unacknowledged by parents' social networks (Lee and
Slade, 1996).

5 See Robinson and Mahon (1997) for an extensive review of outcomes as well as
measurement and conceptual issues and inconsistencies across studies.

6 The autonomic nervous system is responsible for all of the automatic functions
within the human body, including breathing and regulating blood pressure,
body temperature, digestion, and more.

Chapter 7   Death and Destruction

1 According to the American Heritage Dictionary (2004), jaundice is a "yellowish
discoloration of the whites of the eyes, skin, and mucous membranes caused
by deposition of bile salts in these tissues. It occurs as a symptom of various
diseases, such as hepatitis, that affect the processing of bile."

2 Some historians argue that the flu came to the US from Asia and that there may
have been two different outbreaks in 1918 (Marks and Beatty, 1976).

3 On March 23, 2008, the Associated Press reported that the number of US soldiers killed in Iraq had hit the 4,000 mark.

4 It is also of note that much of the research on bereavement during wartime
comes from Israel and focuses on the experiences of Israeli parents after losing
a soldier in the ongoing conflict between Israel and Palestine (see, for example,
Beder, 2004). Little recent literature exists on the American experience of this
type of loss.

Chapter 10   Life after Death

1 Unless otherwise quoted the scholars mentioned in this section are also mentioned in Becker's book.

2 Constructionist sociologists believe that society is socially constructed in interaction among members of society, and that there are no absolute truths but
only humanly created realities.

3 Freud would have said that religious beliefs were a buffer to "mask" one's
upcoming death. Marx would have agreed, as he called religion the opium of
the masses.

References

AAP (American Academy of Pediatrics) (2005) The changing concept of sudden infant death syndrome: diagnostic coding shifts, controversies regarding the sleeping environment, and new variables to consider in reducing risk. *Pediatrics*, 116: 1245–56.

Abel-Smith, B. (1964) *The Hospital: 1800–1948*. London: Heinemann.

Abelson, R. (2005) Possible conflicts for doctors are seen on medical devices. *New York Times*. September 22.

Ackerkecht, E. H. (1955) *A Short History of Medicine*. New York: Ronald Press.

Ad Hoc Committee of the Harvard Medical School to Examine the Definition of Brain Death (1968) A definition of irreversible coma. *Journal of the American Medical Association*, 205: 337–40.

Adherents (2005) Major religions of the world ranked by number of adherents. http://www.adherents.com/Religions_By_Adherents.html (accessed April 10, 2006).

Alexander, L. (1949) Medical science under dictatorship. *New England Journal of Medicine*, 241, July 14: 39–47.

Alvarez. L. (2006) The reach of war: the survivors; for some families, notification of army deaths repeats pain. *New York Times*, April 7.

Angell, M. (1994) After Quinlan: the dilemma of the persistent vegetative state. *New England Journal of Medicine*, 330, May 26: 1524–5.

Angell, M. (1996) Euthanasia in the Netherlands: good news or bad? *New England Journal of Medicine*, 335, November 28: 1676–8.

Annin, P., and Peyser, M. (1996) A father's sorrow. *Newsweek*, September 2: 54.

Anspach, R. (1993) *Deciding Who Lives: Fateful Choices in the Intensive-Care Nursery*. Berkeley: University of California Press.

Arens, D. A. (1982) Widowhood and well-being: an examination of sex differences within a causal model. *International Journal of Aging and Human Development*, 15: 27–40.

Arias, E. (2006) *United States Life Tables, 2003*. National Vital Statistics Report, vol. 54, no.14. Hyattsville, MD: National Center for Health Statistics.

Ariès, P. (1962) *Centuries of Childhood: A Social History of Family Life*. New York: Random House.

Ariès, P. (1974) *Western Attitudes toward Death from the Middle Ages to the Present*, trans. P. Ranum. Baltimore: Johns Hopkins University Press.

Ariès, P. (1981) *The Hour of our Death*, trans. H. Weaver. New York: Vintage.

ASCE (American Society of Civil Engineers), Hurricane Katrina External Review Panel (2007) *The New Orleans Hurricane Protection System: What Went Wrong and Why: A Report*. Reston, VA: American Society of Civil Engineers.

Associated Press (2005) Pope laid to rest after emotional ceremony. http://www. msn.com/id/3305285/ (accessed November 26, 2007).

Atran, S. (2006) The moral logic and growth of suicide terrorism. *Washington Quarterly*, 29 (2): 127–47.

Attig, T. (1996) *How We Grieve: Re-Learning the World*. New York: Oxford University Press.

Avery, G. (1994) *Behold the Child: American Children and their Books 1621–1922*. Baltimore: Johns Hopkins University Press.

Ayers, T. S., Cara, L. K., Sandler, I. N., and Stokes, J. (2003) Adolescent bereavement. In T. P. Gullotta and M. Bloom (eds), *Encyclopedia of Primary Prevention and Health Promotion*. New York: Kluwer Academic/Plenum Press, 221–9.

Balk, D. E., and Corr, C. A. (1996) Adolescents, developmental tasks, and encounters with death and bereavement. In C. A. Corr and D. E. Balk (eds), *Handbook of Adolescent Death and Bereavement*. New York: Springer, 3–24.

Bank, S. P., and Kahn, M. D. (1982) *The Sibling Bond*. New York: Basic Books.

Barboza, D. (2006) China turns out mummified bodies for displays. *New York Times*, August 8.

Barron, J. (2005) For families of fallen soldiers, the 2nd knock brings $12,000. *New York Times*, January 26.

Barry, J. M. (2004) The site of origin of the 1918 influenza pandemic and its public health implications. *Journal of Translational Medicine*, 2 (3); http://www. translational-medicine.com/content/2/1/3.

Basler, B. (2004) Green graveyards – a natural way to go. http://bulletin.aarp. org/yourworld/family/articles/green_graveyards_a.html (accessed August 8, 2006).

Bass, B., and Jefferson, J. (2003) *Death's Acre: Inside the Legendary Forensic Lab the Body Farm, where the Dead Do Tell Tales*. New York: Putnam.

Bates, S. (2007) The new death. *Wall Street Journal*, October 19: W13.

Baughman, W., Bruh, J., and Gould, F. (1973) Euthanasia: criminal, tort, constitutional and legislative considerations. *Notre Dame Lawyer*, 48: 1206–60.

BBC News (2001) "Near death experiences" probed. http://news.bbc.co.uk/2/hi/ health/1685311.stm (accessed June 6, 2008)

Beauvoir, S. de (1965) *A Very Easy Death*. New York: Pantheon Books.

Becker, E. (1973) *The Denial of Death*. New York: Free Press.

Beder, J. (2002) Grief: anticipatory. In R. Kastenbaum (ed.), *Macmillan Encyclopedia of Death and Dying*, vol. 1. New York: Macmillan, 353–5.

Beder, J. (2003) War, death, and bereavement: how we can help. *Families in Society: The Journal of Contemporary Human Services*, 84: 163–7.

Beder, J. (2004) *Voices of Bereavement: A Casebook for Grief Counselors*. New York: Routledge.

Ben-Ari, E. (2005) Epilogue: a good military death? *Armed Forces & Society*, 31: 651–64.

Bendann, E. (1930) *Death Customs*. New York: Knopf.

Bennett, K. M. (1997) Widowhood in elderly women: the medium and long-term effects on mental and physical health. *Mortality*, 2: 137–48.

Bennett, K. M. (2005) Was life worth living? Older widowers and their explicit discourses of the decision to live. *Mortality*, 10: 144–54.

Berenson, A. (2006) Hope, at $4,200 a dose. *New York Times*, October 1.

Berger, P. (1969) *The Sacred Canopy*. New York: Anchor Books.

Berry, D. (2006) Tracing the path of a corpse, from the street to dignity. *New York Times*, August 27.

Blackmore, S. J. (2004) *Consciousness*. Oxford: Oxford University Press.

Bodnar, J. C., and Kiecolt-Glaser, J. K. (1994) Caregiver depression after bereavement: chronic stress isn't over when it's over. *Psychology and Aging*, 9: 372–80.

Bodyworlds2 (2005) The anatomical exhibition of real human bodies. http://www.bodyworlds.com (accessed March 3, 2006).

Bowlby, J., and Parkes, C. M. (1970) Separation and loss within the family. In E. J. Anthony (ed.), *The Child and the Family*. New York: Wiley, 197–216.

Bowman, L. (1977). The effects of city civilization. In C. Jackson (ed.), *Passing: The Vision of Death in America*. Westport, CT: Greenwood Press, 153–73.

Breslow, L. (1990) The future of public health: prospects in the United States for the 1990s. *Annual Review of Public Health*, 2: 1–28.

Brewin, T. B. (1991) Three ways of giving bad news. *The Lancet*, 337: 1207–10.

Brinkley, D. (2006) *The Great Deluge: Hurricane Katrina, New Orleans, and the Mississippi Gulf Coast*. New York: HarperCollins.

Britt, R. (2008) People said to believe in aliens and ghosts more than God. http://www.livescience.com/strangenews/081124-britain-supernatural.html (accessed December 1, 2008).

Brosco, J. P. (1999) The early history of the infant mortality rate in America: a reflection upon the past and a prophecy of the future. *Pediatrics*, 103: 478–85.

Brown, N. O. (1959) *Life against Death: The Psychoanalytic Meaning of History*. New York: Viking Books.

Brown, P. L. (2007) Cemeteries seek breathing clientele. *New York Times*, May 25.

Brunvand, J. H. (1984) *The Chocking Doberman and Other "New" Urban Legends*. New York: W. W. Norton.

Buckman, R. (1992) *How to Break Bad News: A Guide for Health Care Professionals*. Baltimore: Johns Hopkins University Press.

Budge, E. A. W. (1961) *Osiris: The Egyptian Religion of Resurrection*. New Hyde Park, NY: University Books.

Bugen, L. (1979) *Death and Dying*. Dubuque, IA: W. C. Brown.

Burelli, D. F., and Cornwell, J. R. (2005) Military death benefits: status and proposals. Washington, DC: Library of Congress, Congressional Research Service.

Campbell, G. (2006) Children and slavery in the New World: a review. *Slavery & Abolition*, 27: 261–85.

Campbell, M. L. (1994) Breaking bad news to patients. *Journal of the American Medical Association*, 271: 1052.

Capron, M. A. (2001) Brain death: well settled yet still unresolved. *New England Journal of Medicine*, 344, April 19: 1244–6.

Carnelley, K. B., Wortman, C. B., and Kessler, R. C. (1999) The impact of widowhood on depression: findings from a prospective survey. *Psychological Medicine*, 29: 1111–23.

Carr, D., and Utz, R. L. (2002) Late-life widowhood in the United States: new directions in research and theory. *Ageing International*, 27: 65–88.

Carr, D., House, J. S., Kessler, R. C., Nesse, R., Sonnega, J., and Wortman, C. B. (2000) Marital quality and psychological adjustment to widowhood among older adults: a longitudinal analysis. *Journal of Gerontology: Social Sciences*, 55B: 197–207.

CDC (Centers for Disease Control) (1999) Achievements in public health, 1900–1999: healthier mothers and babies. *Morbidity and Mortality Weekly Report*, 48: 849–58.

CDC (Centers for Disease Control) (2005) *Plague Fact Sheet*. Atlanta: US Government

Department of Health and Human Services, Centers for Disease Control and Infection.

CDC (Centers for Disease Control) (2007) A glance at the HIV/AIDS epidemic. CDC HIV/AIDS Fact Sheet. http://www.cdc.gov/hiv/resources/factsheets/PDF/At-A-Glance.pdf.

CDC (Centers for Disease Control) (2008) *Sickle-Cell Disease: Health Care Professionals: Data and Statistics*; http://www.cdc.gov/ncbddd/sicklecell/hcp_data.htm (accessed May 5, 2008).

Charmaz, K. (1975) The coroners' strategies for announcing death. In L. Lofland (ed.), *Toward a Sociology of Death*. Beverly Hills, CA: Sage, 61–82.

Charmaz, K. (1980) *The Social Reality of Death*. Reading, MA: Addison-Wesley.

Chickering, R. (1999) The use and abuse of a concept. In M. F. Boemeke, R. Chickering, and S. Forster (eds), *Anticipating Total War: The German and American Experiences, 1874–1914*. Cambridge: Cambridge University Press, 13–28.

Chomsky, N. (2003) *Hegemony or Survival: America's Quest for Global Dominance*. New York: Macmillan.

Choron, J. (1964) *Death and Modern Man*. New York: Collier

CIA (Central Intelligence Agency) (2007) Rank order: infant mortality rate. In *The World Factbook*; https://www.cia.gov/library/publications/the-world-factbook/rankorder/2091rank.html (accessed December 28, 2007).

Cicourel, A. (1964) *Method and Measurement in Sociology*. New York: Free Press.

Clark, K. (2008) Counting Iraqi civilian casualties. *The World: Global Perspectives for an American Audience*; http://www.theworld.org/taxonomy_by_date/1/20080324 (accessed May 14, 2008).

Clark, R. E., and LaBeff, E. E. (1982) Death telling: managing the delivery of bad news. *Journal of Health and Social Behavior*, 23: 366–80.

Clausewitz, C. von (2005) *On War*, trans. J. J. Graham. New York: Taylor & Francis.

Cline, S. (1996) *Lifting the Taboo: Women, Death and Dying*. London: Abacus.

Coale, A. (1986) Population trends and economic development. In J. Menken (ed.), *World Population and the US Population Policy: The Choice Ahead*. New York: W. W. Norton, 96–104.

Colby, W. H. (2002) *Long Goodbye: The Deaths of Nancy Cruzan*. Carlsbad, CA: Hay House.

Comfort, A. (1964) *The Process of Ageing*. New York: Signet.

Conference of the Medical Royal Colleges and their Faculties in the United Kingdom (1976) Diagnosis of brain death. *British Medical Journal*, 2, October 11: 1187–8.

Cook, J. A. (1988) Dad's double binds: rethinking fathers' bereavement from a men's studies perspective. *Journal of Contemporary Ethnography*, 17: 285–308.

Coombs, R., and Powers, P. (1977) Socialization for death: the physician's role. In L. Lofland (ed.), *Toward a Sociology of Death*. Beverly Hills, CA: Sage, 15–36.

Corsaro, W. A. (2005) *The Sociology of Childhood*. Thousand Oaks, CA: Pine Forge Press.

Coser, L. A. (1977) *Masters of Sociological Thought*. New York: Harcourt Brace Jovanovich.

Cote, M. (2000) *Death and the Meaning of Life: Selected Spiritual Writings of Leo Tolstoi*. Huntington, NY: Troitsa Books.

Coulehan, J. L., and Block, M. (1997) *The Medical Interview: Mastering Skills for Clinical Practice*. 3rd edn, Philadelphia: F. A. Davis.

Cox, M., Garret, E., and Graham, J. A. (2005) Death in Disney films: implications for children's understanding of death. *Omega: Journal of Death and Dying*, 50: 267–80.

Coyle, N., and Sculco, L. (2003) Communication and the patient/physician relationship: a phenomenological inquiry. *Journal of Supportive Oncology*, 1: 206–15.

Craven, J., and Wald, F. (1975) Hospice care for dying patients. *American Journal of Nursing*, 75: 1816–22.

Davidson, M. (1993) Indecent proposals? *New Physician*, October: 135.

Davies, B. (1991) Long-term outcomes of adolescent sibling bereavement. *Journal of Adolescent Research*, 6: 83–96.

Davies, R. (2004) New understanding of parental grief: literature review. *Journal of Advanced Nursing*, 46: 506-12.

Davis, F. (1972) *Illness, Interaction and the Self*. Belmont, CA: Wadsworth.

DeBaggio, T. (2000) Loss of memory, loss of hope. *New York Times*, 25 June.

Defoe, D. (2001) *A Journal of the Plague Year*. New York: Modern Library.

Densmore, F. (1929) *Chippewa Customs*. Washington, DC: US Government Printing Office.

DeSalle, R. (ed.) (1999) *Epidemic! The World of Infectious Disease*. New York: New Press.

Descartes, R. (1958) *Philosophical Writings*, trans. N. K. Smith. New York: Modern Library.

Dethlefsen, E., and Deetz, J. (1977) Death's heads, cherubs, and willow trees. In C. Jackson (ed.), *Passing: The Vision of Death in America*. Westport, CT: Greenwood Press, 48–60.

Devita-Raeburn, E. (2004) *The Empty Room: Surviving the Loss of a Brother or Sister at Any Age*. New York: Scribner.

Dicum, G. (2006) Green is the new dead. *Grist Magazine*, July 27; http://www.grist.org/news/maindish/2006/07/27dicum/index.html (accessed August 10, 2006).

DiJoseph, S. (2006) Illegal harvesting and sale of body parts, tissues and organs: Dr Frankenstein would have been proud. http://www.newsinferno.com/archives/1064 (accessed February 24, 2006).

Doka, K. (1989) Disenfranchised grief. In K. Doka (ed.), *Disenfranchised Grief: Recognizing Hidden Sorrow*. Lexington, MA: Lexington Books, 3–12.

Doka, K., and Martin, T. (2001) Take it like a man: masculine response to loss. In D. Lund (ed.), *Men Coping with Grief*. Amityville, NY: Baywood, 37–48.

Donate Life (2005) Organ & tissue donation: statistics. http://www.donatelifeny.org/organ/2005.html (accessed April 28, 2006).

Durkheim, E. (1951) *Suicide*. New York: Free Press.

Durkheim, E. (1965) *The Elementary Forms of the Religious Life*. New York: Free Press.

Dyregrov, A., and Dyregrov, K. (1999) Long-term impact of sudden infant death: a 12 to 15 year follow-up. *Death Studies*, 23: 635–61.

Earle M. A. (1977) Death ritual in colonial New York. In C. Jackson (ed.), *Passing: The Vision of Death in America*. Westport, CT: Greenwood Press, 30–41.

Ebon, M. (1969) *The Psychic Reader*. New York: World.

Eckholm, E. (2007) In turnabout, infant deaths climb in south. *New York Times*, April 22.

Ein, J. (2004) The future of the "death care" industry. *Forbes*, October 8; http://www.forbes.com/business/2004/10/08/cz_1008findsvpdeathcare.html (accessed March 22, 2007).

Elder, G. H., Jr. (1994) Time, human agency, and social change: perspectives on the life course. *Social Psychology Quarterly*, 57: 4–15.

Ellis, J. B., and Stump, J. E. (2000) Parents' perceptions of their children's death concept. *Death Studies*, 24: 65–70.

Ethical Perspectives (2002) The Belgian Act on Euthanasia of May, 28th 2002. 9(2–3): 182–8.

Ezzati, M., Friedman, A., Kulkarni, S., and Murray, C. (2008) The reversal of fortunes: trends in county mortality and cross-county mortality disparities in the United States. *PLoS* [Public Library of Science] *Medicine*, 4: 557–62.

Fahler, J. (1958) Does hypnosis increase psychic powers? *Tomorrow*, autumn.

Fallowfield, L. (1993) Giving sad and bad news. *The Lancet*, 341: 476–8.

Faust, D. G. (2008) *This Republic of Suffering: Death and the American Civil War*. New York: Knopf.

Feifel, H. (1977) *New Meanings of Death*. New York: McGraw-Hill.

Fenner, E. D. (1854) *History of the Epidemic Yellow Fever, at New Orleans, LA, in 1853*. New York: Hall, Clayton.

Ferree, M. M. (1990) Beyond separate spheres: feminism and family research. *Journal of Marriage and the Family*, 52: 866–84.

Ferrell, B., and Coyle, N. (2002) An overview of palliative nursing care. *American Journal of Nursing*, 102 (5): 26–31.

Field, M. J., and Behrman, R. E. (eds) (2003) *When Children Die: Improving Palliative and End-of-Life Care for Children and their Families*. Washington, DC: National Academies Press.

Field, N. P., and Sundin, E. C. (2001) Attachment style in adjustment to conjugal bereavement. *Journal of Social and Personal Relationships*, 18: 347–61.

Final Exit (2005) Continental Europe. http://www.finalexit.org/lawseurope-frame.html (accessed March 6, 2006).

Fish, W. C. (1986) Differences of grief intensity in bereaved parents. In T. A. Rando (ed.), *Parental Loss of a Child*. Champaign, IL: Research Press, 418–23.

Flannelly, K. J., Galek, K., and Handzo, G. F. (2005) To what extent are the spiritual needs of hospital patients being met? *International Journal of Psychiatry in Medicine*, 35: 319–23.

Florian, V. (1990) Meaning and purpose in life of bereaved parents whose son fell during active military service. *Omega: Journal of Death and Dying*, 20 (2): 91–102.

Flory, J., Young-Xu, Y., Gurol, I., Levinsky, N., Ash, A., and Emanuel, E. (2004) Place of death: US trends since 1980. *Health Affairs*, 23: 194–200.

Foderaro, L. W. (2008) Military kin struggle with loss and a windfall. *New York Times*, March 22.

Fodor, N. (1964) *Between Two Worlds*. West Nyack, NY: Parker.

Fontana, A. (1977) *The Last Frontier: The Social Meaning of Growing Old*. Beverly Hills, CA: Sage.

Fontana, A., and Collins, C. (1995) The forgotten other: women in Vietnam. *Studies in Symbolic Interaction*, 18: 197–215.

Fox, E., Kamakahi, J. J., and Capek, S. M. (1999) *Come Lovely and Soothing Death: Right to Die Movement in the United States*. New York: Twayne.

Fox, R. (1979) *Essays in Medical Sociology*. New York: Wiley.

Freud, S. ([1919] 1959) Mourning and melancholia. *Collected Papers*, vol. 4. New York: Basic Books.

Freund, P., McGuire, M., and Podhurst, L. (2003) *Health, Illness, and the Social Body: A Critical Sociology*. 4th edn, Upper Saddle River, NJ: Prentice-Hall.

Fried, T., van Doorn, C., O'Leary, J., Tinetti, M., and Drickamer, M. (1999) Older persons' preference for site of terminal care. *Annals of Internal Medicine*, 131: 109–12.

Friedlander, L. (1913) *Roman Life and Manners under the Early Empire*, vol. 1. London: Routledge.

Fuchs, V. R. (1998) *Who Shall Live? Health, Economics, and Social Choice*. River Edge, NJ: World Scientific.

Fulton, R. (2003) Anticipatory mourning: a critique of the concept. *Mortality*, 8: 342–51.

Fulton, R., and Fulton, J. (1971) A psychosocial aspect of terminal illness: anticipatory grief. *Omega: Journal of Death and Dying*, 2: 91–9.

Fuhrman, M. (2005) *Silent Witness: The Untold Story of Terri Schiavo's Death*. New York: HarperCollins.

Gallup Organization (1997) *Knowledge and Attitudes related to Hospice Care*. Arlington, VA: National Hospice Association.

Gates Foundation (2006) Powerful new HIV prevention methods in sight, but major hurdles remain, say experts. http://www.gatesfoundation.org/press-releases/Pages/male-circumcision-microbicides-hiv-prevention-060815.aspx (accessed January 22, 2009).

Gawande, A. (2007) The way we age now. *New Yorker*, April 30.

Gaylin, W. (1974). Harvesting the dead. *Harper's*, September: 23–8.

Gibbs, C. E. (1976) *Caring for the Grieving*. Corte Madera, CA: Omega Books.

Gibson, C. (2006) Our 10 greatest natural disasters. *American Heritage*, 57 (4) 26–37.

Giddens, A. (1991) *Modernity and Self-Identity*. Cambridge: Polity.

Gilanshah, F. (1993) Islamic customs regarding death. In D. P. Irish, K. F. Lundquist, and V. Jenkins Nelsen (eds), *Ethnic Variations in Dying, Death and Grief*. Washington, DC: Taylor & Francis, 137–46.

Gillotti, C., and Applegate, J. (2000) Explaining illness as bad news: individual differences in explaining illness-related information. In B. Whaley (ed.), *Explaining Illness: Research, Theory and Strategies*. New York: Lawrence Erlbaum Associates, 101–20.

Ginzburg, K., Geron, Y., and Zahava, S. (2002) Patterns of complicated grief among bereaved parents. *Omega: Journal of Death & Dying*, 45: 119–33.

Giovanola, J. (2005) Sibling involvement at the end of life. *Journal of Pediatric Oncology Nursing*, 22: 222–6.

Glaser, B., and Strauss, A. (1965) *Awareness of Dying*. Chicago: Aldine.

Govinda, L. A. (1960) Foreword. In *The Tibetan Book of the Dead*, ed. W. Y. Evans-Wentz. New York: Oxford University Press.

Goffman, E. (1952) On cooling the mark out: some aspects of adaptation to failure. *Psychiatry: Journal for the Study of Interpersonal Relations*, 15: 451–63.

Gomez, C. F. (1991) *Euthanasia and the Case of the Netherlands*. New York: Free Press.

Gordon, J. (2002) Undertakers go animal. http://www.jrn.columbia.edu/student-work/cns/2002-04-17/389.asp (accessed August 7, 2006).

Graham, C. (2001). Mourners breaking new ground in storage of ashes. *Las Vegas Review-Journal*, June 24: 5A.

Gramelspacher, G., Zhou, X., Hanna, M., and Tierney, W. (1997) Preferences of physicians and their patients for end-of-life care. *Journal of General Internal Medicine*, 12: 346–51.

Gregg, C. T. (1985) *Plague: An Ancient Disease in the Twentieth Century*. Rev. edn, Albuquerque: University of New Mexico Press.

Greve, F. (2006) Some in hospice win reprieves, statistics show. *Wall Street Journal*, July 7: 24A.

Grmeck, M. (1990) *History of AIDS: Emergence and Origin of a Modern Pandemic*. Princeton, NJ: Princeton University Press.

Groopman J. (2002) Dying words. *New Yorker*, October 28: 62–70.

Groopman, J. (2004) The grief industry. *New Yorker*, January 26.

Groopman, J. (2008) Buying a cure: what business know-how can do for disease. *New Yorker*, January 28.

Gross, J. (2008) For the elderly, being heard about life's end. *New York Times*, May 5.

Güner, O. (2005) Poverty in traditional Islamic thought: is it virtue or captivity? *Studies in Islam and the Middle East Journal*, January: 1–12.

Habenstein, R., and Lamers, W. (1955) *The History of Funeral Directing in America*. Milwaukee: Bulfin.

Hackett, M. (2006) Babies sleep safest on their backs: race, resistance, and the consequences of cultural competency. Paper presented at the annual meeting of the American Sociological Association.

Hammond, J. (2000) *The American Puritan Elegy: A Literary and Cultural Study*. Cambridge: Cambridge University Press.

Hampson, L. A., and Emanuel, E. J. (2005) The prognosis for changes in end-of-life care after the Schiavo case. *Health Affairs*, 24: 972–5.

Hardt, D. V. (1979) *Death: The Final Frontier*. Englewood Cliffs, NJ: Prentice-Hall.

Harlow, S. D., Goldberg, E. L., and Comstock, G. W. (1991) A longitudinal study of the prevalence of depressive symptomatology in elderly widowed and married women. *Archives of General Psychiatry*, 48: 1065–8.

Harrington, A. (1969) *The Immortalist*. New York: Random House.

Harris, N. (1977) The cemetery beautiful. In C. Jackson (ed.), *Passing: The Vision of Death in America*. Westport, CT: Greenwood Press, 103–11.

Hastings, S. (2000) Self-disclosure and identity management by bereaved parents. *Communication Studies*, 51: 352–71.

Hays, J. (1998) *The Burdens of Disease: Epidemics and Human Response in Western History*. New Brunswick, NJ: Rutgers University Press.

Hays, J., Gold, D., Flint, E., and Winer, E. (1997) Patient preference for place of death: a qualitative approach. In B. de Vries (ed.), *End of Life Issues: Interdisciplinary and Multidimensional Perspectives*. New York: Springer, 3–21.

Hays, S. (1998) *The Cultural Contradictions of Motherhood*. New Haven, CT: Yale University Press.

Hazzard, A., Weston, J., and Gutterres, C. (1992) After a child's death: factors related to parental bereavement. *Developmental and Behavioral Pediatrics*, 13: 24–30.

Heidegger, M. (1962) *Being and Time*. New York: Harper.

Henig, R. M. (2005) Will we ever arrive at the good death? *New York Times*, August 7.

Herlihy, D. (1997) *The Black Death and the Transformation of the West*. Cambridge, MA: Harvard University Press.

Hinduism Today (1987) Uproar over Rajput "sati." http://www.hinduismtoday. com/archives/1987/12/1987-12-04.shtml (accessed September 14, 2007).

Hirst, Paul Q. (2002) Another century of conflict? War and the international system in the 21st century. *International Relations*, 16: 327–42.

Homer (1965) *The Odyssey*, trans. R. Lattimore. New York: Harper.

Hoyert D. L., Kochanek K. D., and Murphy S. L. (1999) *Deaths: Final Data for 1997*. National Vital Statistics Report, vol. 47, no. 20. Hyattsville, MD: US Department of Health and Human Services, National Center for Health Statistics.

Hoyert, D., Heron, M., Murphy, S., and Kung, H.-C. (2006) *Death: Final Data for 2003*. Hyattsville, MD: US Department of Health and Human Services, National Center for Health Statistics.

Humphry, D. (2001) August 2. Swiss assisted suicide branching out. http://www.finalexit.org/swissframe.html (accessed February 10, 2005).

Huntington, R., and Metcalf, P. (1979) *Celebrations of Death*. New York: Cambridge University Press.

Huxley, A. ([1932] 1989. *Brave New World*. New York: Harper & Row.

Hyperstrategy (2007) The death care industry. http://www.hyperstrategy.com/c4.htm (accessed March 22, 2007).

igovernment (2007) Anti-sati law falls through. http://www.igovernment.in/site/anti-sati-law-falls-through/

Illich, I. (1976) *Medical Nemesis*. New York: Pantheon Books.

Institute of Medicine (2003) *When Children Die: Improving Palliative and End-of-Life Care for Children and their Families*. Washington, DC: National Academies Press.

Ionesco, E. (1968) *Fragments of a Journal*. New York: Grove Press.

Iwashyna, T. J., and Chang, V. W. (2002) Racial and ethnic differences in place of death: United States. *Journal of the American Geriatric Society*, 50: 1113–17.

Jackson, C. (ed.) (1977) *Passing: The Vision of Death in America*. Westport, CT: Greenwood Press.

Jackson, K. T., and Vergara, C. J. (1989) *Silent Cities: The Evolution of the American Cemetery*. New York: Princeton Architectural Press.

Jameson, F. (1991) *Postmodernism, or The Cultural Logic of Late Capitalism*. Durham, NC: Duke University Press.

Janoff-Bulman, R., and Berg, M. (1998) Disillusionment and the creation of value: from traumatic losses to existential gains. In J. H. Harvey (ed.), *Perspectives on Loss: A Sourcebook*. Philadelphia: Taylor & Francis, 35–47.

Johnson, N. P., and Mueller, J. (2002) Updating the accounts: global mortality of the 1918–1920 "Spanish" influenza pandemic. *Bulletin of the History of Medicine*, 76: 105–15.

Jonas, H. (1974) *Philosophical Essays*. Englewood Cliffs, NJ: Prentice-Hall.

Kant, I. (1949) *Critique of Practical Reason*. Chicago: University of Chicago Press.

Kant, I. (1956) *Critique of Pure Reason*. London: Macmillan.

Kanter, R. (1977) *Men and Women of the Corporation*. New York: Basic Books.

Kaplan, K. J. (1998) The case of Dr Kevorkian and Mr Gale: a brief historical note. *Omega: Journal of Death and Dying*, 36: 169–76.

Kastenbaum, R. (1997) Hospice care in the United States. In C. Saunders and R. Kastenbaum (eds), *Hospice Care on the International Scene*. New York: Springer, 101–13.

Kauffman, J. (1989) Intrapsychic dimensions of disenfranchised grief. In K. Doka (ed.), *Disenfranchised Grief: Recognizing Hidden Sorrow*. Lexington, MA: Lexington Books, 25–30.

Kavenaugh, R. (1972) *Facing Death*. Los Angeles: Nash.

Kayser-Jones, J., Schell, E., Lyons, W., Kris, A. E., Chan, J., and Beard, R. L. (2003) Factors that influence end-of-life care in nursing homes: the physical environment, inadequate staffing, and lack of supervision. *The Gerontologist*, 43: 76–84.

Keefe-Cooperman, K. (2005) A comparison of grief as related to miscarriage and termination for fetal abnormality. *Omega: Journal of Death and Dying*, 50: 281–300.

Keene, J. R., and Prokos, A. H. (2008) Widowhood and the end of spousal caregiving: wear and tear or relief? *Ageing & Society*, 28: 1–20.

Kelly, J. (2005) *The Great Mortality: An Intimate History of the Black Death, the Most Devastating Plague of All Time*. New York: HarperCollins.

Kennet, L. (1987) *GI: The American Soldier in World War II*. New York: Scribners.

Klass, D. (1988) *Parental Grief: Solace and Resolution*. New York: Springer.

Klass, D. (1993a) Solace and immortality: bereaved parents' continuing bond with their children. *Death Studies*, 17: 343–68.

Klass, D. (1993b) The inner representation of the dead child and the world views of bereaved parents. *Omega: Journal of Death and Dying*, 26: 255–73.

Kleinman, J. C. (1990) The slowdown in the infant mortality decline. *Paediatric and Perinatal Epidemiology*, 4: 373–81.

Koerner, B. (2002) (October 1). What's the deal with the bright light you see before dying? http://www.slate.com/id/2071835/ (accessed February 6, 2009).

Kohn, J. (1976) Hospice building speaks on many emotional levels to patients' family. *Modern Healthcare*, October.

Kramer, B. J., and Lambert, J. D. (1999) Caregiving as a life course transition among older husbands: a prospective study. *The Gerontologist*, 39: 658–67.

Kreicbergs, U., Valdimarsdottir, U., Onelov, E., Henter, J., and Steineck, G. (2004) Talking about death with children who have severe malignant disease. *New England Journal of Medicine*, 351: 1175–86.

Kübler-Ross, E. (1969) *On Death and Dying*. New York: Macmillan.

Kübler-Ross, E. (1978) Out of the body. In R. Fulton, E. Markusen, G. Owen, and J. Scheiber (eds), *Death and Dying: Challenge and Change*. Reading, MA: Addison-Wesley.

Lamerton, R. C. (1975) The need for hospices. *Nursing Times*, January 23: 155–7.

Lamprecht, F., and Sack, M. (2002) Posttraumatic stress disorder revisited. *Psychosomatic Medicine*, 64: 222–37.

Lapidus, I. M. (1996) The meaning of death in Islam. In H. Spiro, M. McCrea Curnen, and W. L. Palmer (eds), *Facing Death: Where Culture, Religion, and Medicine Meet*. New Haven, CT: Yale University Press, 148–59.

Larson, E. V., and Savych, B. (2006) *Misfortunes of War: Press and Public Reactions to Civilian Deaths in Wartime*. Santa Monica, CA: RAND Project Air Force.

Lasch, C. (1995) *Haven in a Heartless World*. New York: W. W. Norton.

Lassel, M. (2005) Your number's up. *Metropolitan Home*, May.

Lauer, M., Mulhern, R., Wallskog, J., and Camitta, B. (1983) A comparative study of parental adaptation following a child's death at home or in the hospital. *Pediatrics*, 71: 107–12.

Lautzenheiser, S. (2007) The last responders. Unpublished paper, Las Vegas, Office of the Coroner.

Layne, L. L. (1990) Motherhood: lost cultural dimensions of miscarriage. *Women & Health*, 16 (3/4): 69–98.

Lee, C., and Slade, P. (1996) Miscarriage as a traumatic event: a review of the literature and new implications for intervention. *Journal of Psychosomatic Research*, 40: 235–44.

Lee, F. (1993) Being polite and keeping mum: how bad news is communicated in organizational hierarchies. *Journal of Applied Social Psychology*, 23: 1124–9.

Lee, G. R., DeMaris, A., Bavin, S., and Sullivan, R. (2001) Gender differences in the depressive effect of widowhood in later life. *Journal of Gerontology*, 56B: S36–61.

Lee, R. (2003) The demographic transition: three centuries of fundamental change. *Journal of Economic Perspectives*, 17: 167–90.

Legal Information Institute (2006) Supreme Court collection: Gonzales v. Oregon http:/www.law.cornell.edu.supct/html/04-623.ZO.html (accessed April 3, 2006).

Leitenberg, M. (2005) *Deaths in War and Conflicts between 1945 and 2000*. Ithaca, NY: Cornell University, Peace Studies Program, Occasional Paper #29.

Lendrum, S., and Syme, G. (1992) *The Gift of Tears: A Practical Approach to Loss and Bereavement Counseling*. London: Routledge.

Lepore, J. (2006) *New York Burning: Liberty, Slavery, and Conspiracy in Eighteenth-Century Manhattan*. New York: Vintage.

Levesque, L., Cosette, S., and Laurin, L. (1995) Multidimensional examination of the psychological and social well-being of caregivers of a demented relative. *Research on Aging*, 17: 332–60.

Levy, S. B., and Marshall, B. (2004) Antibacterial resistance worldwide: causes, challenges, and responses. *Nature Medicine*, December, Supplement 12 (10): S110–S121.

Lewin, T. (2007) A move for birth certificates for stillborn babies. *New York Times*, May 22.

Lewis, P. (1987) *Organizational Communication: The Essence of Effective Management*. New York: Wiley.

Lexchin, J. (2001) Lifestyle drugs: issues for debate. *Canadian Medical Association Journal*, May 15: 164–74.

Leydon, G. (2008) "Yours is potentially serious but most of these are cured": optimistic communication in UK outpatient oncology consultations. *Psycho-Oncology*, 17: 1081–8.

Lindemann, E. (1944) The symptomatology and management of acute grief. *American Journal of Psychiatry*, 101: 141–8.

Lindsey, J. R. (2007) America and the new dynamics of war. *Peace Review*, 19: 255–60.

Lofland, L. (1978) *The Craft of Dying*. Beverly Hills, CA: Sage.

Lopata, H. (1979) *Women as Widows: Support Systems*. New York: Elsevier.

Lopata, H. (1986) Becoming and being a widow: reconstruction of the self and support systems. *Journal of Geriatric Psychiatry*, 19: 203–14.

McCarthy, E. P., et al. (2003) Hospice use among Medicare managed care and fee-for-service patients dying with cancer. *Journal of the American Medical Association*, 289: 2238–45.

McCarthy, J. R. (2007) "They all look as if they're coping, but I'm not": the relational power/lessness of "youth" in responding to experiences of bereavement. *Journal of Youth Studies*, 10: 285–303.

McCown, D., and Davies, B. (1995) Patterns of grief in young children following the death of a sibling. *Death Studies*, 19: 41–53.

McKinlay, J. B., and McKinlay, S. J. (1977) The questionable contribution of medical measures to the decline of mortality in the United States in the twentieth century. *Milbank Memorial Fund Quarterly/Health and Society*, Summer, 405–28.

McLeroy, K. R., and Crump, C. (1994) Health promotion and disease prevention: a historical perspective. *Generations*, 18: 9–18.

McNeil, D. G. (2007) Child mortality at record low; further drop seen. *New York Times*, September 13.

McNeill, W. H. (1976) *Plagues and Peoples*. Garden City, NY: Anchor Press.

McNeill, W. H. (1993) Patterns of disease emergence in history. In S. S. Morse (ed.), *Emerging Viruses*. Oxford: Oxford University Press, 29–36.

McNulty, E. G., and Holderby, R. A. (1983) *Hospice: A Caring Challenge*. Springfield, IL: Charles C. Thomas.

Magner, L. (2005) *A History of Medicine*. 2nd edn, Boca Raton, FL: Taylor & Francis.

Mahon, M., and Page, M. L. (1995) Childhood bereavement after the death of a sibling. *Holistic Nursing Practice*, 9: 15–26.

Marks, G., and Beatty, W. K. (1976) *Epidemics*. New York: Charles Scribner's Sons.

Martin, L., and Kinsella, K. (1994) Research on the demography in developing countries. In L. Martin and S. Preston (eds), *Demography of Aging*. Washington, DC: National Academy Press, 356–404.

Marx, K. ([1867] 1967) *Capital: A Critique of Political Economy*, 3 vols. New York: International.

Mather, C. (1689) *Right Thoughts in Sad Hours*. London: James Astwood.

Mathews, T. J., Curtin, S. C., and MacDorman, M. F. (2000) *Infant Mortality Statistics from the 1998 Period Linked Birth/Infant Death Data Set*. National Vital Statistics Report, 48: 1–25.

Maynard, D. (2003) *Bad News, Good News: Conversational Order in Everyday Talk and Clinical Settings*. Chicago: University of Chicago Press.

Meckel, R. A. (1990) *Save the Babies: American Public Health Reform and the Prevention of Infant Mortality, 1850–1929*. Baltimore: Johns Hopkins University Press.

Meggitt, M. J. (1965) *Desert People*. Chicago: University of Chicago Press.

Memorial Sloan-Kettering Cancer Center (2008) Multiple myeloma. http://www.mskcc.org/mskcc/html/3371.cfm (accessed June 11, 2008).

Mendes de Leon, C. F., Kasl, S. V., and Jacobs, S. (1994) A prospective study of widowhood and changes in symptoms of depression in a community sample of the elderly. *Psychological Medicine*, 24: 613–24.

Merleau-Ponty, M. (1962) *The Phenomenology of Perception*, trans. C. Smith. London: Routledge & Kegan Paul.

Meyer, E. C., Burns, J. P., Griffith, J. L., and Truog R. D. (2002) Parental perspectives on end-of-life care in the pediatric intensive care unit. *Critical Care Medicine*, 30: 226–31.

Middleton, W., Raphael, B., Martinek, N., and Misso, V. (1993) Pathological grief reactions. In M. Stroebe, W. Stroebe, and R. Hansson (eds), *Handbook of Bereavement: Theory, Research and Intervention*. New York: Cambridge University Press, 44–61.

Miech, R. A., and Shanahan, M. J. (2000) Socioeconomic status and depression over the life course. *Journal of Health and Social Behavior*, 41: 162–76.

Miller, F., and Annas, G. (1988) Letters: 'It's over, Debbie'. *Journal of the American Medical Association*, 259: 2094–8.

Miller, P. A., Forbes, S., and Boyle, D. K. (2001) End-of-life care in the intensive care unit: a challenge for nurses. *American Journal of Critical Care*, 10: 230–7.

Minelli, L. A. (2006) Some information about Dignitas: address to the Liberal Party Convention, Brighton, September 20. http://www.dignitas.ch/media_dignitas/Referat_Brighton20092006.pdf (accessed September 17, 2007).

Miniño, A. M., Heron, M., Murphy, S., and Kochanek, K. D. (2007) *Deaths: Final Data for 2004*. National Vital Statistics Report, vol. 55, no. 19. Hyattsville, MD: National Center for Health Statistics.

Mintz, S., and Kellogg, S. (1988) *Domestic Revolutions: A Social History of American Family Life*. New York: Free Press.

Mirsky, S. (2008) Cemetery science: the geology of mausoleums. http://www.sciam.com/podcast/episode.cfm?id=cemetery-science-the-geology-of-mau0810-30 (accessed December 8, 2008).

Mishlove, J. (1975) *The Roots of Consciousness*. New York: Random House.

Mitchell, S., Teno, J., Miller, S., and Mor, V. (2005) A national study of the location of death for older persons with dementia. *Journal of the American Geriatric Society*, 53: 299–305.

Mitford. J. (1963) *The American Way of Death*. New York: Simon & Schuster.

Mitscherlich, A., and Mielke, F. (1949) *Doctors of Infamy*. New York: Henry Schuman.

Moinpour, C. M., and Polissar, L. (1989) Factors affecting place of death of hospice and non-hospice cancer patients. *American Journal of Public Health*, 79: 1549–51.

Mollaret, P., and Goulon, M. (1959) Le coma dépassé (mémoire préliminaire). *Revue Neurologique* [Paris], 1001: 3–5.

Moller, D. W. (1996) *Confronting Death: Values, Institutions and Human Mortality*. Oxford: Oxford University Press.

Moody, R. (1975) *Life after Life*. New York: Bantam Books.

Moody, R. (1977) *Reflections on Life after Life*. New York: Bantam Books.

Moore, C. H. (1963) *Ancient Beliefs in the Immortality of the Soul*. New York: Cooper Square.

Morgan, J. D. (ed.) (1990) *The Dying and the Bereaved Teenager*. Philadelphia: Charles Press.

Moss, T. (1974) *The Probability of the Impossible*. Los Angeles: J. P. Tarcher.

Mostert, M. P. (2002) Useless eaters: disability as genocidal marker in Nazi Germany. *Journal of Special Education*, 33: 155–68.

Munson, R. (2002) *Raising the Dead*. Oxford: Oxford University Press.

Murphy, S. A. (1996) Parent bereavement stress and preventive intervention following the violent deaths of adolescent or young adult children. *Death Studies*, 20: 441–52.

Murphy, S. A., Johnson, L. C., and Weber, N. A. (2002) Coping strategies following a child's violent death: how parents differ in their responses. *Omega: Journal of Death & Dying*, 45: 99–119.

Naik, G. (2002) Swiss group serves grim task by providing visitors' suicide. *Wall Street Journal*, November 22; http://www.calbaptist.edu/dskubik/euthanasia.htm (accessed January 23, 2009).

Nakashima, M., and Canda, E. R. (2005) Positive dying and resiliency in later life: a qualitative study. *Journal of Aging Studies*, 19: 109–25.

Nathan, H. M., Conrad, S. L., Held, P. J., McCullough, K. P., Pietroski, R. E., Sminoff, L. A., and Ojo, A. O. (2003) Organ donation in the United States. *American Journal of Transplantation*, 3 (4): 29–40

National Funeral Directors Association (2006) Trends and Statistics. http://www.nfda.org.

NCHS (National Center for Health Statistics) (2002) *Vital Statistics of the United States, Mortality*. Hyattsville, MD: National Center for Health Statistics.

NCHS (National Center for Health Statistics) (2007) Health, United States, 2007, with Chartbook on Trends in the Health of Americans. Hyattsville, MD: National Center for Health Statistics.

Neely, M. E. (2007) *The Civil War and the Limits of Destruction*. Cambridge, MA: Harvard University Press.

Neubauer, B. V., and Hamilton, C. L. (1990) Racial differences in attitudes toward hospice care. *Hospice Journal*, 6: 37–48.

New Orleans Public Library (2008) Yellow fever deaths in New Orleans, 1817–1905. http://nutrias.org/facts/feverdeaths.htm (accessed February 1, 2008).

New York Times (2006) The Last Word: Art Buchwald. www.nytimes.com/packages/html/obituaries/BUCHWALD_FEATURE/blocker.html (accessed May 15, 2008).

Nguyen, V., and Ash, J. M. (2002) The last days: the actively dying patient. In B. Kinzbrunner, N. Weinreb, and B. Weiss (eds), *20 Common Problems in End-of-Life Care*. New York: McGraw-Hill, 241–56.

Nguyen, V., and Weinreb, N. (2002) How to inform the patient: conveying bad news. In B. Kinzbrunner, N. Weinreb, and B. Weiss (eds), *20 Common Problems in End-of-Life Care*. New York: McGraw-Hill, 47–56.

NHPCO (National Hospice and Palliative Care Organization) (2007) NHPCO facts and figures: hospice care in America. http://www.nhpco.org/research (accessed May 5, 2008).

Norris, F. H., and Murrell, S. A. (1987) Older adult family stress and adaptation before and after bereavement. *Journal of Gerontology: Social Sciences*, 42: 606–12.

Nossiter, A., and Hauser, C. (2006) 3 arrested in hospital deaths after Katrina. New York Times, July 18.

NYS Department of State (2006) Cemetery regulation in New York State. http://www.dos.state.ny.us/cnsl/cemreg.html (accessed August 7, 2006).

Oddi, L. F., and Cassidy, V. R. (1998) The message of SUPPORT: Study to Understand Prognosis and Preferences for Outcomes and Risks of Treatment: change is long overdue. *Journal of Professional Nursing*, 14: 165–74.

Office of the Executive Director (2005) *HIV/AIDS Facts and Figures: A Quarterly Report: Fourth Quarter*. San Francisco: San Francisco AIDS Foundation.

Olshaunsky, S. J., and Ault, B. (1986) The fourth stage of the epidemiologic transition: the age of delayed degenerative diseases. *Milbank Quarterly*, 64: 355–91.

Oltjenbruns, K. A. (1996) Death of a friend during adolescence: issues and impacts. In C. A. Corr and D. E. Balk (eds), *Handbook of Adolescent Death and Bereavement*. New York: Springer, 196–216.

Omran, A. R. (1974) Changing patterns of health and disease during the process of national development. In A. R. Omran (ed.), *Community Medicine in Developing Countries*. New York: Springer, 259–74.

Opinion Research Business (2008) New analysis "confirms" 1 million+ Iraq casualties. http://www.opinion.co.uk/Newsroom_details.aspx?NewsId=88 (accessed March 24, 2008).

Oregon Department of Health and Human Services (2007) Summary of Oregon's Death with Dignity Act, 2006. http://www.oregon.gov/DHS/ph/pas/docs/year9.pdf (accessed September 17, 2007).

Orwell, G. (1956) *The Orwell Reader*. New York: Harcourt, Brace & World.

Osgood File (1999) Green burial. http://www.acfnewsource.org/environment/green_burial.html (accessed August 10, 2006).

Osterweiss, M., and Champagne, D. S. (1979) The US hospice movement: issues in development. *American Journal of Public Health*, 69: 429–96.

Ozawa, M. N., Downs, S. W., and Frigo, D. (1984) Income and personal resources: correlates of psychological adjustment to widowhood. *Journal of Sociology and Social Welfare*, 11: 598–610.

Padfield, P. (1966) *The Titanic and the Californian*. New York: John Day.

Parkes, C. M. (1965) Bereavement and mental illness. *British Journal of Medical Psychology*, 38: 388–97.

Parkes, C. M. (2001) *Bereavement: Studies of Grief in Adult Life*. 3rd edn, London: Routledge.

Parkes, C. M. (2002) Grief: lessons from the past, visions for the future. *Death Studies*, 2: 367–85.

Parkes, C. M. (2006) *Love and Loss: The Roots of Grief and its Complications*. New York: Routledge.

Parsons, T. (1951) *The Social System*. Glencoe, IL: Free Press.

Paterson, D. S., Trachtenberg, F. L., Thompson, E. G., Belliveau, R. A., Beggs, A. H., Darnall, R., Chadwick, A. E., Krous, H. F., and Kinney, H. C. (2006) Multiple serotonergic brainstem abnormalities in sudden infant death syndrome. *Journal of the American Medical Association*, 296: 2124–32.

Payer, L. (1996) *Medicine and Culture*. New York: Henry Holt.

Payne, S., Hillier, R., Langley-Evans, A., and Roberts, T. (1996) Impact of witnessing death on hospice patients. *Social Science Medicine*, 43: 1785–94.

Payutto, P. A. (1994) *Buddhist Economics: A Middle Way for the Market Place*, trans. Dhammavijaya and B. Evans. 2nd edn, Bangkok: Buddhadhamma Foundation.

Pear, R. (2001) Bill establishing patients' rights passes in senate. *New York Times*, June 30.

Pear, R. (2008) Gap in life expectancy widens for the nation. *New York Times*, March 23.

Perls, T. T., and Fretts, R. C. (2001) The evolution of menopause and human life span. *Annals of Human* Biology, 28: 237– 45.

Pew Research Center (2006) Strong public support for right to die. http://people-press.org/reports/display-php3?ReportID=266 (accessed March 13, 2006).

Pharoah, P. O. D., and Morris, J. N. (1979) Postneonatal mortality. *Epidemiological Review*. 1: 170–83.

Pickett, K. E., Luo, Y., and Lauderdale, D. S. (2005) Widening social inequalities in risk for sudden infant death syndrome. *American Journal of Public Health*, 95: 1975–81.

Pine, V. (1975) *Caretaker of the Dead*. New York: Irvington.

Pine, V. (1989) Death, loss and disenfranchised grief. In K. Doka (ed.), *Disenfranchised Grief: Recognizing Hidden Sorrow*. Lexington, MA: Lexington Books, 13–24.

Plato (1969) *The Last Days of Socrates*. Baltimore: Penguin Books.

Plato (1973) *The Republic*. New York: Oxford University Press.

Pogash, C. (2006) Colma, Calif., is a town of 2.2 square miles, most of it 6 feet deep. *New York Times*, December 9.

Powell, J. H. (1993) *Bring out your Dead: The Great Plague of Yellow Fever in Philadelphia in 1793*. Philadelphia: University of Pennsylvania Press.

Prescott, H. M. (2004) Stories of childhood health and disease. In R. A. Meckel and H. M. Prescott (eds), *Children and Youth in Sickness and in Health*. Westport, CT: Greenwood Press, 25–41.

Prokos, A. H., and Keene, J. R. (2005) The long-term effects of spousal caregiving on survivors' well-being in widowhood. *Social Science Quarterly*, 86: 664–82.

Promessa Organic (2008) http://www.promessa.se/index_en.asp (accessed March 30, 2008).

Prothero, S. (2001) *Purified by Fire: A History of Cremation in America*. Berkeley: University of California Press.

Puckle, B. S. (1926) *Funeral Customs*. London: T. Werner Laurie.

Quality Standards Subcommittee of the American Academy of Neurology (1995) Practice parameters for determining brain death in adults (summary statement), *Neurology*, 45: 1012–14.

Quigley, C. (1996) *The Corpse: A History*. Jefferson, NC: McFarland.

Quinlan, J. D. (2005) *My Joy, my Sorrow: Karen Ann's mother remembers*. Cincinnati: St Anthony Messenger Press.

Rando, T. A. (1985) Bereaved parents: particular difficulties, unique factors, and treatment issues. *Social Work*, 1: 19–23.

Rando, T. A. (1986a) *Parental Loss of a Child*. Champaign, IL: Research Press.

Rando, T. A. (1986b) The unique issues and impact of the death of a child. In T. A. Rando (ed.), *Parental Loss of a Child*. Champaign, IL: Research Press, 5–43.

Rando, T. A. (1991) Parental adjustment to the death of a child. In D. Papadatou and C. Papadatos (eds), *Children and Death*. New York: Hemisphere.

Rando, T. A. (ed.) (2000) *Clinical Dimensions of Anticipatory Mourning: Theory and Practice in Working with the Dying, their Loved Ones, and their Caregivers*. Champaign, IL: Research Press.

Range, L. (2002) Grief: traumatic. In R. Kastenbaum (ed.), *Macmillan Encyclopedia of Death and Dying*, vol. 1. New York: Macmillan, 379–82.

Richardson, R. (1987) *Death, Dissection and the Destitute*. London: Routledge & Kegan Paul.

Riches, G., and Dawson, P. (1996a) Communities of feeling: the culture of bereaved parents. *Mortality*, 1: 143-162.

Riches, G., and Dawson, P. (1996b) "An intimate loneliness": evaluating the impact of a child's death on parental self-identity and marital relationships. *Journal of Family Therapy*, 18: 1–22.

Riches G., and Dawson P. (1998) Lost children, living memories: the role of photographs in processes of grief and adjustment among bereaved parents. *Death Studies*, 22: 121–40.

Riches G., and Dawson P. (2000) *An Intimate Loneliness: Supporting Bereaved Parents and Siblings*. Buckingham: Open University Press.

Rinaldi, A., and Kearl, M. C. (1990) The hospice farewell: ideological perspectives of its professional practitioners. *Omega: Journal of Death and Dying*, 21: 283–300.

Rinehart, R. (ed.) (2004) *Contemporary Hinduism: Ritual, Culture and Practice*. Santa Barbara, CA: ABC-CLIO.

Ring, K. (1980) *Life at Death: A Scientific Investigation of the Near-Death Experience*. New York: Coward, McCann & Geoghegan.

Ringler, L. L., and Hayden, D. C. (2000) Adolescent bereavement and social support: peer loss compared to other losses. *Journal of Adolescent Research*, 1: 209–30.

Roach, M. (2003) *Stiff: The Curious Lives of Human Cadavers*. New York: W. W. Norton.

Robinson, L., and Fontana, A. (1989) Managing reality: the nurse and the birthing process. *Free Inquiry in Creative Sociology*, 17: 57–63.

Robinson, L., and Mahon, M. M. (1997) Sibling bereavement: a concept analysis. *Death Studies*, 21: 477–99.

Rodriquez, K. L., Gambino F. J., Butow, P. N., Hagerty, R. G., and Arnold, R. M. (2008) It's going to shorten your life: framing of oncologist–patient communication about prognosis. *Psycho-Oncology*, 17: 219–25.

Romanoff, B. D., and Terenzio, M. (1998) Rituals and the grieving process. *Death Studies*, 22: 697–711.

Ronel, N., and Lebel, U. (2006) When parents lay their children to rest: between anger and forgiveness. *Journal of Social & Personal Relationships*, 23: 507–22.

Rosen, C. (2008) A life worth living. *Wall Street Journal*, June 27: W11.

Rosen, F. (2004) *Cremation in America*. New York: Prometheus Books.

Rosen, G. (1963) The hospital: historical sociology of a community institution. In E. Friedson (ed.), *The Hospital in Modern Society*. New York: Free Press, 1–36.

Rosenblatt, P. C. (2000) *Parent Grief: Narratives of Loss and Relationship*. Philadelphia: Taylor & Francis.

Rossman, P. (1977) *Hospice: Creating New Models of Care for the Terminally Ill*. New York: Association Press.

Roth, A. (2007) Final salute to "Fighting Fifth." http://www.signonsandiego.com/news/military/20070216-9999-lz1n16salute.html (accessed February 16, 2007).

Rothaupt, J. W., and Becker, K. (2007) A literature review of Western bereavement theory: from decathecting to continuing bonds. *Family Journal*, 15: 6–15.

Rousseau, J.-J. ([1762] 1979) *Emile: or, On education*, trans. A. Bloom. New York: Basic Books.

Rubin, S. S. (1990) Death of the future? An outcome study of bereaved parents in Israel. *Omega: Journal of Death and Dying*, 20: 323–39.

Rubin, S. S. (1992) Adult child loss and the two-track model of bereavement. *Omega: Journal of Death and Dying*, 24: 183–202.

Sack, K. (2007) The short end of the longer life. *New York Times*, April 27.

Sanders, C. M. (1993) Risk factors in bereavement outcome. In M. Stroebe, W. Stroebe, and R. O. Hansson (eds), *Handbook of Bereavement: Theory, Research, and Intervention*. Cambridge: Cambridge University Press, 255–70.

Schantz, M. S. (2008) *Awaiting the Heavenly Country: The Civil War and America's Culture of Death*. Ithaca, NY: Cornell University Press.

Schiff, H. S. (1977) *The Bereaved Parent*. New York: Penguin Books.

Schlissel, L. (1982) *Women's Diaries of the Westward Journey*. New York: Schocken Books.

Schoendorf, K. C, and Kiely, J. L. (1997) Birth weight and age-specific analysis of the 1990 US infant mortality drop: was it surfactant? *Archives of Pediatric and Adolescent Medicine*, 51: 129–34.

Schutz, A. (1971) *Collected Papers I*. The Hague: Martinus Nijhoff.

Schwab, R. (1996) Gender differences in parental grief. *Death Studies*, 20: 103–13.

Schwab, R. (1998) A child's death and divorce: dispelling the myth. *Death Studies*, 22: 445–68.

Scott, S., and Duncan, C. J. (2001) *Biology of Plagues: Evidence from Historical Populations*. Cambridge: Cambridge University Press.

Seale, C. (1991) Communication and awareness about death: a study of a random sample of dying patients. *Social Science and Medicine*, 32: 943–52.

Sebba, J. (2004) A word a day. http://wordsmith.org/awad/awadmail137.html (accessed November 18, 2008).

Segerberg, O., Jr. (1974) *The Immortality Factor*. New York: E. P. Dutton.

Seligman, C. G. (1910) *The Melanesians of British New Guinea*. Cambridge: Cambridge University Press.

Selzer, R. (1974) *Rituals of Surgery: Short Stories*. New York: Simon & Schuster.

Servaty-Seib, H., and Pistole, M. H. (2006) Adolescent grief: relationship category and emotional closeness. *Omega: Journal of Death and Dying*, 54: 147–67.

Shelley, M. W. ([1818] 1983) *Frankenstein*. Mattituck, NY: Amereon House.

Shibles, W. (1974) *Death: An Interdisciplinary Analysis*. White Water, WI: Language Press.

Siebold, C. (1992) *The Hospice Movement: Easing Death's Pains*. New York: Twayne.

Simmerling, M. (2007) Beyond scarcity: poverty as a contraindication for organ transplantation. *Virtual Mentor*, 9: 441–5.

Simmons, L. (1960) Aging in pre-industrial societies. In C. Tibbits (ed.), *Handbook of Social Gerontology*. Chicago: University of Chicago Press.

Singer, N. (2006) Do my knees look fat to you? *New York Times*, June 15.

Slaughter, V. (2005) Young children's understanding of death. *Australian Psychologist*, 40: 179–86.

Smith, J., and Haddad, Y. (2002) *The Islamic Understanding of Death and Resurrection*. Oxford: Oxford University Press.

Smith, L. F. (1998) Medical paradigms for counseling: giving clients bad news. *Clinical Law Review*, 4: 391.

Solzhenitsyn, A. (1968) *Cancer Ward*, trans. N. Bethell and D. Burg. New York: Farrar, Straus & Giroux.

Sourkes, B. (1995) *Armfuls of Time: The Psychological Experience of the Child with a Life-Threatening Illness*. Pittsburgh: University of Pittsburgh Press.

Speece, M. W., and Brent, S. B. (1984) Children's understanding of death: a review of three components of a death concept. *Child Development*, 55: 1671–86.

Spiro, H., McCrea, C. M., and Palmer, W. L. (eds) (1996) *Facing Death: Where Culture, Religion, and Medicine Meet*. New Haven, CT: Yale University Press.

Stannard, D. E. (1973) Death and dying in puritan New England. *American Historical Review*, 78: 1305–30.

Stannard, D. E. (1974) Death and the puritan child. *American Quarterly*, 26: 456–76.

Starr, P. (1982) *The Social Transformation of American Medicine*. New York: Basic Books.

Steckel, R. H. (1986) A dreadful childhood: the excess mortality of American slaves. *Social Science History* 10: 427–65.

Steinberg, T. (2006) *Acts of God: The Unnatural History of Natural Disaster in America*. New York: Oxford University Press.

Stepanek, M. (2008) FAQs. http://www.mattieonline.com (accessed January 11, 2008).

Stoddard, S. (1978) *The Hospice Movement: A Better Way of Caring for the Dying*. New York: Vintage Books.

Strauss, A., and Glaser, B. (1970a) *Anguish: A Case History of a Dying Trajectory*. Mill Valley, CA: Sociology Press.

Strauss, A., and Glaser, B. (1970b) Patterns of dying. In O. J. Brim, H. Freeman, S. Levine, and N. Scotch (eds), *The Dying Patient*. New York: Russell Sage Foundation.

Stroebe, M. (2001) Introduction: concerns and issues in contemporary research on bereavement. In M. Stroebe, R. Hansson, W. Stroebe, and H. Schut (eds), *Handbook of Bereavement Research: Consequences, Coping and Care*. Washington, DC: American Psychological Association, 3–22.

Stroebe, M., and Schut, H. (2001a) Models of coping with bereavement: a review. In M. Stroebe, R. Hansson, W. Stroebe, and H. Schut (eds), *Handbook of Bereavement Research: Consequences, Coping and Care*. Washington, DC: American Psychological Association, 375–403.

Stroebe, M., and Schut, H. (2001b) Meaning making in the dual process model of coping with bereavement. In R. Neimeyer (ed), *Meaning Reconstruction & the Experience of Loss*. Washington, DC: American Psychological Association, 33–54.

Stroebe, M., and Stroebe, W. (1991) Does "grief work" work? *Journal of Consulting and Clinical Psychology*, 59: 479–82.

Stroebe, M., Gergen, M., Gergen, K., and Stroebe, W. (1995) Broken hearts or broken bonds: love and death in historical perspective. In A. DeSpelder and A. Strickland (eds), *The Path Ahead*. Mountain View, CA: Mayfield.

Stroebe, W., and Stroebe, M. (1987) *Bereavement and Health*. New York: Cambridge University Press.

Stroebe, W., and Stroebe, M. (1993) Determinants of adjustment to bereavement in younger widows and widowers. In M. Stroebe, W. Stroebe, and R. O. Hansson (eds), *Handbook of Bereavement: Theory, Research and Intervention*. New York: Cambridge University Press, 208–26.

Sudnow, D. (1967) *Passing On: On The Social Organization of Dying*. Englewood Cliffs, NJ: Prentice-Hall.

SUPPORT Principal Investigators (1995) A controlled trial to improve care for seriously ill hospitalized patients: the study to understand prognoses and preferences for outcomes and risks of treatments (SUPPORT). *Journal of the American Medical Association*, 274: 1591–8.

Svendsen, L. (1997) The black death. http://www.duluth.umn.edu/cla/faculty/tbacig/hmcl1005/plague/ (accessed July 20, 2007).

Swissinfo (2003) Swiss more tolerant of euthanasia. http://www.swissinfo.html?siteSect=41&sid=3963860 (accessed February 10, 2005).

Takahashi, Y. (1995) Recent trends in suicidal behavior in Japan. *Psychiatry and Clinical Neurosciences*, 49 (Suppl. 1): S105–9.

Talbot, K. (2002) *What Forever Means after the Death of a Child*. London: Brunner-Routledge.

Tang, S. T. (2003) When death is imminent: where terminally ill patients with cancer prefer to die and why. *Cancer Nursing*, 26: 245–51.

Tart, C. (1968) A psychophysiological study of OBEs in a selected subject. *Journal of the American Society for Psychic Research*, 62: 3–27.

Taubenberger, J. K., and Morens, D. M. (2006) 1918 influenza: the mother of all pandemics. *Emerging Infectious Diseases*. January. http://www.cdc.gov/ncidod/EID/vol12no01/05-0979.htm (accessed July 6, 2007).

Taylor, L. (1983) *Mourning Dress: A Costume and Social History*. London: Allen & Unwin.

Teno, J. M., Clarridge, B. R., Casey, V., Welch, L. C., Wetle, T., Shield, R., and Mor, V. (2004) Family perspectives on end-of-life care at the last place of care. *Journal of the American Medical Association*, 291: 88–93.

Thomasma, D. (2003) Telling the truth to patients: a clinical ethics exploration. In T. Beauchamp and L. Walters (eds), *Contemporary Issues in Bioethics*. Belmont, CA: Thomson/Wadsworth, 128–32.

Thompson, N. (1997) Children, death, and ageism. *Child and Family Social Work*, 2: 59–65.

Thompson, T. (2000) The nature and language of illness explanation. In B.

Whaley (ed.), *Explaining Illness: Research, Theory and Strategies*. Mahwah, NJ: Lawrence Erlbaum, 3–39.

Tigay, J. H. (2007) Hair: holiness in mourning. *Jewish Heritage Online Magazine*, http://www.jhom.com/topics/hair/mourning.html (accessed September 4, 2007).

Time (1975) Death companionship. February 17: 68.

Tolle, S., Rosenfeld, A., Tilden, V., and Park, Y. (1999) Oregon's low in-hospital death rates: what determines where people die and satisfaction with decision on place of death? *Annals of Internal Medicine*, 130: 681–5.

Toller, P. W. (2005) Negotiation of dialectical contradictions by parents who have experienced the death of a child. *Journal of Applied Communication Research*, 33: 46–66.

Trilling, L. (1972) *Sincerity and Authenticity*. Cambridge, MA: Harvard University Press.

Truog, R. D., Christ, G., Browning, D. M., and Meyer, E. C. (2006) Sudden traumatic death in children: we did everything, but your child didn't survive. *Journal of the American Medical Association*, 295: 2646–54.

Turner, R., and Edgley, C. (1976) Death as theatre: a dramaturgical analysis of the American funeral. *Sociology and Social Research*, 60: 377–93.

UC Atlas of Global Inequality (2007) Cause of death. http://ucatlas.ucsc.edu/cause.php (accessed October 15, 2007).

Umberson, D., Wortman, C. B., and Kessler, R. C. (1992) Widowhood and depression: explaining long-term gender differences in vulnerability. *Journal of Health and Social Behavior*, 33: 10–24.

UNAIDS (Joint United Nations Programme on HIV/AIDS) (2005) *Aids Epidemic Update*, December. Geneva: UNAIDS

UNICEF (United Nations Children's Fund) (2003) *The State of the World's Children 2004: Girls, Education, and Development*. New York: UNICEF.

US Census Bureau (1999) *World Population at a Glance: 1998 and Beyond*. International Brief, 98-104. Washington, DC: US Census Bureau.

US Department of Defense (2009) Global war on terrorism: casualties by military service component – active, guard, and reserve, October 7, 2001, through January 17. http://siadapp.dmdc.osd.mil/personnel/CASUALTY/gwot_component.pdf (accessed January 27, 2009).

US Department of Labor (2008) Health plans and benefits: Employee Retirement Income Security Act – ERISA. http://www.dol.gov/dol/topic/health-plans/erisa.htm (accessed April 8, 2008).

US Department of Veterans Affairs (2007) Fact sheet: America's wars. http://www1.va.gov/opa/fact/amwars.asp (accessed March 18, 2008).

US Living Will Registry (2007) Advance directive forms. http://www.uslivingwillregistry.com/forms/shtm (accessed 21 September 2007).

Utz, R. L. (2002) The economic consequences of widowhood: does income loss impact psychological well-being? Paper presented at the annual meeting of the Gerontological Society of America, Boston, November 22–6.

van Lommel, P., van Wees, R., Meyers, V., and Elferrinch, I. (2001) Near-death experiences in survivors of cardiac arrest; a prospective study in the Netherlands. *The Lancet*, 358: 2039–45.

Vanio, J., and Cutts, F. (1998) *Yellow Fever*. Geneva: World Health Organization.

Veatch, R. M. (1976) *Death, Dying, and the Biological Revolution: Our Last Quest for Responsibility*. New Haven, CT: Yale University Press.

Verhagen, E., and Sauer, P. (2005) The Groninger protocol: euthanasia in severely ill newborns. *New England Journal of Medicine*, 352: 959–62.

Videojug (2008) Cemeteries. http://videojug.com/interview/cemeteries (accessed June 20, 2008).

Vinitzky-Seroussi, V., and Ben-Ari, E. (2000) "A knock on the door": managing death in the Israeli Defense Forces. *Sociological Quarterly*, 41: 391–411.

Walker, B., and Warren, R. (2007) Katrina perspectives. *Journal of Health Care for the Poor and Underserved*, 18: 233–40.

Wallace, R. (1978) The elegies and enigmas of romantic Père-Lachaise. *Smithsonian*, November: 108–17.

Wallis, C. L. (1954) *Stories on Stone: a Book of American Epitaphs*. New York: Oxford University Press.

Waltari, M. (1949) *The Egyptian*. New York: G. T. Putnam's Sons.

Walter, T. (1999) *On Bereavement: The Culture of Grief*. Philadelphia: Open University Press.

Warner, W. L. (1959) *The Living and the Dead*. New Haven: Yale University Press.

Waugh, E. (1948) *The Loved One*. Boston: Little, Brown.

WDSU (2007) 'Dark cloud' lifted from Pou, attorney says. http://www.wdsu.com/news/13744299/detail.html (accessed 21 September 2007).

Weber, M. (1974) *The Theory of Social and Economic Organization*. New York: Free Press.

Weese-Mayer, D. E. (2006) Sudden infant death syndrome: is serotonin the key factor? *Journal of the American Medical Association*, 296: 2143–4.

Weitzen, S., Teno, J., Fennel, M., and Mor, V. (2003) Factors associated with site of death: a national study of where people die. *Medical Care*, 41: 323–35.

Weyer, E. (1932) *The Eskimos*. New Haven, CT: Yale University Press.

Whaley, B. (ed) (2000) *Explaining Illness: Research, Theory and Strategy*. Mahwah, NJ: Lawrence Erlbaum.

WHO (World Health Organization) (2001) Yellow fever. http://www.who.int/mediacentre/factsheets/fs100/en/.

WHO (World Health Organization) (2003) Influenza. Fact Sheet no. 2011. http://www.who.int/mediacentre/factsheets/fs211/en/.

WHO (World Health Organization) (2006a) *World Health Statistics 2006*. Geneva: World Health Organization.

WHO (World Health Organization) (2006b) *The World Health Report 2006: Working Together for Health*. Geneva: World Health Organization.

Wijdicks, E. F. M. (2001) The diagnosis of brain death. *New England Journal of Medicine*, 344: 1215–21.

Wilde, O. (1974) *The Picture of Dorian Gray*. New York: Oxford University Press.

Willinger, M., Hoffman, H., and Wu, K. (1998) Factors associated with the transition to non-prone sleep positions of infants in the United States: the national infant sleep position study. *Journal of the American Medical Association*, 280: 329–39.

Willinger, M., Ko, C. W., Hoffman, H. J., Kessler R. C., and Corwin, M. J. (2000) Factors associated with caregivers' choice of infant sleep position, 1994–1998: the national infant sleep position study. *Journal of the American Medical Association*, 283: 2135–42.

Wines, M. (2006) AIDS cited in the climb in South Africa's death rate. *New York Times*, September 8.

Wittgenstein, L. (1958) *Philosophical Investigations*. New York: Macmillan.

Wood, J. (1976) The structure of concern: the ministry in death-related situations. In L. Lofland (ed.), *Toward a Sociology of Death and Dying*. Beverly Hills, CA: Sage, 135–50.

Woodlawn Cemetery (2008) http://www.thewoodlawncemetery.org/landscape. html (accessed December 8, 2008).

Woodson, M. (2003) Green burials. http://www.colorfulcoffins.com/burial.html (accessed November 18, 2008).

Worden, W. J. (1991) *Grief Counseling and Grief Therapy: A Healthbook for the Mental Health Practitioner.* 2nd edn, New York: Springer.

Worden, J. W. (1996) *Children and Grief.* New York: Guilford Press.

Worden, W. J. (2002) *Grief Counseling and Grief Therapy: A Healthbook for the Mental Health Practitioner.* 3rd edn, New York: Springer.

Worden, J. W., Davies, B., and McCown, D. (1998) Comparing parent loss with sibling loss. *Death Studies,* 23: 1–15.

Worldchanging. 2004. Alternatives to traditional burials. http://www.world-changing.com/archives/001657.html (accessed March 8, 2006).

Wortman, C. B., and Silver, R. C. (2001) The myths of coping with loss revisited. In M. Stroebe, R. Hansson, W. Stroebe, and H. Schut (eds), *Handbook of Bereavement Research: Consequences, Coping and Care.* Washington, DC: American Psychological Association, 405–30.

Wright, R. (2005) *Chronology of Public Health in the United States.* Jefferson, N.C.: McFarland.

Wyness, M. (2006) *Childhood and Society.* New York: Palgrave.

Yahil, L. (1987) *The Holocaust: The Fate of European Jewry.* New York: Oxford University Press.

Yanuck, J. (1953) The Garner fugitive slave case. *Mississippi Valley Historical Review* 40: 47–66

Youngner, S. J., Arnold, R. M., and Schapiro, R. (1999) *The Definition of Death: Contemporary Controversies.* Baltimore: Johns Hopkins University Press.

Zamboni, G., Budriesi, C., and Nichelli, P. (2005) Seeing oneself: a case of autoscopy. *Neurocase,* 11: 212–15.

Zisook, S., and Shuchter, S. R. (1991) Depression through the first year after the death of a spouse. *American Journal of Psychiatry,* 148: 1346–52.

Zoepf, K. (2007) A dishonorable affair. *New York Times,* September 23.

Zuger, A. (2005) For a retainer, lavish care by "Boutique Doctors." *New York Times,* October 30.

Zuger, A. (2006) Doctors learn how to say what no one wants to hear. *New York Times,* January 10.

Index